LUXURY HOME PLANS

LUXURIOUS LIVING ROOMS

Discover elegance on a grand scale with spacious rooms, built-in entertainment centers, magnificent molding details, and exciting shapes. You'll find a variety of high-impact ceiling treatments, from soaring vaults with balcony views to rustic beams. Atrium, French, and sliding glass doors combine with a generous supply of windows for a magnificent unity of interior and exterior spaces.

SPECIAL FEATURES

Library lofts overlooking two-story rooms, towering fireplaces, impressive foyers, and built-in bars are among the magnificent amenities you'll find. Notice the elegance of traditional Palladium windows, the clerestories high overhead, the glass doors of every description, all designed to take advantage of surrounding grounds and natural sunlight. It's all here. Enjoy.

BEAUTIFUL BEDROOMS

Your inner sanctum deserves special attention, and these bedrooms benefit from a careful hand. Here, you'll find walk-in closets, gracious ceilings adorned with elegant moldings, and built-in shelves for extra storage. Many master suites feature fireplaces for a cozy atmosphere, and adjoining decks for enjoying your first cup of coffee on a sunny spring morning.

EFFICIENT KITCHENS

Range-top islands with built-in grills; a wealth of storage space, and sunny appeal make our step-saving kitchens a gourmet's dream come true. Many adjoin cheerful breakfast rooms for a wide-open atmosphere that keeps the cook in the action and makes mealtime so much easier.

WELL-APPOINTED BATHS

Imagine the luxury of both a garden tub and step-in shower at your disposal. Add double vanities, roomy, mirrored dressing areas, overhead skylights and loads of linen storage and you've got the perfect combination of amenities.

For Order Information see pages 252 through 255

© Copyright 1992 by The L.F. Garlinghouse Company, Inc., Middletown, Connecticut. All rights reserved. None of the contents of this publication may be reproduced in any form or by any means without the written permission of the publisher. All home plans and designs contained in this publication and their construction drawings are included under the copyright. Printed in the USA.

Library of Congress Number: 92-72606

ISBN: 0-938708-41-4

Cover Design by: Kimberly M. Guillemin

Y0-CZQ-120

FIRST FLOOR — 1,957 sq. ft.
- FIRST FLOOR — 1,957 sq. ft.
- SECOND FLOOR — 1,603 sq. ft.
- BASEMENT — 2,238 sq. ft.
- GARAGE — 840 sq. ft.

TOTAL LIVING AREA — 3,560 sq. ft.

CONVENIENCE AND BEAUTY BUILT IN

- Enjoy ingenious plan of gracious brick beauty
- Step inside Foyer from covered-entry porch with open staircase leading upstairs
- Towering Great Room features amenities such as built-in bar, entertainment center and direct access to rear patio
- Tucked away from busy areas, book-lined Study offers perfect place for quiet pursuits
- Across Kitchen counter, Breakfast Room is just steps away from glass-walled sun Porch, perfect for year round activities
- Upstairs Master Bedroom encompasses half of second floor with two walk-in closets and spacious private Bath
- Guests enjoy comfort second to none in private Guest Room featuring trayed ceiling, picture window, spacious closets, and personal full Bath

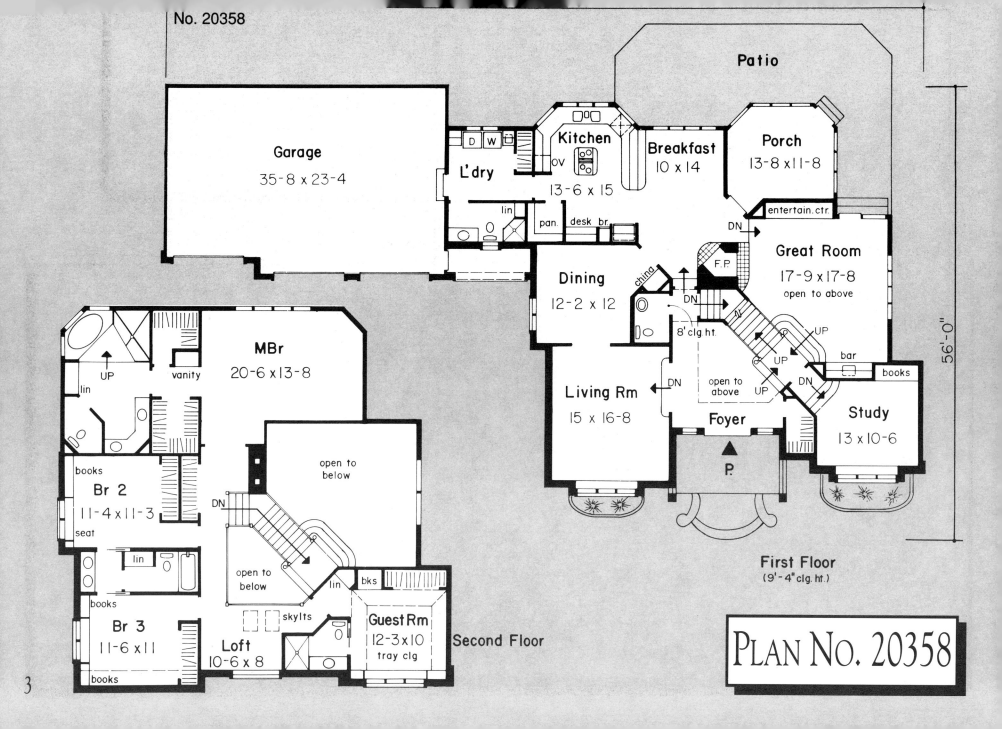

No. 20358

Patio

Garage
35-8 x 23-4

Kitchen
13-6 x 15

L'dry

Breakfast
10 x 14

Porch
13-8 x 11-8

D W OV

lin

pan. desk br.

entertain. ctr.

DN

Great Room
17-9 x 17-8
open to above

Dining
12-2 x 12

china

F.P.

DN

8' clg. ht.

UP

UP

bar

Living Rm
15 x 16-8

DN

open to
above

UP

DN

books

Foyer

Study
13 x 10-6

P.

56'-0"

First Floor
(9'-4" clg. ht.)

MBr
20-6 x 13-8

UP

vanity

lin

open to
below

DN

books

Br 2
11-4 x 11-3

seat

lin

open to
below

lin

bks

books

Br 3
11-6 x 11

skylts

Guest Rm
12-3 x 10
tray clg

Loft
10-6 x 8

Second Floor

books

3

PLAN No. 20358

Master Suite Dominates Second Floor

- ☐ Master Bedroom features private Sitting Room dominated by bright bay window for quiet time
- ☐ Master Bath includes his-n-hers walk-in closets, basins, and commodes
- ☐ Two additional Bedrooms on second floor include ample closet space and share a Bath
- ☐ Formal Dining Room has easy access to well-planned Kitchen

- ☐ U-shaped Kitchen overlooks pleasant Breakfast Nook
- ☐ Great Room includes beamed ceiling and bookcase-framed fireplace for welcoming warmth
- ☐ Relax on patio overlooking backyard in cool evenings
- ☐ Entrance from 3-car Garage leads to convenient half-Bath and Laundry Room

- ☐ First floor — 1,669 sq. ft.
- ☐ Second floor — 1,450 sq. ft.
- ☐ Basement — 1,653 sq. ft.
- ☐ Garage — 823 sq. ft.

Total living area — 3,119 sq. ft.

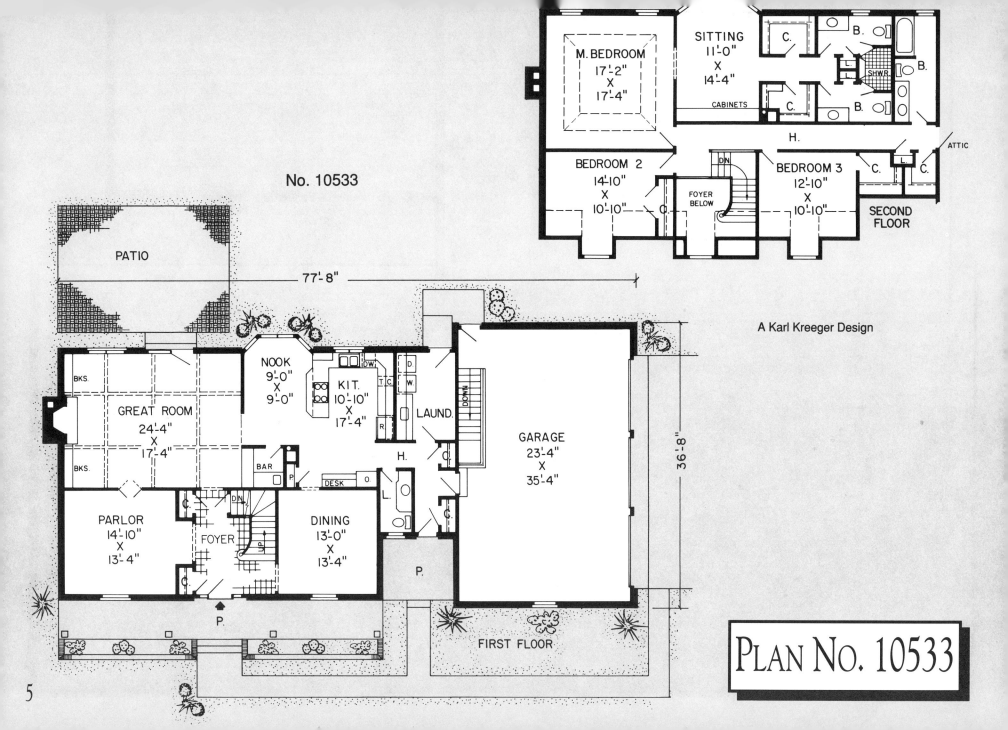

No. 10533

SITTING
11'-0"
X
14'-4"

M. BEDROOM
17'-2"
X
17'-4"

C.

B.

B.

SHWR

B.

CABINETS

C.

H.

BEDROOM 2
14'-10"
X
10'-10"

DN

FOYER
BELOW

BEDROOM 3
12'-10"
X
10'-10"

C.

C.

C.

ATTIC

SECOND
FLOOR

A Karl Kreeger Design

PATIO

77'-8"

36'-8"

BKS.

GREAT ROOM
24'-4"
X
17'-4"

BKS.

NOOK
9'-0"
X
9'-0"

DW

KIT.
10'-10"
X
17'-4"

T.C.

D.

W.

R

LAUND.

DOWN

GARAGE
23'-4"
X
35'-4"

BAR

P.

DESK

O.

H.

L.

C.

C.

PARLOR
14'-10"
X
13'-4"

DN

FOYER

P.

DINING
13'-0"
X
13'-4"

C.

P.

P.

FIRST FLOOR

PLAN NO. 10533

5

LUXURY ON A GRAND SCALE

- Built-in bookcase and window seat in Library extend inviting welcome to readers of all ages
- Whirlpool Bath entices occupants of Master Suite to soothe away tensions of the day
- Walk-in closet with shelving and skylight over double vanities add exciting features to Master Suite
- Fireplaced Living Room adjacent to eating areas for total ease in entertaining close friends or TV snacking

- Spacious Kitchen with food preparation island includes planning desk, pantry, and lots of counter space
- Skylit Sun Room bordering Hearth Room shares view and direct access to outdoor deck
- Three Bedrooms on second floor connected by hall and balcony overlooking two-story Foyer
- Great cedar closet on second level provides excellent out-of-season storage

- FIRST FLOOR — 2,508 SQ. FT.
- SECOND FLOOR — 1,107 SQ. FT.
- BASEMENT — 2,508 SQ. FT.
- GARAGE — 835 SQ. FT.

TOTAL LIVING AREA — 3,615 SQ. FT.

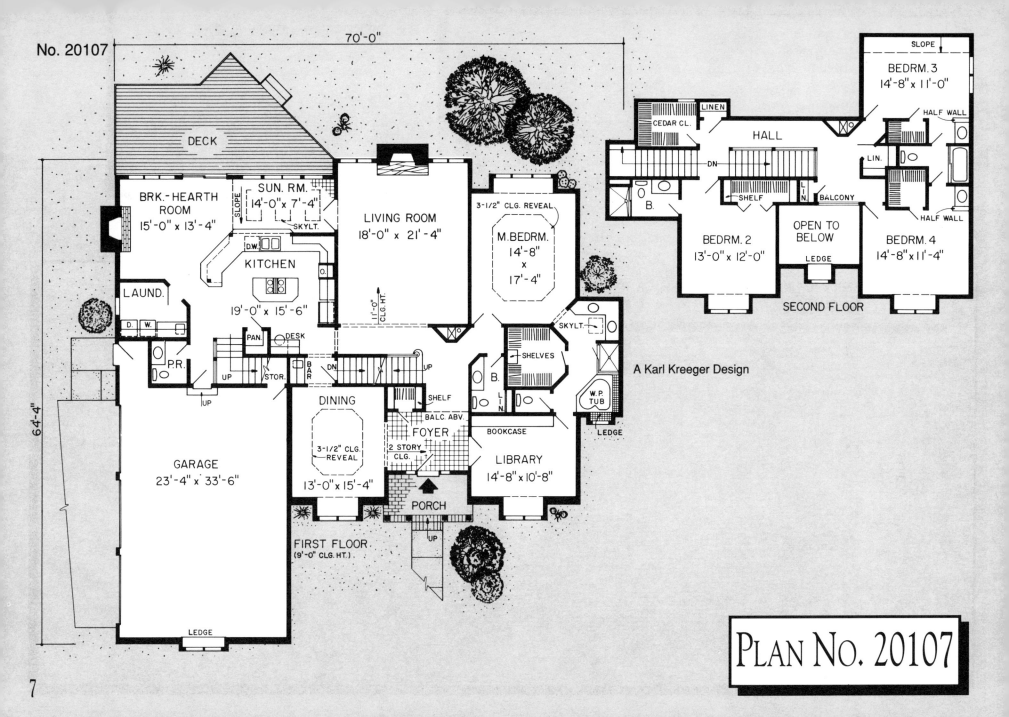

No. 20107

70'-0"

64'-4"

DECK

BRK.-HEARTH ROOM
15'-0" x 13'-4"

SUN. RM.
14'-0" x 7'-4"
SKYLT.
SLOPE

KITCHEN
19'-0" x 15'-6"
D.W.

LAUND.
D. W.

P.R.

PAN. DESK

UP
STOR.

UP

GARAGE
23'-4" x 33'-6"

LEDGE

DINING
3-1/2" CLG. REVEAL
13'-0" x 15'-4"

BAR
DN
UP

SHELF

BALC. ABV.

FOYER
2 STORY CLG.

PORCH

UP

FIRST FLOOR
(9'-0" CLG. HT.)

LIVING ROOM
18'-0" x 21'-4"

11'-0" CLG. HT.

M.BEDRM.
14'-8"
x
17'-4"

3-1/2" CLG. REVEAL

SKYLT.

SHELVES

B.

LIN.

BOOKCASE

LIBRARY
14'-8" x 10'-8"

W.P. TUB

LEDGE

A Karl Kreeger Design

SLOPE

BEDRM. 3
14'-8" x 11'-0"

CEDAR CL.
LINEN

HALL

DN

SHELF
LIN.

B.

BALCONY

LIN.

HALF WALL

HALF WALL

BEDRM. 2
13'-0" x 12'-0"

OPEN TO BELOW

LEDGE

BEDRM. 4
14'-8" x 11'-4"

SECOND FLOOR

PLAN NO. 20107

ACCENT ON LUXURY

- Gracefully curved staircase in soaring two-story Foyer invites admiration from all who enter

- Enormous Great Room extends warm greeting with fireplace and built-in bar

- Guest Bedroom possessing personal Bath and spacious closet

- Roomy Kitchen offers plenty of counter space, cupboards, and built-in desk for convenience

- Sunny Breakfast Room in unique hexagonal shape adjacent to Kitchen leads to outside deck

- Large Library off grand Foyer provides built-in bookcases and quiet getaway area

- Generous Master Bedroom on second floor emcompasses large walk-in closets, and private Bath with skylight

- Two more full baths and three Bedrooms with walk-in closets occupy remainder of second level

- FIRST FLOOR — 2,526 SQ. FT.
- SECOND FLOOR — 2,062 SQ. FT.
- BASEMENT — 2,493 SQ. FT.
- GARAGE — 976 SQ. FT.

TOTAL LIVING AREA — 4,588 SQ. FT.

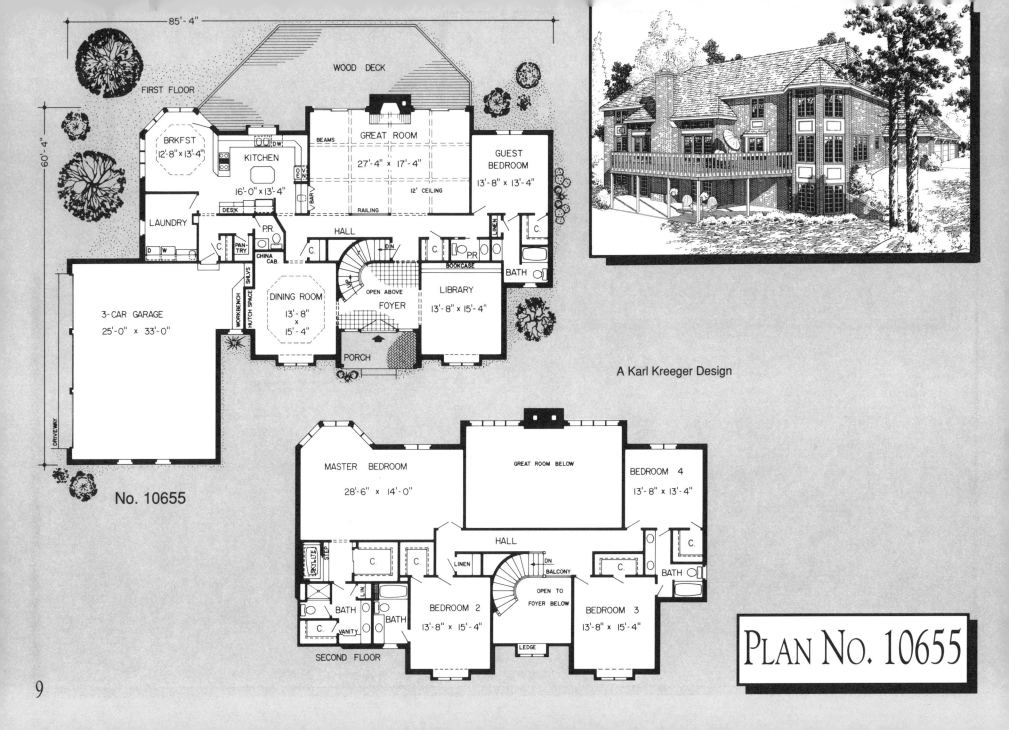

85'-4"

FIRST FLOOR

60'-4"

WOOD DECK

BRKFST
12'-8" x 13'-4"

KITCHEN
16'-0" x 13'-4"

GREAT ROOM
27'-4" x 17'-4"
12' CEILING

BEAMS

RAILING

GUEST
BEDROOM
13'-8" x 13'-4"

LINEN

C.

BAR

OVEN

DW

LAUNDRY

D W

C.

PAN-
TRY

CHINA
CAB.

DESK

PR.

HALL

C.

DN

OPEN ABOVE

C.

PR.

BOOKCASE

BATH

3-CAR GARAGE
25'-0" x 33'-0"

WORKBENCH
HUTCH SPACE
SHLVS

DINING ROOM
13'-8"
x
15'-4"

FOYER

LIBRARY
13'-8" x 15'-4"

DRIVEWAY

PORCH

A Karl Kreeger Design

No. 10655

MASTER BEDROOM
28'-6" x 14'-0"

GREAT ROOM BELOW

BEDROOM 4
13'-8" x 13'-4"

C.

HALL

SKYLITE

STEP

C.

C.

LINEN

DN
BALCONY

C.

BATH

BATH

LIN

BEDROOM 2
13'-8" x 15'-4"

OPEN TO
FOYER BELOW

BEDROOM 3
13'-8" x 15'-4"

C.

VANITY

BATH

LEDGE

SECOND FLOOR

PLAN NO. 10655

9

ENJOY BACKYARD VIEWS

- ☐ Skylit Sunporch leading to backyard patio offers peaceful relaxation while enjoying backyard beauty

- ☐ Large Kitchen provides ample counter space, pantry, and desk

- ☐ Easy access to Breakfast Nook and Dining Room from Kitchen

- ☐ Fireplaced Great Room exhibits warm characteristics with wood-beamed ceiling

- ☐ Private Study affords quiet solitude

- ☐ Recessed ceilings in Dining Room and Master Bedroom create distinctive angles throughout the first floor

- ☐ Master Bedroom includes oversized personal Bath with double basins

- ☐ Office area adjacent to Master Bedroom situated to induce minimum disturbance for working at home

- ☐ Second floor contains three additional Bedrooms, two full Baths and lots of closet space

- ☐ FIRST FLOOR — 2,069 SQ. FT.
- ☐ SECOND FLOOR — 821 SQ. FT.
- ☐ BASEMENT — 2,045 SQ. FT.
- ☐ GARAGE — 562 SQ. FT.

TOTAL LIVING AREA — 2,890 SQ. FT.

No. 10550
A Karl Kreeger Design

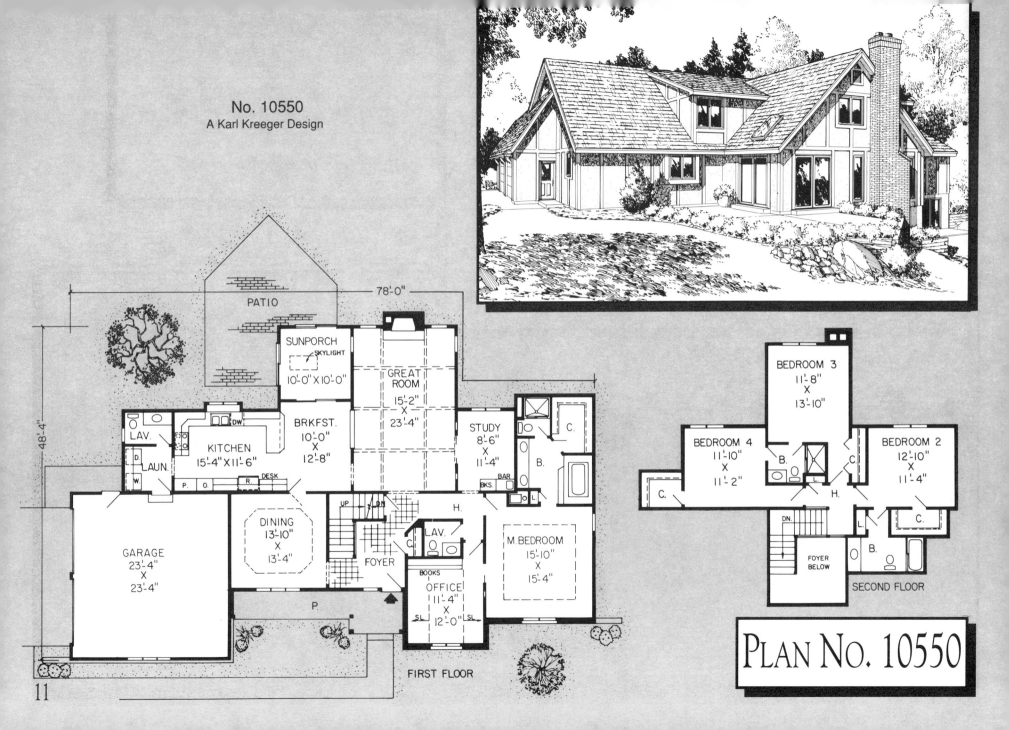

PLAN No. 10550

FIRST FLOOR

78'-0"

48'-4"

PATIO

SUNPORCH
SKYLIGHT
10'-0" X 10'-0"

GREAT ROOM
15'-2" X 23'-4"

BRKFST.
10'-0" X 12'-8"

STUDY
8'-6" X 11'-4"

C.

B.

BAR

BKS.

KITCHEN
15'-4" X 11'-6"

LAV.

LAUN.
D. W.

DW

P. O. DESK R.

H.

DINING
13'-10" X 13'-4"

UP DN

C.

LAV.

FOYER

M. BEDROOM
15'-10" X 15'-4"

GARAGE
23'-4" X 23'-4"

P.

BOOKS

OFFICE
11'-4" X 12'-0"
SL SL

SECOND FLOOR

BEDROOM 3
11'-8" X 13'-10"

BEDROOM 4
11'-10" X 11'-2"

BEDROOM 2
12'-10" X 11'-4"

B.

C.

C.

H.

L.

DN

FOYER BELOW

B.

C.

L.

11

Spacious Gem Reflects Contemporary Flair

- ☐ Unrestricted plan combines vaulted ceilings and expansive window treatments throughout for light, airy feeling in all rooms

- ☐ Open staircase in dramatic two-story entry leads to three Bedrooms

- ☐ Master Bedroom nestled in secluded position for privacy

- ☐ Oversized raised tub, double vanities, and expansive walk-in closet in Master suite invites total relaxation

- ☐ Living Room, Dining Room, and skylit Sun Room each claim passive solar features with heat-holding tile floors

- ☐ Two fireplaces send warmth radiating throughout house when temperatures drop

- ☐ Three-level outdoor deck area accessible from three different rooms

- ☐ Additional Bedroom can be utilized as Den for quiet study, homework, or reading place

☐ FIRST FLOOR — 1,886 SQ. FT.

☐ SECOND FLOOR — 1,127 SQ. FT.

☐ BASEMENT — 1,686 SQ. FT.

☐ GARAGE — 2-CAR

TOTAL LIVING AREA — 3,013 SQ. FT.

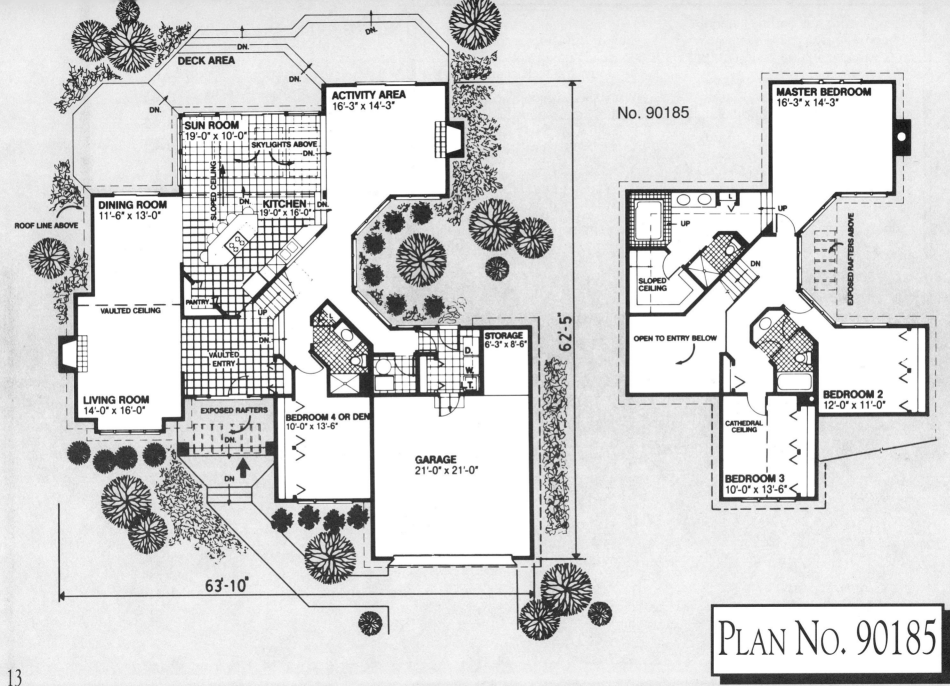

DECK AREA

DN.

SUN ROOM
19'-0" x 10'-0"

SKYLIGHTS ABOVE

ACTIVITY AREA
16'-3" x 14'-3"

No. 90185

MASTER BEDROOM
16'-3" x 14'-3"

DINING ROOM
11'-6" x 13'-0"

ROOF LINE ABOVE

SLOPED CEILING

KITCHEN
19'-0" x 16'-0"

VAULTED CEILING

PANTRY

UP

VAULTED ENTRY

DN.

LIVING ROOM
14'-0" x 16'-0"

EXPOSED RAFTERS

DN.

BEDROOM 4 OR DEN
10'-0" x 13'-6"

STORAGE
6'-3" x 8'-6"

D.
W.
L.T.

GARAGE
21'-0" x 21'-0"

62'-5"

63'-10"

UP

UP

SLOPED CEILING

DN

OPEN TO ENTRY BELOW

EXPOSED RAFTERS ABOVE

BEDROOM 2
12'-0" x 11'-0"

CATHEDRAL CEILING

BEDROOM 3
10'-0" x 13'-6"

PLAN No. 90185

13

B. LeBold

SPACIOUS SPLENDOR

- ☐ FIRST FLOOR — 1,688 SQ. FT.
- ☐ SECOND FLOOR — 1,500 SQ. FT.
- ☐ BASEMENT — 1,688 SQ. FT.
- ☐ GARAGE — 814 SQ. FT.

TOTAL LIVING AREA — 3,188 SQ. FT.

- ☐ Towering arch provides intriguing entry for sun-filled family home
- ☐ Step inside soaring Foyer with sunken Study and Living Room on either side
- ☐ Past powder room, open feeling accentuated by glass walls of Breakfast, Family, and Dining Rooms overlooking backyard
- ☐ Off fireplaced Family Room, Three-Season Porch opens to angular deck wrapping around active areas
- ☐ Efficient Kitchen with stovetop island flows into Breakfast Room and ensures ease in mealtime service
- ☐ Enjoy view overlooking Foyer below from balcony on second floor
- ☐ Grandiose Master Suite occupies entire wing featuring many luxurious amenities
- ☐ Master Suite also includes two walk-in closets, Dressing Room, double vanities, and Sitting Room

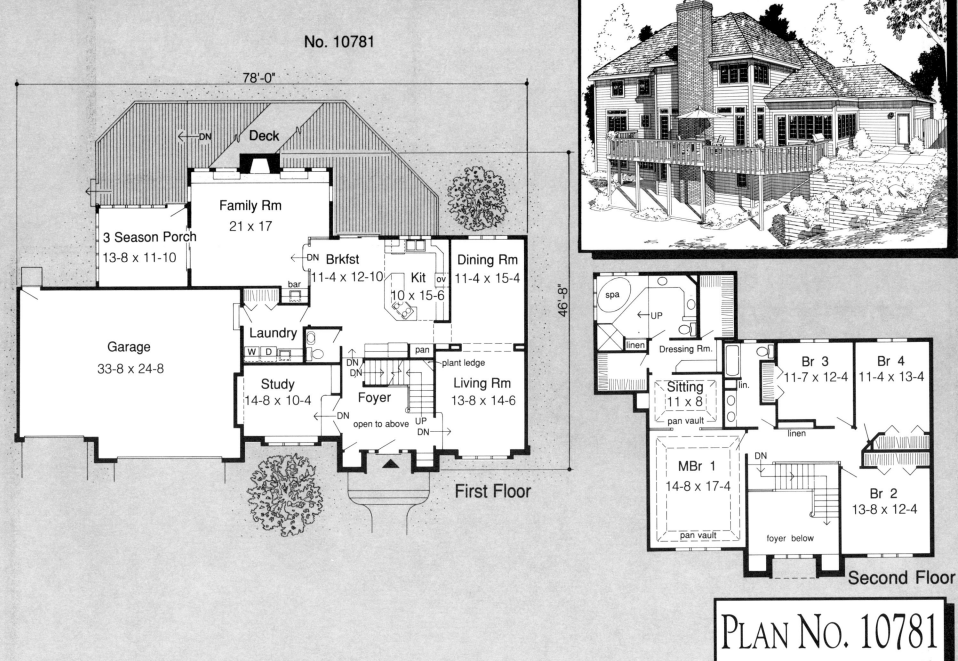

No. 10781

78'-0"

Deck
DN

Family Rm
21 x 17

3 Season Porch
13-8 x 11-10

DN Brkfst
11-4 x 12-10

bar

Kit
10 x 15-6

Dining Rm
11-4 x 15-4

ov

Garage
33-8 x 24-8

Laundry

W D

Study
14-8 x 10-4

DN
DN

Foyer

pan

plant ledge

Living Rm
13-8 x 14-6

open to above

UP
DN

DN

46'-8"

First Floor

spa

UP

linen

Dressing Rm.

Sitting
11 x 8
pan vault

lin.

Br 3
11-7 x 12-4

Br 4
11-4 x 13-4

linen

MBr 1
14-8 x 17-4

pan vault

DN

foyer below

Br 2
13-8 x 12-4

Second Floor

PLAN NO. 10781

15

LARGE COVERED PATIO FOR OUTDOOR ENJOYMENT

- Double entry enhanced by brickwork arches and curved steps
- Gracefully angled staircase leading to second floor draws pleasant attention in extensive Foyer
- Master Bedroom sports two walk-in closets, private Bath, and a private fireplace
- Fireplaced Living Room shares bar with comfortable Family Room
- Sunny Eating Nook adjacent to Kitchen for convenience
- Dining Room contains features amicable to formal entertaining
- Three Bedrooms upstairs each have personal access to full Bath
- Ample Library on second level provides safe keeping of book collection

- FIRST FLOOR — 2,277 SQ. FT.
- SECOND FLOOR — 851 SQ. FT.
- GARAGE — 493 SQ. FT.

TOTAL LIVING AREA — 3,128 SQ. FT.

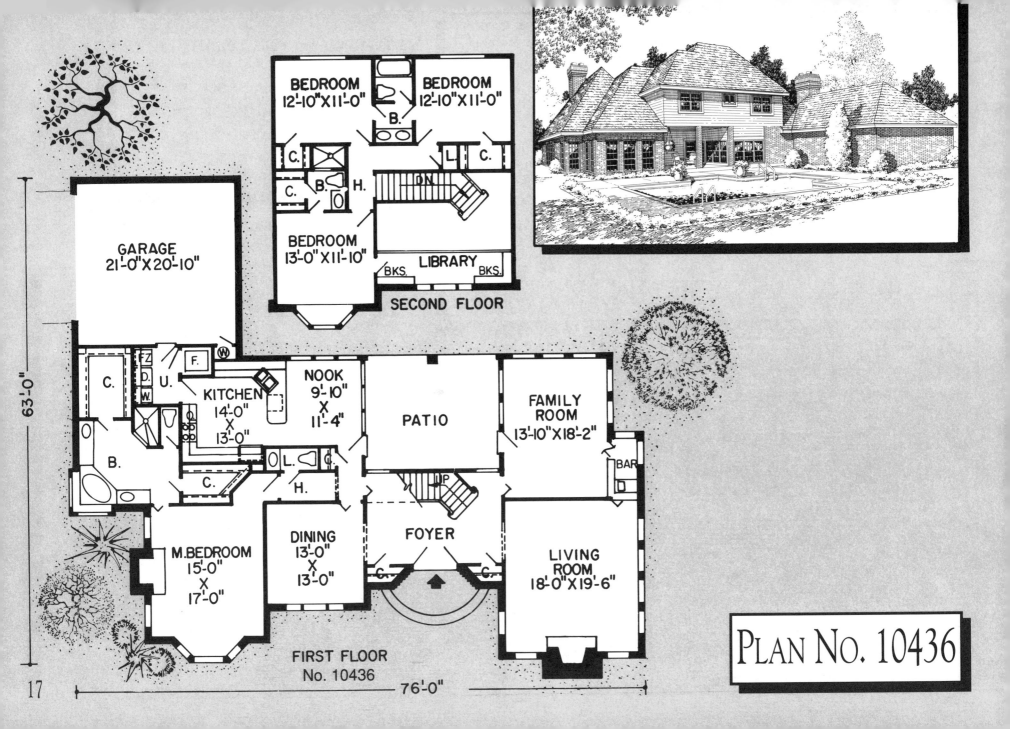

BEDROOM
12'-10"X11'-0"

BEDROOM
12'-10"X11'-0"

B.

C.
C.

L. C.

B.
C.

H.

DN

BEDROOM
13'-0"X11'-10"

BKS. LIBRARY BKS.

SECOND FLOOR

GARAGE
21'-0"X20'-10"

63'-0"

FZ
D.
W.
U.

F.
W.

C.

KITCHEN
14'-0"
X
13'-0"

NOOK
9'-10"
X
11'-4"

PATIO

FAMILY
ROOM
13'-10"X18'-2"

BAR

B.

L.
C.

C.

H.

UP

DINING
13'-0"
X
13'-0"

FOYER

M.BEDROOM
15'-0"
X
17'-0"

C.

C.

LIVING
ROOM
18'-0"X19'-6"

FIRST FLOOR
No. 10436

76'-0"

PLAN No. 10436

17

CONTEMPORARY CASTLE

- ☐ Enjoy poolside socialization made easy via nearby Kitchen through genial Breakfast Nook
- ☐ Usher guests into glass-walled Dining Room for more formal entertaining
- ☐ Family Room and Living Room share wetbar and fireplace
- ☐ Entire wing devoted to Master Bedroom blends into quiet sanctuary
- ☐ Recessed ceilings add polished touch to Master Bedroom

- ☐ Lavish walk-in closet features built-in chest for storage of those special items in Master Suite
- ☐ Take pleasure from private patio accessed through Sitting Room contiguous to Master Bedroom
- ☐ Three additional Bedrooms, two Baths and lots of closet space occupy second level
- ☐ Study Area with sundeck monopolizes remainder of second-floor space

- ☐ FIRST FLOOR — 2,740 SQ. FT.
- ☐ SECOND FLOOR — 948 SQ. FT.
- ☐ GARAGE — 522 SQ. FT.

TOTAL LIVING AREA — 3,688 SQ. FT.

No. 10697

POOL

GARAGE
22'-6"x21'-0"

PATIO

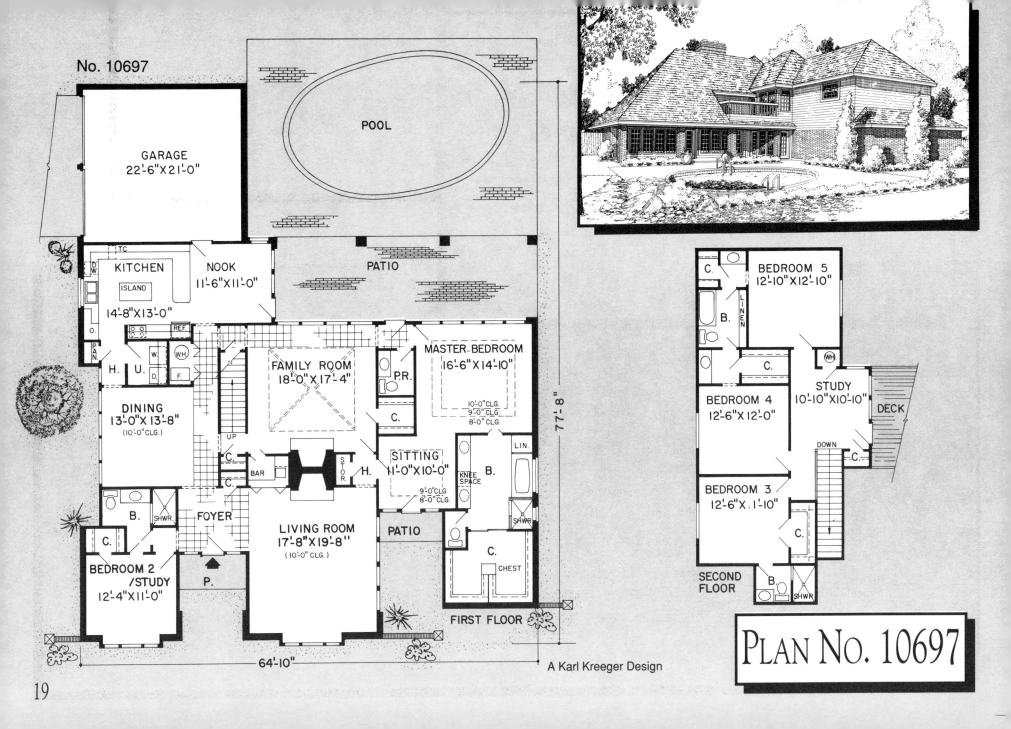

KITCHEN
14'-8"x13'-0"
ISLAND
TC
DW
O.

NOOK
11'-6"x11'-0"

PATIO

REF.
PAN.
H.U.
W D F
WH

MASTER BEDROOM
16'-6"x14'-10"
P.R.
C.
10'-0" CLG.
9'-0" CLG.
8'-0" CLG.

DINING
13'-0"x13'-8"
(10'-0"CLG.)

FAMILY ROOM
18'-0"x17'-4"

UP
C.
BAR
C.
STOR.
H.
SITTING
11'-0"x10'-0"
9'-0" CLG.
8'-0" CLG.
LIN.
B.
KNEE SPACE

77'-8"

C.
B.
SHWR.
FOYER

LIVING ROOM
17'-8"x19'-8"
(10'-0" CLG.)

PATIO
SHWR.

BEDROOM 2
/STUDY
12'-4"x11'-0"
P.

C.
CHEST

FIRST FLOOR

64'-10"

A Karl Kreeger Design

C.
BEDROOM 5
12'-10"x12'-10"
LINEN
B.
C.

WH
STUDY
10'-10"x10'-10"
DECK

BEDROOM 4
12'-6"x12'-0"
DOWN
C.

BEDROOM 3
12'-6"x11'-10"
C.

SECOND FLOOR
B.
SHWR

PLAN No. 10697

19

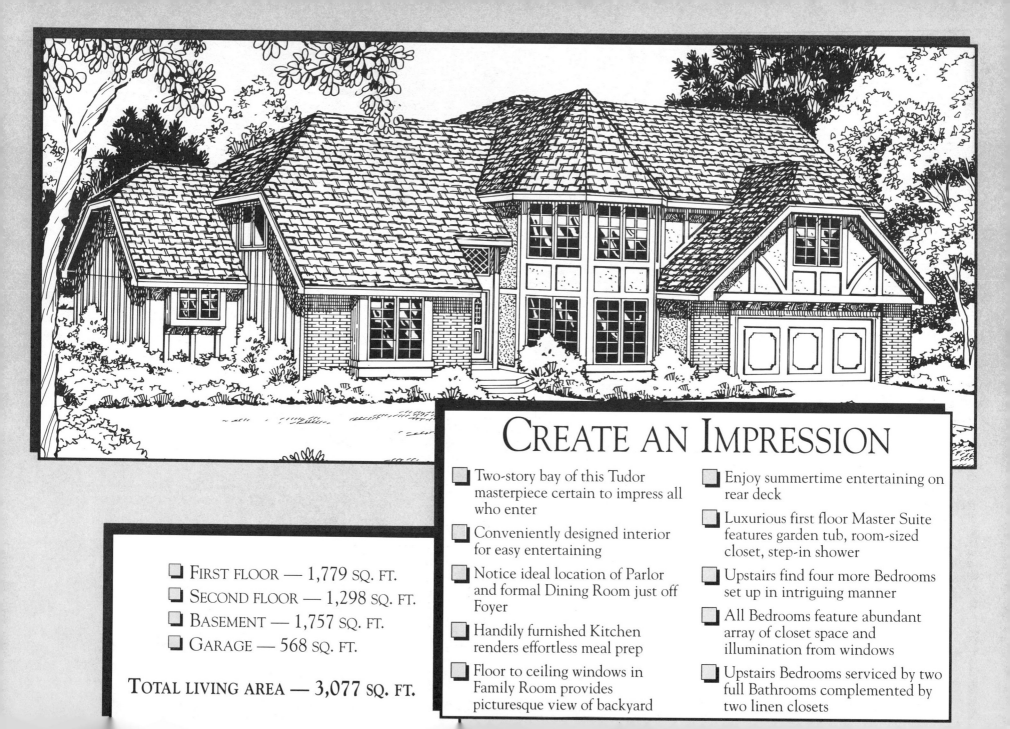

CREATE AN IMPRESSION

- Two-story bay of this Tudor masterpiece certain to impress all who enter
- Conveniently designed interior for easy entertaining
- Notice ideal location of Parlor and formal Dining Room just off Foyer
- Handily furnished Kitchen renders effortless meal prep
- Floor to ceiling windows in Family Room provides picturesque view of backyard

- Enjoy summertime entertaining on rear deck
- Luxurious first floor Master Suite features garden tub, room-sized closet, step-in shower
- Upstairs find four more Bedrooms set up in intriguing manner
- All Bedrooms feature abundant array of closet space and illumination from windows
- Upstairs Bedrooms serviced by two full Bathrooms complemented by two linen closets

- FIRST FLOOR — 1,779 SQ. FT.
- SECOND FLOOR — 1,298 SQ. FT.
- BASEMENT — 1,757 SQ. FT.
- GARAGE — 568 SQ. FT.

TOTAL LIVING AREA — 3,077 SQ. FT.

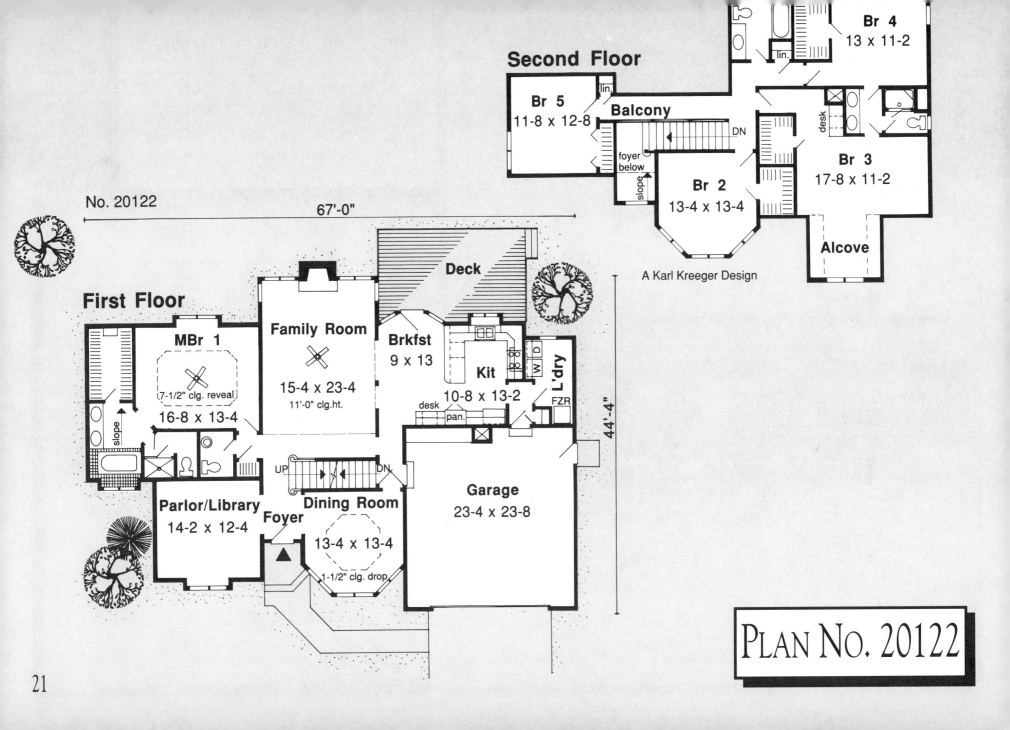

Second Floor

Br 5
11-8 x 12-8

Balcony

Br 4
13 x 11-2

lin.

lin.

desk

DN

foyer below

slope

Br 2
13-4 x 13-4

Br 3
17-8 x 11-2

Alcove

A Karl Kreeger Design

No. 20122

67'-0"

First Floor

Deck

MBr 1

Family Room

Brkfst
9 x 13

7-1/2" clg. reveal

15-4 x 23-4
11'-0" clg.ht.

Kit

L'dry

slope

16-8 x 13-4

10-8 x 13-2

W D

FZR

desk

pan.

44'-4"

UP

DN

Parlor/Library
14-2 x 12-4

Dining Room

Garage
23-4 x 23-8

Foyer

13-4 x 13-4
1-1/2" clg. drop

PLAN NO. 20122

ELEGANT SOPHISTICATION

- Foyer has stately columns, elaborate circular staircase and convenient half Bath nearby

- Columnar elegance carried through main entrance separating Dining Room, Foyer and Guest Room quarters

- Dining Room includes unique feature of built-in lighted hutch

- Sunken fireplaced Family Room leading to deck has built-in bookshelves and plenty of light from soaring two-story windows

- Island Kitchen has unusual Butlery, Pantry, plenty of cupboard space and opens to Nook completely surrounded by windows

- Master Bedroom features fireplace, built-in dresser, multi-windowed Sitting Room leading to private deck and luxurious Master Bath

- Exercise Room over Garage has elegant window works with small step-out balcony on either side affording undisturbed activity

- FIRST FLOOR — 3,403 SQ. FT.
- SECOND FLOOR — 2,774 SQ. FT.
- GARAGE — 1,043 SQ. FT.

TOTAL LIVING AREA — 6,177 SQ. FT.

No. 92109

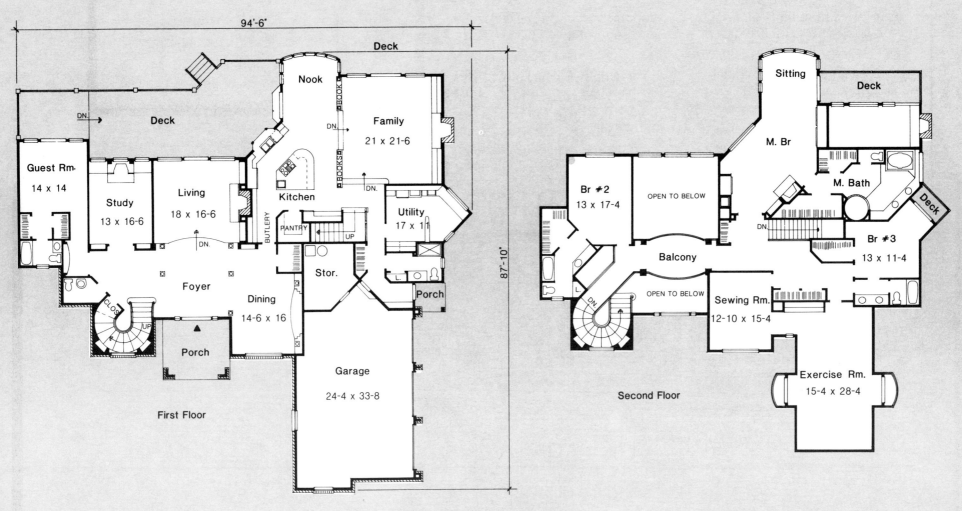

94'-6"

Deck

Deck

DN.

Guest Rm.
14 x 14

Study
13 x 16-6

Living
18 x 16-6

Nook

Kitchen

BUTLERY

PANTRY

Family
21 x 21-6

DN.

DN.

BOOKS

BOOKS

Utility
17 x 11

87'-10"

Foyer

CLOS.

UP

DN.

UP

Dining
14-6 x 16

Stor.

Porch

Porch

Garage
24-4 x 33-8

First Floor

Sitting

Deck

M. Br

Br #2
13 x 17-4

OPEN TO BELOW

M. Bath

Deck

DN.

Br #3
13 x 11-4

Balcony

OPEN TO BELOW

L

DN.

Sewing Rm.
12-10 x 15-4

Exercise Rm.
15-4 x 28-4

Second Floor

PLAN NO. 92109

CONTEMPORARY TWO-STORY

- Beautiful Den with built-in bookshelves located off curved Entry features picturesque bay window

- Fireplaced Family Room merges with sunny Dinette and large Kitchen creating open airy feeling

- Three-season porch just off Dinette offers protected outdoor relaxation

- Country Kitchen features large center island with vegetable sink and stove top and corner sink

- Atrium doors open from Kitchen into formal Dining Room and vaulted Living Room

- First-floor Laundry Room conveniently situated off 3-car Garage doubles as mud room

- Master suite on upper level has coffered ceilings, massive walk-in closet and luxurious bath with whirlpool tub

- Three additional Bedrooms sharing full Bath and Cedar Closet occupy remainder of second level

---

- FIRST FLOOR — 1,712 SQ. FT.
- SECOND FLOOR — 1,387 SQ. FT.
- BASEMENT — 1,548 SQ. FT.
- GARAGE — 831 SQ. FT.

TOTAL LIVING AREA — 3,099 SQ. FT.

No. 92303

BR1
23/4 X 13/8

BR2
12/8 X 10/6

BR3
12/4 X 11/2

STAIRS DOWN

CEDAR CLOSET

BR4
11/8 X 18/6

OPEN
TO
BELOW

UPPER LEVEL FLOOR PLAN

WOOD DECK

3S
11/4 X 11/8

FR
17/0 X 14/4

D
11/0 X 13/0

K
14/0 X 14/4

DW

L

STAIRS DOWN

DR
12/4 X 13/8

GAR
35/4 X 21/4

STAIRS UP

E

DEN
11/8 X 13/8

LR
12/4 X 16/4

nice.
Can do w/o
LR+DR
& have nice
house

MAIN LEVEL FLOOR PLAN

PLAN NO. 92303

- FIRST FLOOR — 3,307 SQ. FT.
- SECOND FLOOR — 837 SQ. FT.
- PORCH/PATIO — 382 SQ. FT.
- GARAGE — 646 SQ. FT.

TOTAL LIVING AREA — 4,144 SQ. FT.

GOURMET'S HEAVEN IN KITCHEN

- Kitchen affords 60 square feet of counter space
- Step-saving cooking island adds more culinary area
- Windowed Eating Nook and nearby patio access extend convenience and brilliance to spacious Kitchen
- Large Master Bedroom with walk-in closet situated away from noisy living areas
- Study easily doubles as Guest Room
- Ten-foot ceilings throughout lower level
- Nine-foot ceilings upstairs add to spaciousness created by large rooms
- Double doors usher you into two-story Entry with staircase curving gently to second-level rooms
- Cedar shake roofing contrasts nicely with brick veneer to complement leaded arched windows and false dormers

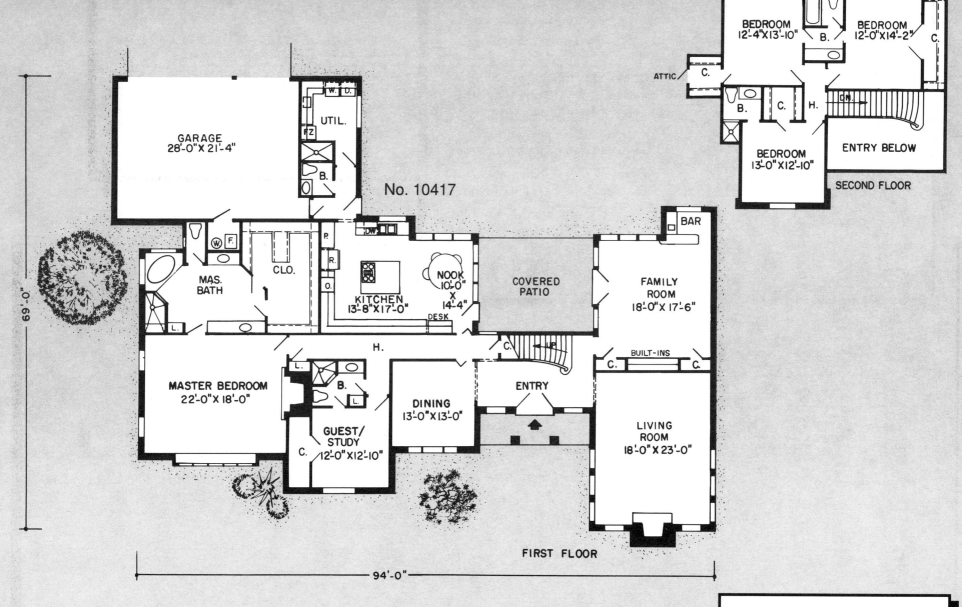

No. 10417

GARAGE
28'-0" X 21'-4"

UTIL.

MAS. BATH

CLO.

KITCHEN
13'-8" X 17'-0"

NOOK
10'-0" X 14'-4"

COVERED PATIO

FAMILY ROOM
18'-0" X 17'-6"

BAR

BUILT-INS

MASTER BEDROOM
22'-0" X 18'-0"

GUEST/ STUDY
12'-0" X 12'-10"

DINING
13'-0" X 13'-0"

ENTRY

LIVING ROOM
18'-0" X 23'-0"

DESK

H.

69'-0"

94'-0"

FIRST FLOOR

BEDROOM
12'-4" X 13'-10"

BEDROOM
12'-0" X 14'-2"

ATTIC

BEDROOM
13'-0" X 12'-10"

ENTRY BELOW

SECOND FLOOR

PLAN No. 10417

GEORGIAN TRADITION

- Elegant home brings best of yesterday to discerning family of today
- Towering columned porch leads to formal central entryway that reminds of times gone by
- Island Kitchen, Living Room and Breakfast/Hearth Room are examples of practical layout in this home of today
- Expansive Master Suite, enhanced by decorative ceiling, features his-n-hers walk-in closets

- Numerous windows add sunny brightness to all rooms in house
- House offers many useful features such as voluminous walk-in closets in all Bedrooms and adjoining Baths
- Large covered porch and sun deck provide convenient areas for outdoor entertaining
- Other unique features include handy bar in book-lined Living Room and two first-floor Baths

- FIRST FLOOR — 1,953 SQ. FT.
- SECOND FLOOR — 1,865 SQ. FT.
- SCREENED PORCH — 180 SQ. FT.
- BASEMENT — 1,929 SQ. FT.
- GARAGE — 864 SQ. FT.

TOTAL LIVING AREA — 3,818 SQ. FT.

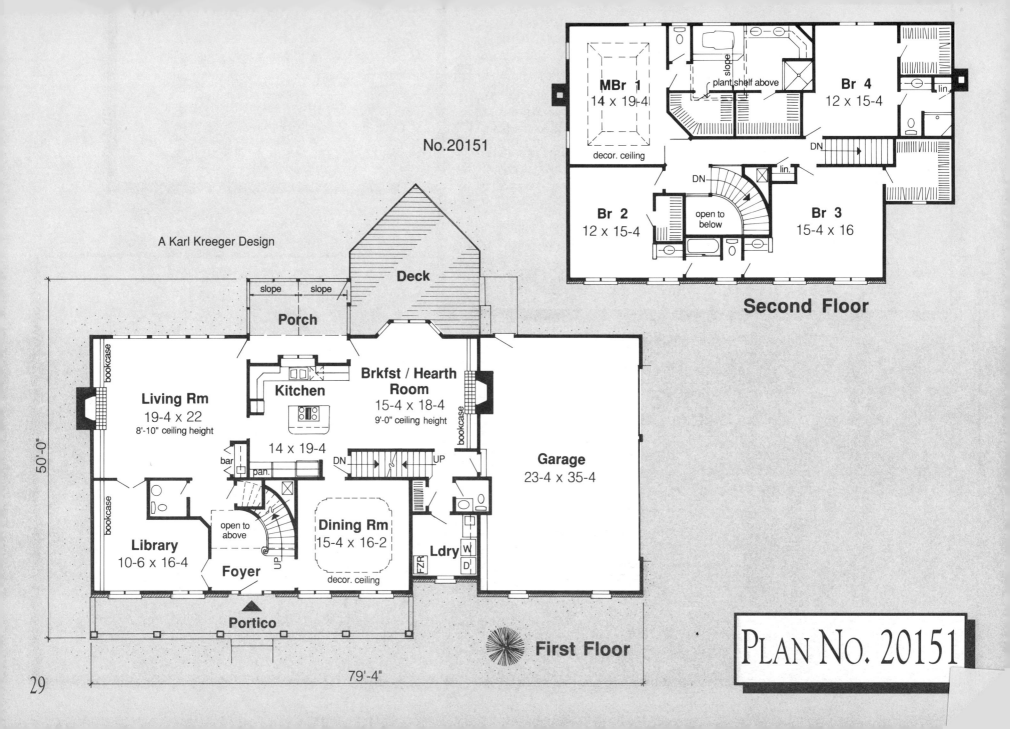

No.20151

Second Floor

MBr 1
14 x 19-4
decor. ceiling

plant shelf above

slope

Br 4
12 x 15-4

lin

DN

Br 2
12 x 15-4

DN

open to
below

lin.

Br 3
15-4 x 16

A Karl Kreeger Design

Deck

slope   slope

Porch

bookcase

Living Rm
19-4 x 22
8'-10" ceiling height

Kitchen

14 x 19-4

Brkfst / Hearth
Room
15-4 x 18-4
9'-0" ceiling height

bar

pan.

DN   UP

Garage
23-4 x 35-4

bookcase

50'-0"

open to
above

UP

Dining Rm
15-4 x 16-2
decor. ceiling

Ldry

W

D

FZR

bookcase

Library
10-6 x 16-4

Foyer

Portico

First Floor

79'-4"

29

PLAN No. 20151

ENERGY-SAVING SUNROOM WARMS TUDOR

- ☐ High two-story Foyer graced by dual-access curving stairway
- ☐ Bookcase-lined Study neighboring Foyer extends quiet solitude for business, homework, or just pleasurable pastime
- ☐ Master bedroom with vaulted ceiling includes private entry into Study
- ☐ Elaborate Master Bath sports two big walk-in closets and esoteric hot tub

- ☐ Proportions of fireplaced Living Room measure up for large gatherings comfortably
- ☐ Kitchen designed for convenience with plenty of counterspace and food preparation island
- ☐ Bright Sun Room extends entire length of Kitchen and Family Room
- ☐ Three good-sized Bedrooms and two full Baths occupy second level
- ☐ Overlook towering Foyer from Loft situated at top of stairs

- ☐ FIRST FLOOR — 3,332 SQ. FT.
- ☐ SECOND FLOOR — 1,218 SQ. FT.
- ☐ SUNROOM — 340 SQ. FT.
- ☐ BASEMENT — 3,672 SQ. FT.
- ☐ GARAGE — 1,137 SQ. FT.

TOTAL LIVING AREA — 4,890 SQ. FT.

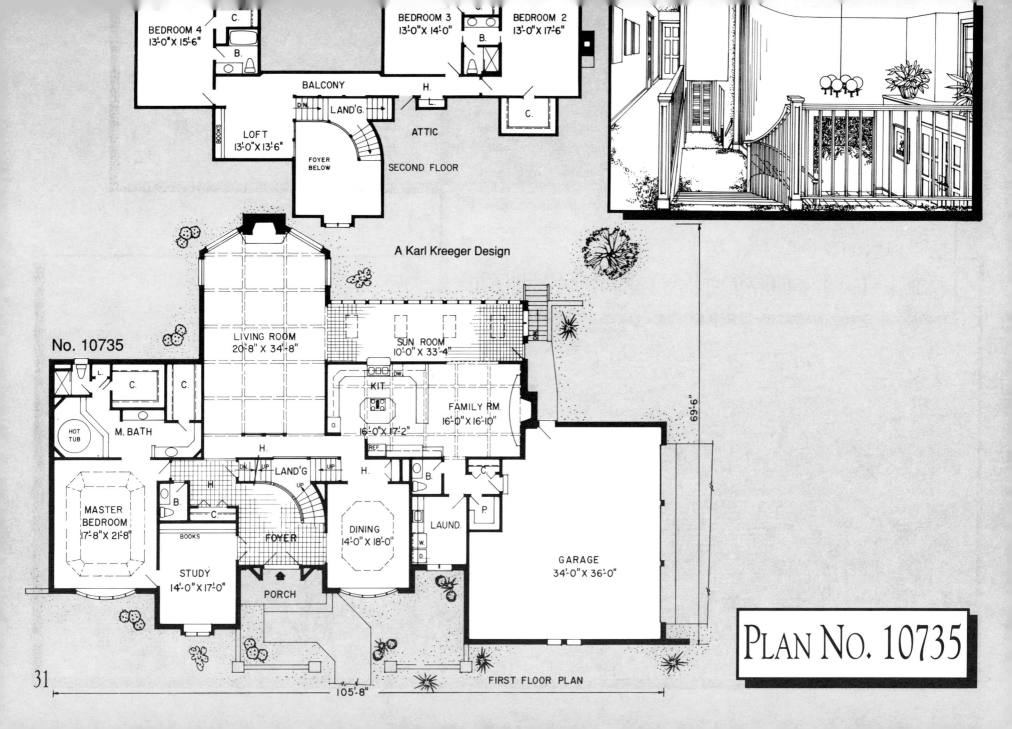

BEDROOM 4
13'-0" X 15'-6"

C.

B.

BEDROOM 3
13'-0" X 14'-0"

B.

BEDROOM 2
13'-0" X 17'-6"

BALCONY

H.

BOOKS

DN.

LAND'G.

ATTIC

C.

LOFT
13'-0" X 13'-6"

FOYER
BELOW

SECOND FLOOR

A Karl Kreeger Design

No. 10735

LIVING ROOM
20'-8" X 34'-8"

SUN ROOM
10'-0" X 33'-4"

DN.

DW.

KIT.

FAMILY RM.
16'-0" X 16'-10"

C.

16'-0" X 17'-2"

REF.

HOT
TUB

M. BATH

C.

C.

H.

DN.

UP

LAND'G

UP

H.

B.

C.

B.

UP

MASTER
BEDROOM
17'-8" X 21'-8"

B.

LAUND.

P.

BOOKS

C.

FOYER

W.

STUDY
14'-0" X 17'-0"

DINING
14'-0" X 18'-0"

D.

GARAGE
34'-0" X 36'-0"

PORCH

69'-6"

PLAN NO. 10735

31

105'-8"

FIRST FLOOR PLAN

Distinctive Entrance Adds Elegance

- ☐ Covered drive and entrance enhance aspects of home
- ☐ Impressive tiled Foyer with curving staircase to second level flows into Great Room
- ☐ Spacious Master Bedroom leads to personal Bath and large walk-in closet
- ☐ Conveniently situated half-Bath and Laundry Room just inside 3-car Garage
- ☐ Two patios offer ample room for outdoor entertaining

- ☐ Three additional Bedrooms sport private Baths and generous closet space
- ☐ Scenic garden courtyard divides Bedrooms three and four
- ☐ Roomy Kitchen features a pantry and an island cooking range
- ☐ Hearth Room just off Kitchen doubles as informal Dining Area and Family Room
- ☐ Great Room features built-in bar and fireplace with sliding glass doors leading to patio

- ☐ FIRST FLOOR — 3,972 SQ. FT.
- ☐ BASEMENT — 3,972 SQ. FT.
- ☐ GARAGE — 924 SQ. FT.

TOTAL LIVING AREA — 3,972 SQ. FT.

No. 10536

PATIO

HEARTH ROOM
15'-4" X 13'-0"

KITCHEN
14'-6" X 16'-0"

GREAT ROOM
19'-0" X 27'-4"

PATIO

BAR

LIBRARY
13'-10" X 13'-4"

CLO.

BATH

CLO.

P.

W.

S.

S.

H.

OV.

C.

L.

H.

RAIL

DN.

L.

H.

L.

MASTER
BEDROOM
16'-6" X 17'-4"

DRIVE

DN.

3-CAR GARAGE
25'-4" X 33'-4"

LAUND.

HUTCH SPACE

W.
D.

FORMAL
DINING
13'-0" X 17'-4"

CHINA

C.

FOYER

C.

BEDROOM #4
13'-0" X 13'-2"

C.

BEDROOM #3
13'-0" X 13'-2"

H.

C.

B.

COVERED
ENTRY

B.

GARDEN
COURT

B.

BEDROOM #2
15'-0" X 13'-4"

B.

66'-8"

108'-8"

COVERED DRIVEWAY

FLOOR PLAN

A Karl Kreeger Design

PLAN NO. 10536

33

ELEGANT DESIGN FOR HILLSIDE SETTING

- Ample Great Room features garden area and large fireplace
- Foyer opens to centralized Great Room
- Lower-level Recreation Room with numerous windows affords easy access to patio via sliding glass doors
- Large walk-in closets in each of the lower-level Bedrooms supply plenty of individual storage space
- Study/TV area offers quiet privacy away from busy activities of others
- Kitchen's roominess enhanced by adjacent Sun Porch
- Island cook center in Kitchen makes meal preparation efficient and easy
- Master Bedroom includes personal Bath and walk-in closet

- MAIN FLOOR — 1,883 SQ. FT.
- LOWER LEVEL — 1,395 SQ. FT.
- SUNPORCH — 131 SQ. FT.
- BASEMENT — 619 SQ. FT.
- GARAGE — 722 SQ. FT.

TOTAL LIVING AREA — 3,278 SQ. FT.

No. 10497

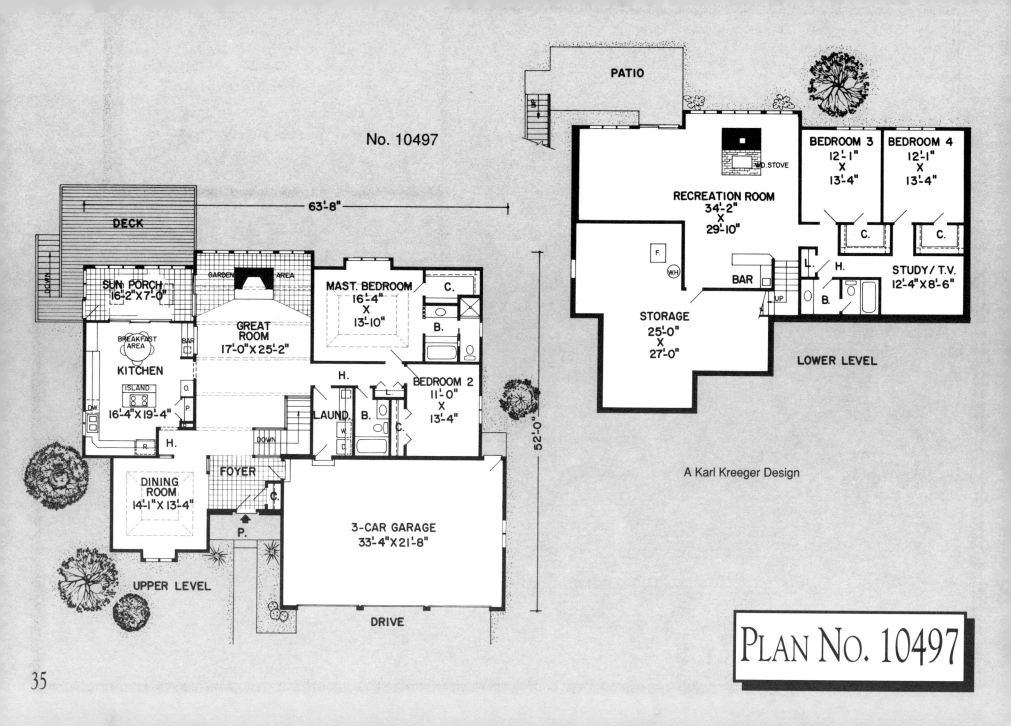

DECK

63'-8"

SUN PORCH
16'-2"X7'-0"

GARDEN AREA

KITCHEN

BREAKFAST
AREA

BAR

ISLAND

16'-4"X19'-4"

DW.

Q.

P.

R.

H.

GREAT
ROOM
17'-0"X25'-2"

MAST. BEDROOM
16'-4"
X
13'-10"

C.

B.

H.

LAUND.

B.

DOWN

FOYER

C.

BEDROOM 2
11'-0"
X
13'-4"

52'-0"

DINING
ROOM
14'-1"X 13'-4"

P.

C.

3-CAR GARAGE
33'-4"X 21'-8"

UPPER LEVEL

DRIVE

PATIO

RECREATION ROOM
34'-2"
X
29'-10"

WD. STOVE

BEDROOM 3
12'-1"
X
13'-4"

BEDROOM 4
12'-1"
X
13'-4"

C.

C.

F.

W.H.

BAR

UP

L.

H.

B.

STUDY/ T.V.
12'-4"X8'-6"

STORAGE
25'-0"
X
27'-0"

LOWER LEVEL

A Karl Kreeger Design

PLAN NO. 10497

SURROUNDED BY MULTI-LEVEL DECKS

- ❏ Enter Utility Room with built-in counter and ample closet space from stucco 3-car Garage

- ❏ Extra lighting and cabinets add to island Kitchen opening to bright sunny Family Room

- ❏ Unique octagonal-shaped Dining Room leads to immense covered deck and steps down to fireplaced Living Room

- ❏ Enjoy view of Foyer below from second floor landing with linen closet

- ❏ Master Bedroom with personal deck features window in walk-in closet and plenty of living and decorating space

- ❏ Master Bath has his-n-hers vanity, linen closet and luxurious circular glass-walled shower

- ❏ Bedroom Two offers good-sized closet and breathtaking view through extra-large window

- ❏ Bedroom Three includes sizeable walk-in closet and opens to shared double vanitied Bath

- ❏ FIRST FLOOR — 2,358 SQ. FT.
- ❏ SECOND FLOOR — 700 SQ. FT.
- ❏ GARAGE — 954 SQ. FT.

TOTAL LIVING AREA — 3,058 SQ. FT.

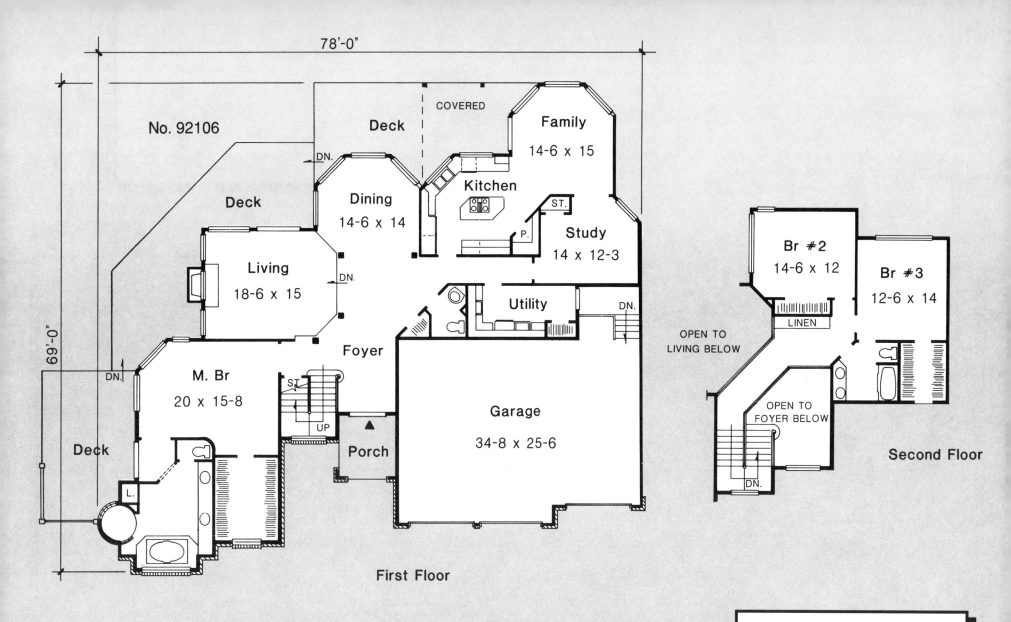

78'-0"

69'-0"

No. 92106

COVERED

Deck

Family
14-6 x 15

Deck

DN.

Dining
14-6 x 14

Kitchen

ST.

Living
18-6 x 15

Study
14 x 12-3

P.

DN.

Utility

DN.

Foyer

Deck

DN.

M. Br
20 x 15-8

ST

UP

Garage
34-8 x 25-6

Porch

L.

First Floor

Br #2
14-6 x 12

Br #3
12-6 x 14

OPEN TO
LIVING BELOW

LINEN

OPEN TO
FOYER BELOW

Second Floor

DN.

PLAN No. 92106

37

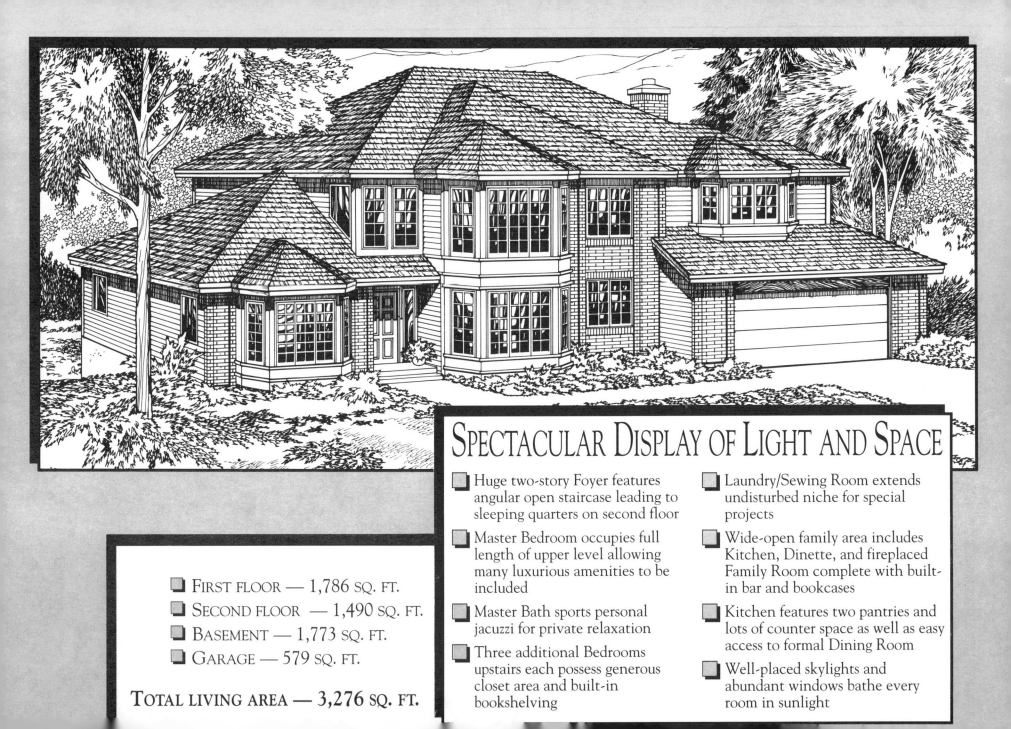

SPECTACULAR DISPLAY OF LIGHT AND SPACE

- Huge two-story Foyer features angular open staircase leading to sleeping quarters on second floor

- Master Bedroom occupies full length of upper level allowing many luxurious amenities to be included

- Master Bath sports personal jacuzzi for private relaxation

- Three additional Bedrooms upstairs each possess generous closet area and built-in bookshelving

- Laundry/Sewing Room extends undisturbed niche for special projects

- Wide-open family area includes Kitchen, Dinette, and fireplaced Family Room complete with built-in bar and bookcases

- Kitchen features two pantries and lots of counter space as well as easy access to formal Dining Room

- Well-placed skylights and abundant windows bathe every room in sunlight

- FIRST FLOOR — 1,786 SQ. FT.
- SECOND FLOOR — 1,490 SQ. FT.
- BASEMENT — 1,773 SQ. FT.
- GARAGE — 579 SQ. FT.

TOTAL LIVING AREA — 3,276 SQ. FT.

No. 10686

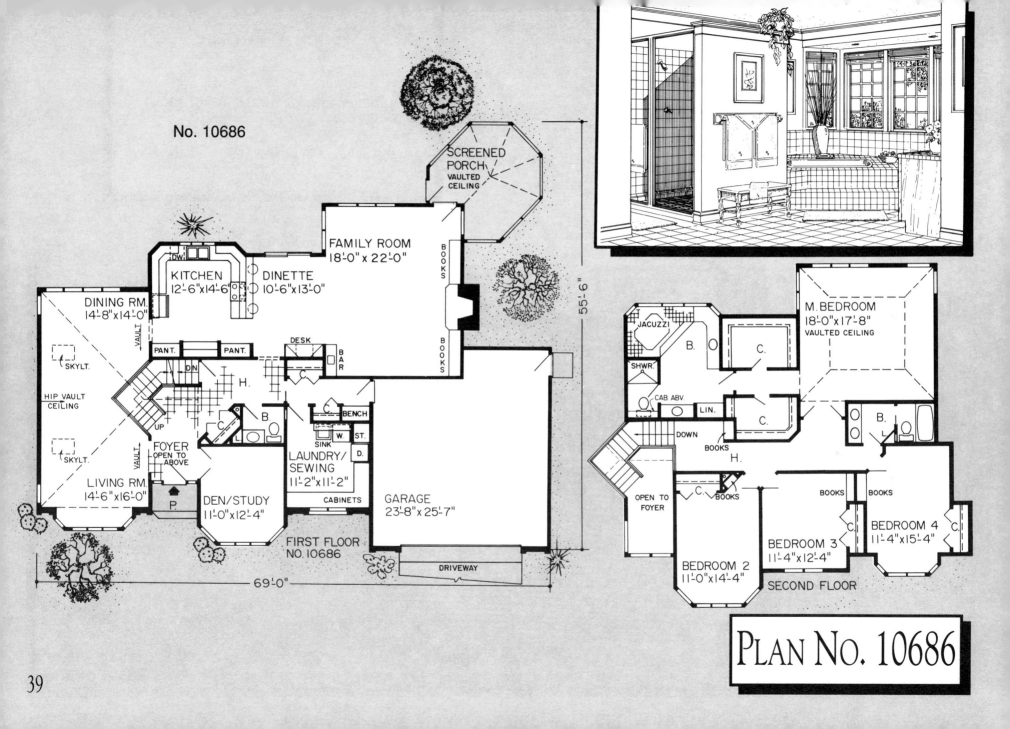

FAMILY ROOM
18'-0" x 22'-0"

SCREENED PORCH
VAULTED CEILING

BOOKS
BOOKS

55'-6"

KITCHEN
12'-6"x14'-6"

DINETTE
10'-6"x13'-0"

DINING RM.
14'-8"x14'-0"

DW

PANT.   PANT.

DESK

BAR

DN

H.

VAULT

SKYLT.

HIP VAULT CEILING

BENCH

UP

C B.

W.

SINK

ST.

D.

LAUNDRY/ SEWING
11'-2"x11'-2"

FOYER
OPEN TO ABOVE

SKYLT.

VAULT

P.

DEN/STUDY
11'-0"x12'-4"

CABINETS

GARAGE
23'-8"x 25'-7"

LIVING RM.
14'-6"x16'-0"

FIRST FLOOR
NO.10686

DRIVEWAY

69'-0"

JACUZZI

B.

C.

M. BEDROOM
18'-0"x17'-8"
VAULTED CEILING

SHWR.

CAB. ABV.

LIN.

C.

DOWN

BOOKS

B.

L

H.

OPEN TO FOYER

C. BOOKS

BOOKS

BOOKS

C.

C.

BEDROOM 3
11'-4"x12'-4"

BEDROOM 4
11'-4"x15'-4"

BEDROOM 2
11'-0"x14'-4"

SECOND FLOOR

PLAN NO. 10686

TIMELESS ELEGANCE

- ☐ Step through Foyer past stairway into massive Living Room characterized by high ceiling, abundant windows, and access to private rear deck

- ☐ Both Living and Hearth Rooms share easy entertaining and cozy atmosphere with two-way access to wetbar and fireplace

- ☐ Steal away to quiet solitude in Parlor/Library for serious contemplation or light conversation with good friends

- ☐ Recessed ceiling, twin walk-in closets and luxurious Bath adorn first floor Master Suite

- ☐ Three ample Bedrooms enjoy walk-in closets and neighboring Baths upstairs

- ☐ Overlook tiled Foyer and Living Room from balcony above

- ☐ Revealed ceiling in Dining Room adds sophistication to formal meals

- ☐ Adjoining Kitchen with handy breakfast bar and nearby pantry is marvel of convenience

- ☐ FIRST FLOOR — 2,080 SQ. FT.
- ☐ SECOND FLOOR — 1,051 SQ. FT.
- ☐ BASEMENT — 2,080 SQ. FT.
- ☐ GARAGE — 666 SQ. FT.

TOTAL LIVING AREA — 3,131 SQ. FT.

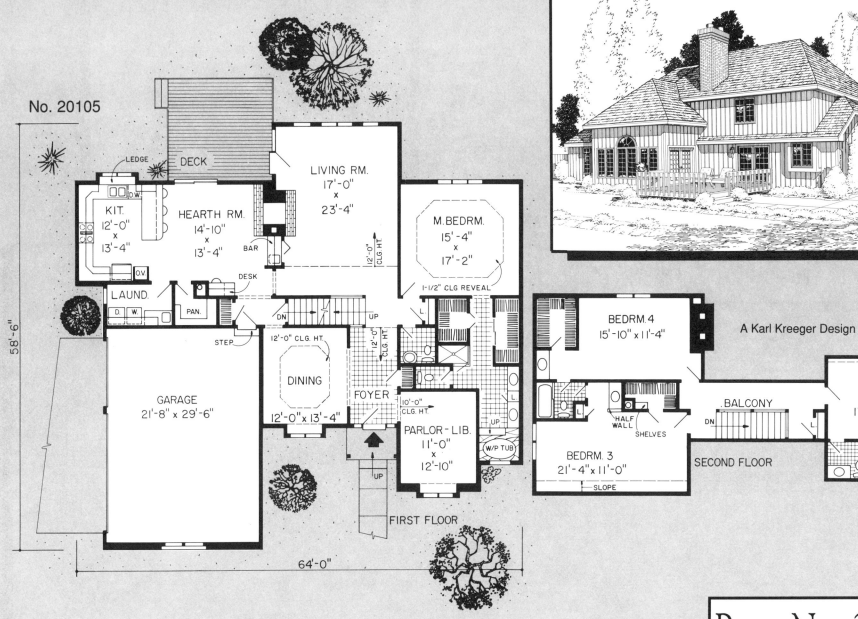

No. 20105

58'-6"

DECK

LEDGE

KIT.
12'-0"
x
13'-4"

D.W.

O.V.

HEARTH RM.
14'-10"
x
13'-4"

BAR

LIVING RM.
17'-0"
x
23'-4"

12'-0" CLG. HT.

M.BEDRM.
15'-4"
x
17'-2"

1-1/2" CLG REVEAL

LAUND.

D.   W.

PAN.

DESK

STEP

DN   UP

12'-0" CLG. HT.

12'-0" CLG. HT.

L.

GARAGE
21'-8" x 29'-6"

DINING
12'-0"x 13'-4"

FOYER

UP

PARLOR - LIB.
11'-0"
x
12'-10"

10'-0"
CLG. HT.

W/P TUB

L.

UP

UP

FIRST FLOOR

64'-0"

BEDRM. 4
15'-10" x 11'-4"

A Karl Kreeger Design

BEDRM. 3
21'-4"x 11'-0"

HALF
WALL

SHELVES

SLOPE

BALCONY

DN

SECOND FLOOR

L.

SLOPE

BEDRM. 2
17'-2" x 11'-0"

TO ATTIC

PLAN NO. 20105

B. LeBold

UPPER DECK AFFORDS ROADSIDE VIEW

- Dominating staircase in Foyer wraps around planter basking in light from skylight far above
- Flanked by Library and Living Room, Foyer leads back to island Kitchen with extra amenities
- Kitchen centrally located to serve formal Dining Area and Breakfast Room
- Warm up informal gatherings at fireplace in Family Room containing large wetbar

- Master Suite on upper floor presents formidable escape spot from remainder of home
- Private deck, oversized double walk-in closet, double vanities and special tub setting render Master Suite truly luxurious
- Three additional Bedrooms on second floor provide ample room for children
- Overlook staircase and planter in Foyer from Sitting Area/Balcony or enjoy roadside view from deck

- FIRST FLOOR — 2,573 SQ. FT.
- SECOND FLOOR — 2,390 SQ. FT.
- BASEMENT — 1,844 SQ. FT.
- CRAWL SPACE — 793 SQ. FT.
- GARAGE — 1,080 SQ. FT.

TOTAL LIVING AREA — 4,963 SQ. FT.

No. 10768

SECOND FLOOR

DECK

DN

UP
BATH
V.

M.BEDRM.
19'-4"
x
19'-0"

SITTING
10'-6" x 7'-2"

S.L.

CHUTE

B.

BEDRM.2
12'-6"
x
14'-10"

BEDRM.3
17'-0"
x
14'-1"

BOOKS

BEDRM.4
12'-4"
x
12'-1"

SKY
LT.

DN

B.
LIN

SITTING / BALC.

DECK

BEDRM.5
17'-0"
x
14'-1"

SEAT

LEDGE
SEAT
FAN

LEDGE
DW

BRKFST.
12'-0"
x
17'-10"

KITCHEN

ISLAND

BRICK
ARCH.
ABV.
MW

DINING
12'-4"
x
18'-4"

UP

DN

CHUTE

L.
D. W.

FAMILY ROOM
15'-0"
x
25'-0"

O.V.

C.

DESK

PANTRY

DN

SCREEN PORCH

52'-6"

CONV. PIT
15'-0"
x
12'-0"

UP

DN

DN

WET
BAR
ICE MACH.
R.

PDR.

DN UP

LIVING ROOM
17'-0"
x
20'-4"

GARAGE
39'-2" x 27'-4"

BENCH COATS

DOOR

LIBRARY
12'-4"
x
11'-4"

FOYER

UP

UP

PORCH

UP

FIRST FLOOR
(9' CLG. HEIGHT)

122'-0"

PLAN No. 10768

43

Plan Separates Formal and Family Areas

- Elegant home easily entertains without dislocating children

- Sunken Study, Living Room, and Dining Room surround central Foyer

- Informal areas in rear of house include island Kitchen with large walk-in pantry

- Pantry adjacent to skylit Breakfast Room and convenient Laundry Room

- Guest Room features spacious walk-in closet and private Bath

- Family Room with vaulted ceiling, built-in bar and entertainment center includes direct access to vaulted Porch

- Ascend curving staircase to find wide-open Balcony Loft for semi-private contemplation

- Master Suite features tray ceiling, large walk-in closet, private Bath, and deck overlooking backyard vista

- Two additional Bedrooms upstairs connected by adjoining Bathroom

- First floor — 2,516 sq. ft.
- Second floor — 1,602 sq. ft.
- Basement — 2,516 sq. ft.
- Garage — 822 sq. ft.

Total living area — 4,118 sq. ft.

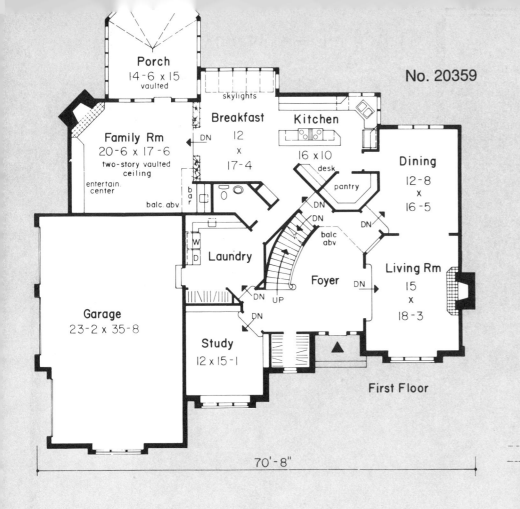

Porch
14-6 x 15
vaulted

No. 20359

skylights

Breakfast
12
x
17-4

Kitchen

16 x 10

desk

Family Rm
20-6 x 17-6
two-story vaulted
ceiling

entertain.
center

balc. abv.

bar

DN

pantry

Dining
12-8
x
16-5

DN

DN

DN

balc
abv

DN

Laundry

W
D

Foyer

UP

DN

DN

DN

Living Rm
15
x
18-3

Garage
23-2 x 35-8

Study
12 x 15-1

First Floor

70'-8"

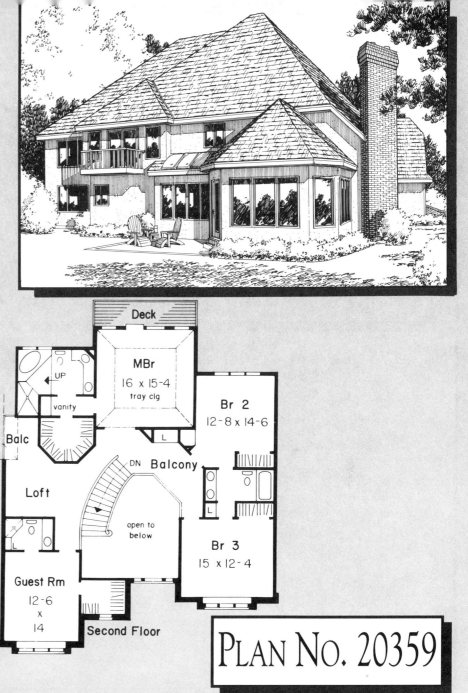

Deck

MBr
16 x 15-4
tray clg

Br 2
12-8 x 14-6

Balc

UP

vanity

DN Balcony

L

Loft

open to
below

L

Br 3
15 x 12-4

L

Guest Rm
12-6
x
14

Second Floor

PLAN NO. 20359

45

FOUR FIREPLACES INSURE COMFORT

- ☐ Gracious brick facade punctuated by arched windows hints at interior elegance

- ☐ Three steps down, sunny fireplaced Gathering Room boasts sliders to beautiful rear terrace

- ☐ Centrally placed island Kitchen just steps away from both Dining Room and handy Laundry room

- ☐ Private sunken Lounge offers occupants comfortable setting for intimate conversation

- ☐ Master suite provides personal retreat occupying entire wing of second floor

- ☐ Step down for huge walk-in closet after reposing luxuriously in raised tub in Master Bath

- ☐ Three additional Bedrooms on second floor furnish plenty of room for children

- ☐ Vast storage area at end of upper floor hallway resolves clutter problems

☐ FIRST FLOOR — 2,126 SQ. FT.
☐ SECOND FLOOR — 1,882 SQ. FT.
☐ BASEMENT — 1,169 SQ. FT.
☐ GARAGE — 2-CAR

TOTAL LIVING AREA — 4,008 SQ. FT.

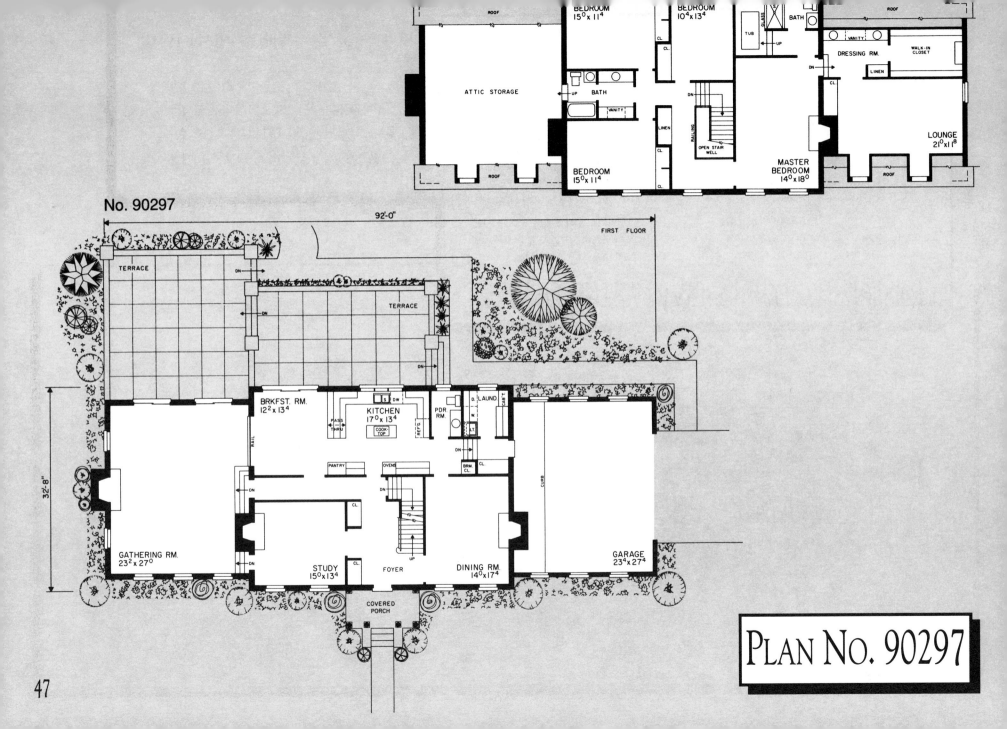

BEDROOM
15⁰ x 11⁴

BEDROOM
10⁴ x 13⁴

GLASS

BATH

TUB

UP

DRESSING RM.

WALK-IN
CLOSET

DN

VANITY

ATTIC STORAGE

UP

BATH

CL.

LINEN

CL.

LINEN

LOUNGE
21⁰ x 11⁸

ROOF

VANITY

RAILING

DN

CL.

OPEN STAIR
WELL

BEDROOM
15⁰ x 11⁴

MASTER
BEDROOM
14⁰ x 18⁰

ROOF

ROOF

No. 90297

92'-0"

FIRST FLOOR

TERRACE

DN

TERRACE

DN

DN

32'-8"

BRKFST. RM.
12² x 13⁴

KITCHEN
17⁰ x 13⁴

S DW

COOK-
TOP

PASS
THRU

REFG.

D. LAUND.

CAB'T

PDR.
RM.

W

DT

RAIL

PANTRY

OVENS

DN

BRM.
CL.

CL.

CL.

DN

CURB

GATHERING RM.
23² x 27⁰

DN

UP

STUDY
15⁰ x 13⁴

CL.

FOYER

DINING RM.
14⁰ x 17⁴

GARAGE
23⁴ x 27⁴

COVERED
PORCH

PLAN No. 90297

47

Soaring Entry Marks Fabulous Design

- Two-story Entry with tiled floor and angular staircase favorably impresses all who enter
- French doors to the den extend cordial welcome for private concentration or pleasurable pastimes
- Step down into sunken Living Room with fireplace bordered by formal Dining Room
- Large Kitchen with work top island blends into Nook for informal family meals
- Sunken Family Room steps up to Kitchen area for convenient late-night snacking
- Master Suite on upper floor features two vanities with individual basins, garden tub, and huge walk-in closet
- Two additional Bedrooms, full Bath, and a Bonus Room occupy remainder of second floor

- FIRST FLOOR — 1,613 SQ. FT.
- SECOND FLOOR — 1,262 SQ. FT.
- BONUS ROOM — 424 SQ. FT.
- GARAGE — 3-CAR

TOTAL LIVING AREA — 2,875 SQ. FT.

No. 90514

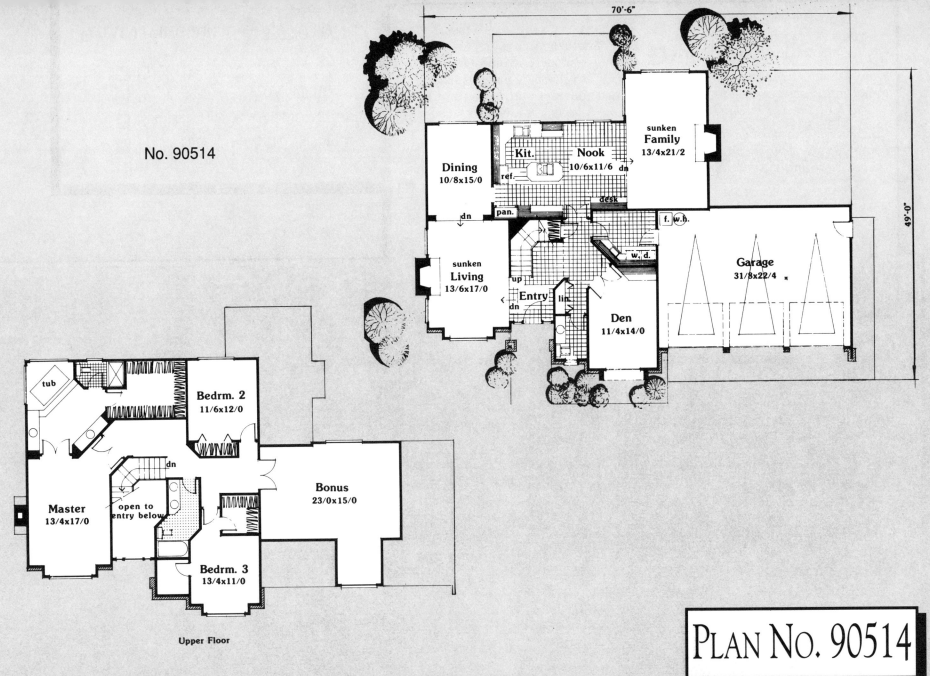

70'-6"

49'-0"

Dining
10/8x15/0

Kit.

ref.

Nook
10/6x11/6

sunken
Family
13/4x21/2

desk

dn

pan.

f. w. h.

sunken
Living
13/6x17/0

w. d.

Garage
31/8x22/4

up

Entry

lin

dn

Den
11/4x14/0

tub

Bedrm. 2
11/6x12/0

dn

Bonus
23/0x15/0

Master
13/4x17/0

open to
entry below

Bedrm. 3
13/4x11/0

Upper Floor

PLAN No. 90514

49

MODERN COLONIAL

- Light streaming in from front window display brightens two-story Entry with angled stairway

- Living Room with arched windows and formal Dining Room frame Entry for convenient ushering of guests

- Oversized country Kitchen featuring central island and eat-in bar situated adjacent to Dining Room and opens to Dinette for ease in mealtime service

- Informal Den offers housing for book collection with built-in shelving and direct access to 3-Season porch

- Elaborate Master Suite highlighted by huge walk-in closet and twin vanities in Master Bath

- Attain ultimate relaxation in whirlpool tub in Master Bath with windows overlooking rear of yard

- Three additional Bedrooms include individual closet space and each adjoins full Bath

- FIRST FLOOR — 2,070 SQ. FT.
- SECOND FLOOR — 1,500 SQ. FT.
- BASEMENT — 1,863 SQ. FT.
- GARAGE — 772 SQ. FT.

TOTAL LIVING AREA — 3,570 SQ. FT.

No. 92304

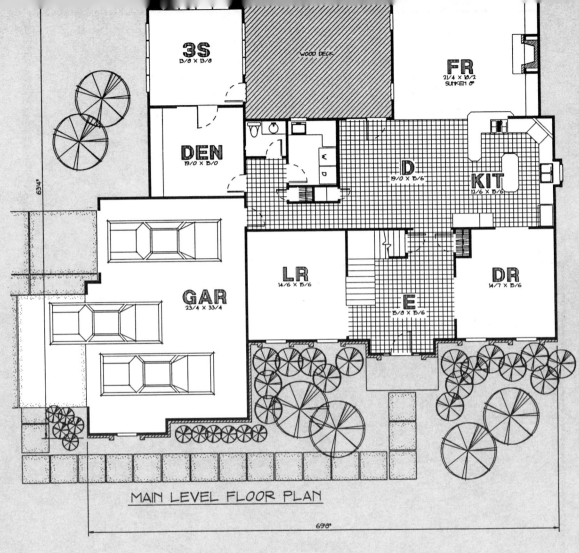

FR
21/4 x 18/2
SUNKEN 8"

3S
13/8 x 13/0

DEN
13/0 x 13/0

D
13/0 x 13/6

KIT
12/6 x 13/6

WOOD DECK

GAR
23/4 x 33/4

LR
14/6 x 13/6

E
13/0 x 13/6

DR
14/7 x 13/6

MAIN LEVEL FLOOR PLAN

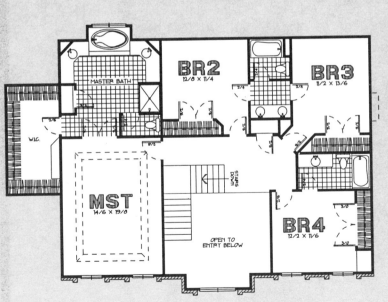

MASTER BATH

W.I.C.

BR2
12/8 x 11/4

BR3
11/2 x 13/6

MST
14/6 x 19/0

STAIRS DOWN

OPEN TO
ENTRY BELOW

BR4
12/2 x 11/6

UPPER LEVEL FLOOR PLAN

PLAN NO. 92304

AT HOME ON A HILLSIDE

- Show guests into beautiful Living Room sharing entry level with private Master Suite

- Dine in elegance overlooking Living Room fireplace

- Comfortable Family Room with built-in bar and close proximity to Kitchen and patio provides excellent choice for casual recess

- Three additional Bedrooms and full Bath located half-flight up away from active areas assures quiet atmosphere

- Master Suite features oversized Dressing Room leading into large walk-in closet

- Raised tub filled with silky bubbles in Master Bath induces true relaxation

- Large Laundry Area with built-in sewing center located adjacent to Master Suite

- Kitchen and handy Powder Room just steps away for convenience

- FIRST FLOOR — 2,388 SQ. FT.
- SECOND FLOOR — 709 SQ. FT.
- BASEMENT — 1,358 SQ. FT.
- GARAGE — 928 SQ. FT.

TOTAL LIVING AREA — 3,097 SQ. FT.

No. 90559

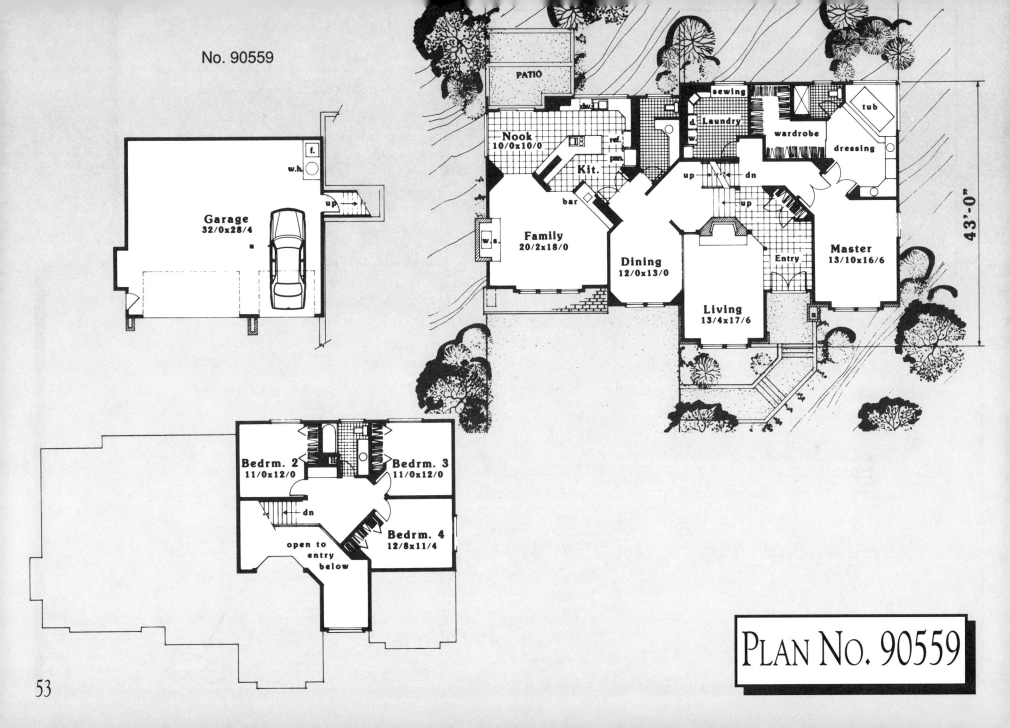

Garage
32/0x28/4

w.h.
f.

up

PATIO

sewing

Nook
10/0x10/0

d
Laundry
w

Kit.

ref.

pan.

wardrobe

tub

dressing

up   dn

bar

Family
20/2x18/0

w.s.

up

Dining
12/0x13/0

Entry

Master
13/10x16/6

Living
13/4x17/6

43'-0"

Bedrm. 2
11/0x12/0

Bedrm. 3
11/0x12/0

dn

Bedrm. 4
12/8x11/4

open to
entry
below

53

PLAN No. 90559

FAMILY HOME WITH FLAIR

- Brick beauty characterized by graceful arches, twin chimneys, and abundant, oversized windows
- Double doors topped by massive transom window opens to two-story Entry
- Sunken formal Living Room and impressive U-shaped stairway, washed with sunlight, flank foyer
- Well-equipped island Kitchen adjoins Nook overlooking backyard
- Fireplaced Family Room only steps away from Kitchen for TV snacking with family
- Private Master Suite sports luxurious raised garden tub, double vanities, and room-size closet
- Three additional Bedrooms on second floor share full Bath with twin basins
- Bonus room over 3-car Garage accessible from second staircase off Family Room or Bedroom hall offers many optional uses

- FIRST FLOOR — 1,626 SQ. FT.
- SECOND FLOOR — 1,473 SQ. FT.
- BONUS — 487 SQ. FT.
- BASEMENT — 1,605 SQ. FT.
- GARAGE — 3-CAR

TOTAL LIVING AREA — 3,586 SQ. FT.

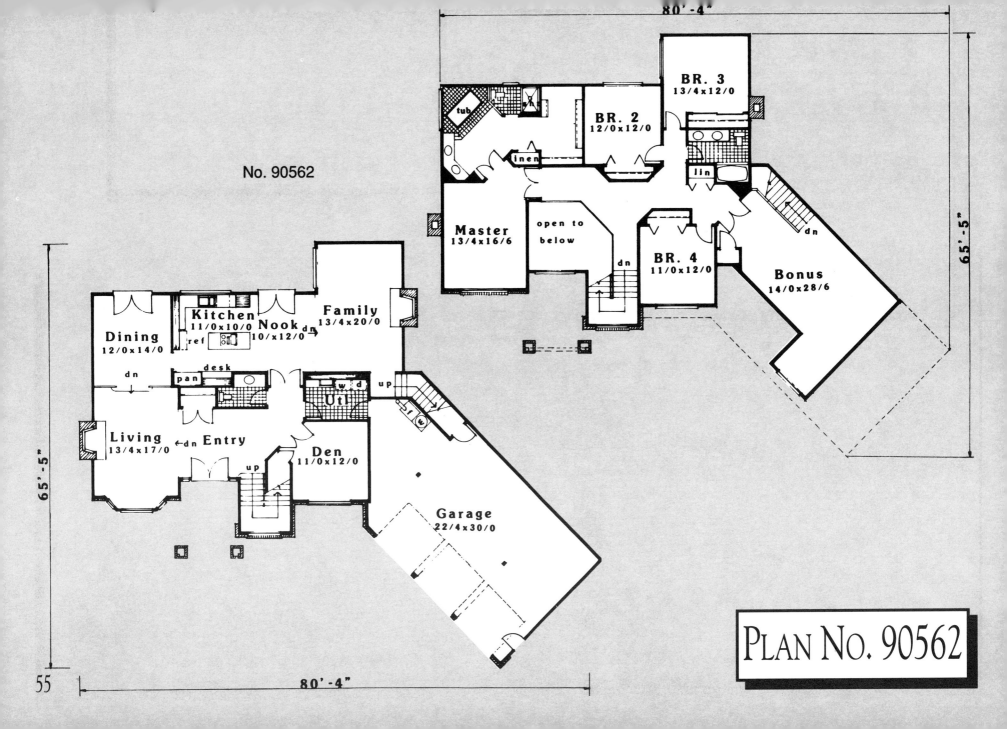

No. 90562

80'-4"

65'-5"

BR. 3
13/4 x 12/0

tub

BR. 2
12/0 x 12/0

linen

lin

Master
13/4 x 16/6

open to below

dn

BR. 4
11/0 x 12/0

dn

Bonus
14/0 x 28/6

65'-5"

Family
13/4 x 20/0

Kitchen
11/0 x 10/0

Nook
10/ x 12/0

dn

Dining
12/0 x 14/0

ref

dn

pan

desk

Utl

w d

up

Living
13/4 x 17/0

dn **Entry**

up

Den
11/0 x 12/0

Garage
22/4 x 30/0

55

80'-4"

PLAN NO. 90562

Porch Recalls Romantic Era

- ☐ Interior spaces characterized by distinctive ceiling treatments, sloping ceilings pierced by skylights, and smart room placements

- ☐ Efficient Kitchen with snack bar easily serves Breakfast Room

- ☐ Hexagonal Breakfast Room enjoys bright sunshine through abundant windows

- ☐ Large cedar closet with access to attic offers safe storage place for valuable items

- ☐ Expansive family area with fireplace exudes welcoming warmth to friends and family

- ☐ Front Parlor off Foyer offers cozy spot to visit with not-so-formal guests

- ☐ Roomy Master Bedroom with private Bath offers plenty of closet space

- ☐ Three Bedrooms on second floor sport lots of individual closet area but share full Bath with double vanities

- ☐ First floor — 1,843 sq. ft.
- ☐ Second floor — 1,039 sq. ft.
- ☐ Basement — 1,843 sq. ft.
- ☐ Garage — 484 sq. ft.

Total living area — 2,882 sq. ft.

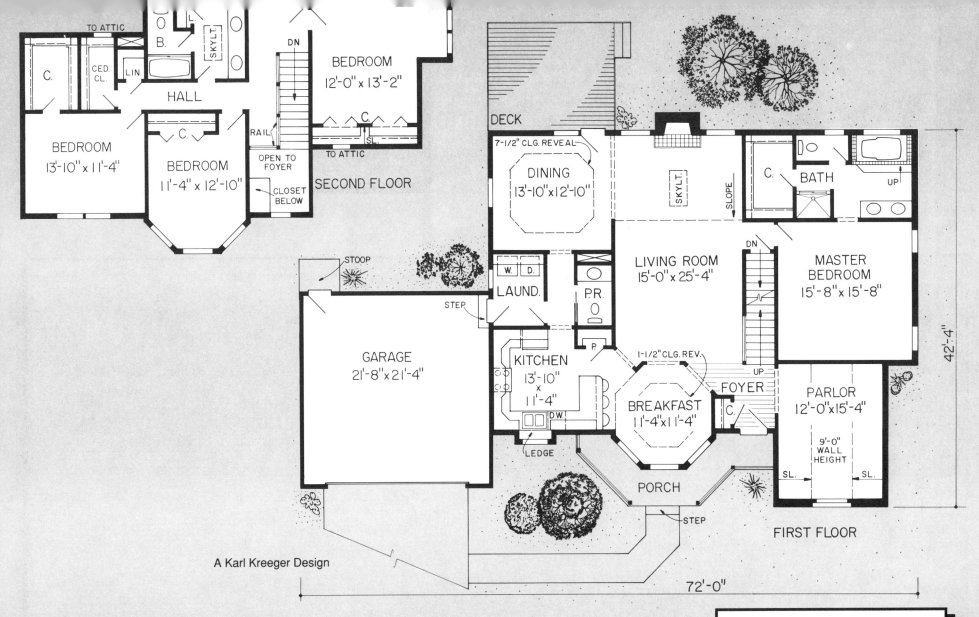

TO ATTIC

C.

CED. CL.

LIN.

B.

SKYLT.

HALL

BEDROOM
13'-10" x 11'-4"

C.

BEDROOM
11'-4" x 12'-10"

RAIL

OPEN TO FOYER

CLOSET BELOW

DN

BEDROOM
12'-0" x 13'-2"

C.

SL.

TO ATTIC

SECOND FLOOR

DECK

7-1/2" CLG. REVEAL

DINING
13'-10" x 12'-10"

SKYLT.

SLOPE

LIVING ROOM
15'-0" x 25'-4"

C.

BATH

UP

W. D.

LAUND.

P.R.

DN

MASTER BEDROOM
15'-8" x 15'-8"

STOOP

STEP

GARAGE
21'-8" x 21'-4"

KITCHEN
13'-10"
x
11'-4"

D.W.

LEDGE

P.

1-1/2" CLG. REV.

BREAKFAST
11'-4" x 11'-4"

C.

FOYER

UP

PARLOR
12'-0" x 15'-4"

9'-0"
WALL
HEIGHT

SL.

SL.

PORCH

STEP

FIRST FLOOR

A Karl Kreeger Design

72'-0"

42'-4"

PLAN No. 20098

TRADITIONAL SPLENDOR

- ❑ Gourmet Kitchen with elegant eating bar comfortably seats seven people

- ❑ Enjoy family barbeques on backyard deck with optional bench and convenience access to Kitchen and Family Room

- ❑ Dining Room on other side of room-sized pantry in close proximity of Kitchen for ease in formal entertaining

- ❑ Six Bedrooms and 4-1/2 baths accommodates large families

- ❑ Bayed sitting area in Master Bedroom provides ideal quiet spot for avid reader

- ❑ Master Bath features plenty of storage space with huge walk-in closet and separate wardrobe

- ❑ Overlook impressive Entry on one side and vaulted Living Room from opposite side of skylit balcony on second floor

- ❑ Daylight basement to rear of home designed for two guest rooms, multipurpose area and full bath

- ❑ FIRST FLOOR — 2,376 SQ. FT.
- ❑ SECOND FLOOR — 1,048 SQ. FT.
- ❑ BASEMENT — 2,376 SQ. FT.
- ❑ GARAGE — 3-CAR

TOTAL LIVING AREA — 3,424 SQ. FT.

No. 91339

BDRM. #3
13'-3" X 11'-0"

WINDOW SEAT

VAULTED CLG.

BDRM. #5
11'-0" X 12'-0"

SEAT

WARDROBE

OPEN RAILING

WARDROBE

LINEN

VANITY

BATH

VANITY

LINEN

(2) 4"x 2" SKYLTS
(OPTIONAL)

OPEN RAILING

WARDROBE

VANITY

OPEN
TO
BELOW

5'0 TUB
W/SHOWER

BATH

VANITY

WARDROBE

SHELF

BDRM. #4
12'-0" X 11'-0"

BDRM. #6
14'-0" X 12'-6"

WINDOW SEAT

OPTIONAL BENCH

D E C K

D E C K

LIVING RM.
15'-0" X 20'-6"

T.C.

DBL. SINK

DW

KITCHEN
14'-0" X 15'-6"

EATING BAR

RANGE

OVEN

REFRIG.

BROOMS

DEN
12'-0" X 11'-0"

MSTR. BDRM.
16'-0" X 16'-6"

FIREPLACE w
GLASS DOORS EACH SIDE

FAMILY RM.
12'-0" X 14'-0"

VANITY

WARDROBE

5'0 TUB
SHOWER

WALK-IN
WARDROBE

**MSTR.
BATH**

VANITY

**COMPUTER
DEN**
7'-0" X 12'-6"

DESK

STORAGE

PANTRY

SHELVES

GUESTS

STORAGE

DN
1R

5'0 TUB
SHOWER

BATH

VANITY

LAUNDRY

WARDROBE

DRYER

WSHR

STORAGE

D.N.K.

2/8 · 4/0

SHOWER

GARAGE
20'-4" X 34'-0"

DINING RM.
12'-0" X 15'-0"

ENTRY

DN
5R

BDRM. #2
14'-0" X 12'-3"

UP
STEP

UP
STEP

PLAN No. 91339

59

STATELY STUCCO MASTERPIECE

- Old world touches manifested in towering palladium windows, columned entry, and curving staircase

- Vaulted Foyer opens to Living Room featuring huge expanses of glass taking advantage of rear view

- Wide open Kitchen with efficient layout flows into Family Room

- Overlook magnificent staircase and vaulted Foyer from Balcony on second floor

- Enjoy direct access to backyard deck via comfortable Family Room with vaulted ceiling, fireplace, and wetbar

- Marvelous Master Suite beckons occupants to luxuriate in first-class accommodations

- Design offers three additional Bedrooms for remainder of family

- Formal Dining Room embellished with built-in buffet and convenient location adjacent to Kitchen

- FIRST FLOOR — 2,125 SQ. FT.
- SECOND FLOOR — 1,103 SQ. FT.
- BASEMENT — 2,125 SQ. FT.
- GARAGE — 3-CAR

TOTAL LIVING AREA — 3,228 SQ. FT.

No. 91414

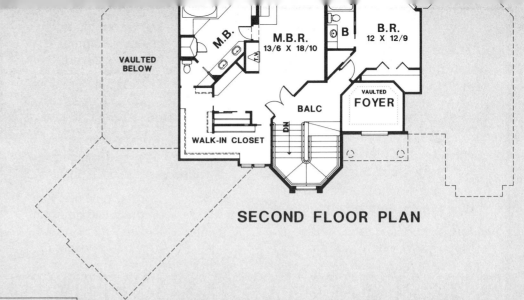

SECOND FLOOR PLAN

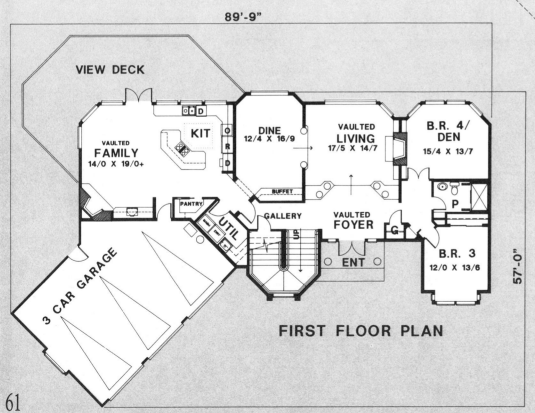

FIRST FLOOR PLAN

PLAN NO. 91414

61

PRIVATE COURT OUTSIDE MASTER BEDROOM

- ☐ Secluded from the rest of first floor, Master Bedroom Suite includes oversized walk-in closet and personal Bath

- ☐ Adjoining luxurious Master Bedroom is private courtyard complete with hot tub

- ☐ Enter cozy Library through French doors from Foyer

- ☐ Comfortable Morning Room features built-in linen closet, china cabinet and desk

- ☐ Focal point of spacious Living Room is warm welcoming fireplace

- ☐ Wine storage area behind bar in Living Room for convenience

- ☐ Walk out to Sun Porch through French doors in Dining Room

- ☐ Overlook Living Room from second-floor railing

- ☐ Three additional Bedrooms, two Baths, and plenty of closet space adorn upstairs level

- ☐ FIRST FLOOR — 2,486 SQ. FT.
- ☐ SECOND FLOOR — 954 SQ. FT.
- ☐ BASEMENT — 2,486 SQ. FT.
- ☐ GARAGE — 576 SQ. FT.

TOTAL LIVING AREA — 3,440 SQ. FT.

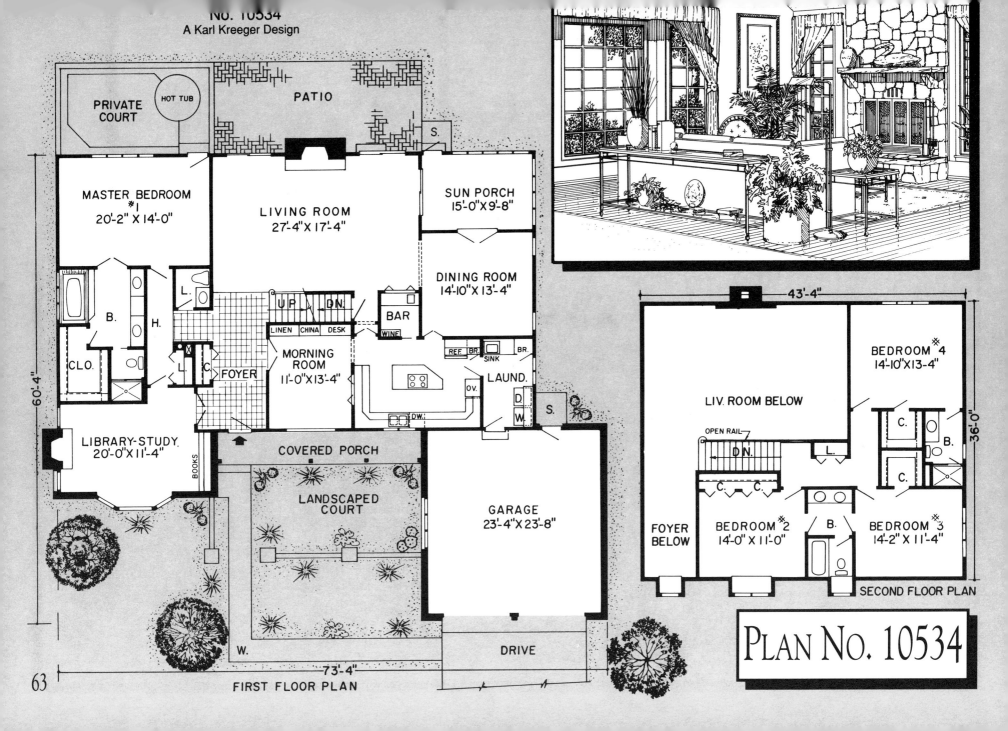

NO. 10534
A Karl Kreeger Design

PRIVATE COURT

HOT TUB

PATIO

S.

MASTER BEDROOM
#1
20'-2" X 14'-0"

LIVING ROOM
27'-4" X 17'-4"

SUN PORCH
15'-0" X 9'-8"

L.

B.   H.

DINING ROOM
14'-10" X 13'-4"

CLO.

UP   DN.

BAR

LINEN CHINA DESK

WINE

L. C.

FOYER

MORNING ROOM
11'-0" X 13'-4"

REF. BR.
SINK BR.

LAUND.

OV.

60'-4"

LIBRARY-STUDY.
20'-0" X 11'-4"

BOOKS

DW.

D.
W.   S.

COVERED PORCH

LANDSCAPED COURT

GARAGE
23'-4" X 23'-8"

W.

DRIVE

73'-4"

FIRST FLOOR PLAN

63

43'-4"

LIV. ROOM BELOW

BEDROOM #4
14'-10" X 13'-4"

OPEN RAIL

DN.

C. B.

L.

C.

36'-0"

C.   C.

B.

FOYER BELOW

BEDROOM #2
14'-0" X 11'-0"

B.

BEDROOM #3
14'-2" X 11'-4"

SECOND FLOOR PLAN

PLAN NO. 10534

FAMILY ROOM LINKED WITH OUTDOORS

- ☐ Angled stairway adds polished touch to two-story Entry

- ☐ Ample wetbar parallel to walk-in pantry links formal Dining Room to spacious Kitchen

- ☐ Efficient layout of Kitchen affords plenty of room for extra amenities such as built-in planning desk and stove-top/breakfast bar island

- ☐ Kitchen contains direct access to Screened Porch for expanded outdoor living space

- ☐ Built-in bookcases frame fireplace in Family Room for congenial display of books and/or collectibles

- ☐ Master Bedroom features two substantial walk-in closets, double vanities, and raised garden tub

- ☐ Two additional Bedrooms with sufficient closet space sharing full Bath occupy remainder of second level

- ☐ Enter home through convenient Laundry Room adjacent to Kitchen from 2-car Garage

- ☐ FIRST FLOOR — 1,642 SQ. FT.
- ☐ SECOND FLOOR — 1,428 SQ. FT.
- ☐ BASEMENT — 1,524 SQ. FT.
- ☐ GARAGE — 612 SQ. FT.

TOTAL LIVING AREA — 3,070 SQ. FT.

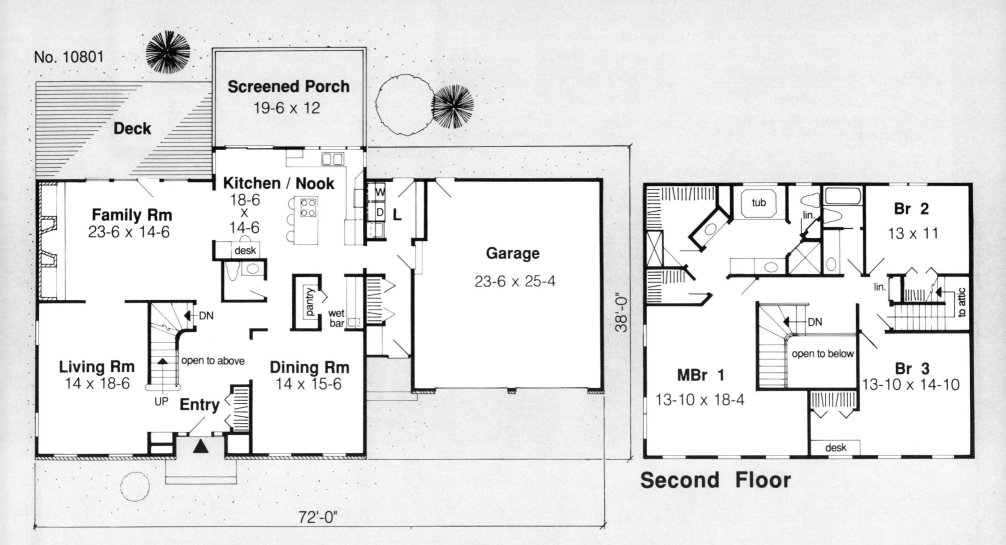

No. 10801

Screened Porch
19-6 x 12

Deck

Kitchen / Nook
18-6
x
14-6

Family Rm
23-6 x 14-6

desk

W
D
L

Garage
23-6 x 25-4

pantry

wet
bar

DN

Living Rm
14 x 18-6

open to above

Dining Rm
14 x 15-6

UP

Entry

38'-0"

72'-0"

First Floor

Second Floor

tub

lin.

Br 2
13 x 11

lin.

to attic

MBr 1
13-10 x 18-4

DN

open to below

Br 3
13-10 x 14-10

desk

PLAN NO. 10801

FIVE FIREPLACES ADD DISTINCTION

- Sprawling portico opens to two-story Foyer with sweeping view of overhead balcony
- Fireplaced Dining and Living Rooms allow for formal entertaining
- Towering Family Room leads out to an expansive rear terrace
- Rear-facing rooms linked to backyard with charming atrium doors
- Centrally located island Kitchen for easy service to active areas

- Huge Master suite has fireplace, luxurious walk-in closets, plush Bath, and extends into unique exercise room
- Upstairs Bedrooms feature twin walk-in closets and private baths
- Design topped with decorative glass-walled cupola to reflect air of elegance
- Guest room has desirable privacy and added comfort of adjoining Bath, perfect for entertaining visitors

- FIRST FLOOR — 4,104 SQ. FT.
- SECOND FLOOR — 979 SQ. FT.
- BASEMENT — 2,110 SQ. FT.
- GARAGE — 2-CAR

TOTAL LIVING AREA — 5,083 SQ. FT.

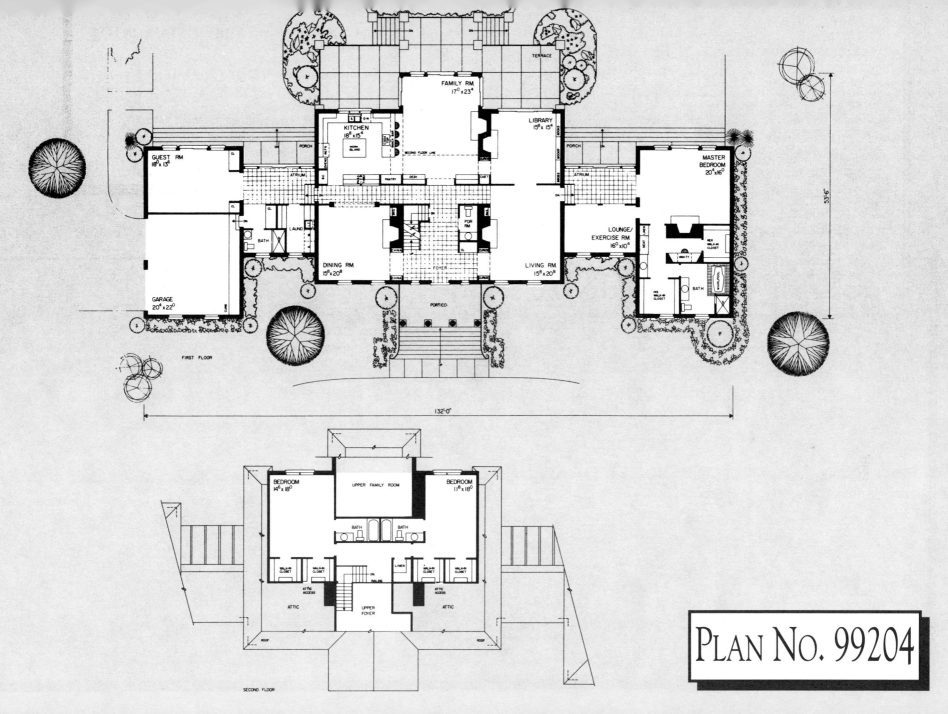

FAMILY RM.
17⁰ x 23⁴

KITCHEN
18⁰ x 15⁴

LIBRARY
15⁸ x 15⁴

TERRACE

GUEST RM
18⁰ x 13⁶

PORCH

ATRIUM

MASTER
BEDROOM
20⁴ x 16⁰

WORK
ISLAND

SECOND FLOOR LINE

PORCH

ATRIUM

CL

PANTRY DESK

CAB'T

DN

HER
WALK-IN
CLOSET

BATH

LAUND.

LOUNGE/
EXERCISE RM.
16⁰ x 10⁴

VANITY

POR.
RM.

WHIRLPOOL

CHINA

HIS
WALK-IN
CLOSET

BATH

DINING RM.
15⁸ x 20⁸

FOYER

LIVING RM.
15⁸ x 20⁸

GARAGE
20⁴ x 22⁰

CHINA

FIRST FLOOR

PORTICO

53'6"

132'-0"

BEDROOM
14⁶ x 18⁰

UPPER FAMILY ROOM

BEDROOM
11⁸ x 18⁰

BATH

BATH

WALK-IN
CLOSET

WALK-IN
CLOSET

LINEN

WALK-IN
CLOSET

WALK-IN
CLOSET

ATTIC
ACCESS

DN

RAILING

ATTIC
ACCESS

ATTIC

UPPER
FOYER

ATTIC

ROOF

ROOF

SECOND FLOOR

PLAN NO. 99204

BAY WINDOWS ABOUND

- Facade of impressive home has bay windows that hint at classic beauty found upon entering
- Two-story Foyer flanked by formal Living Room and Master suite
- Master Suite contains amenities such as spacious walk-in closet and amazing Bathroom
- Step past staircase in Foyer to rear of home to find formal Dining Room with bump-out window overlooking backyard
- Efficient gourmet Kitchen complete with range-top island for simple meal preparation
- Adjoining Breakfast Room abutts cozy fireplaced Hearth Room
- Ascend two-way staircase from either Hearth Room or Foyer for three more Bedrooms
- Each Bedroom has walk-in closet and adjoining Bath
- Note convenient laundry chute that will deliver clothes to first floor Laundry Room effortlessly

- FIRST FLOOR — 2,136 SQ. FT.
- SECOND FLOOR — 873 SQ. FT.
- BASEMENT — 2,130 SQ. FT.
- GARAGE — 720 SQ. FT.

TOTAL LIVING AREA — 3,009 SQ. FT.

No. 20138

A Karl Kreeger Design

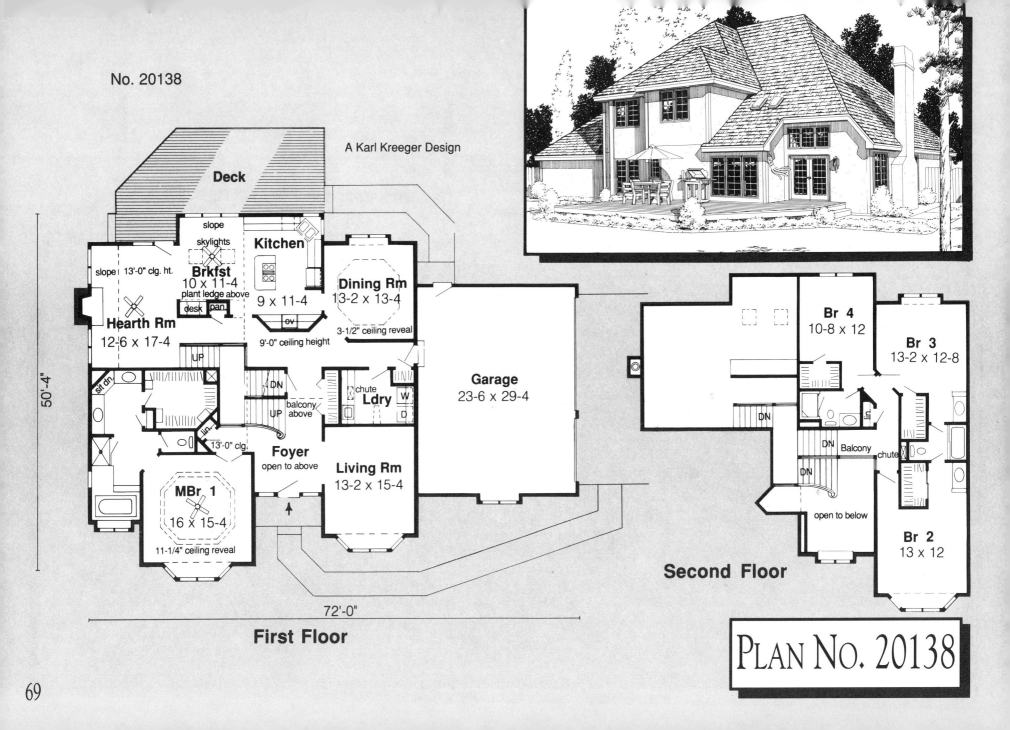

Deck

slope

skylights

Kitchen

Brkfst
10 x 11-4
plant ledge above

9 x 11-4

slope 13'-0" clg. ht.

desk pan.

Hearth Rm
12-6 x 17-4

Dining Rm
13-2 x 13-4

ov

3-1/2" ceiling reveal

9'-0" ceiling height

UP

Garage
23-6 x 29-4

DN

sit dn

chute

Ldry

W

D

balcony above

UP

13'-0" clg

Foyer
open to above

Living Rm
13-2 x 15-4

MBr 1
16 x 15-4

11-1/4" ceiling reveal

50'-4"

72'-0"

First Floor

Second Floor

W

Br 4
10-8 x 12

Br 3
13-2 x 12-8

DN

DN

Balcony

chute

DN

open to below

Br 2
13 x 12

PLAN No. 20138

TODAY'S FEATURES — YESTERDAY'S CHARM

- Clapboard siding and full-length covered Porch give friendly air to classic home with Colonial accent

- Central Entry opens to cozy Den

- Step down to sunken Living Room with fireplace and invite guests into adjoining Dining Room for formal entertaining

- Kitchen with food preparation island features wide-open airy atmosphere with cheerful Nook with bay windows

- Full Bath with double vanities serves two Bedrooms with lots of closet space on second floor

- Open space links Breakfast Nook with Family Room featuring a wetbar and access to three-season Porch and backyard deck

- Master Bedroom suite spans rear of house enjoying huge, walk-in closet

- Relax in raised whirlpool Bath after hard day's work in Master bath

- FIRST FLOOR — 1,622 SQ. FT.
- SECOND FLOOR — 1,156 SQ. FT.
- BASEMENT — 1,156 SQ. FT.
- GARAGE — 632 SQ. FT.

TOTAL LIVING AREA — 2,778 SQ. FT.

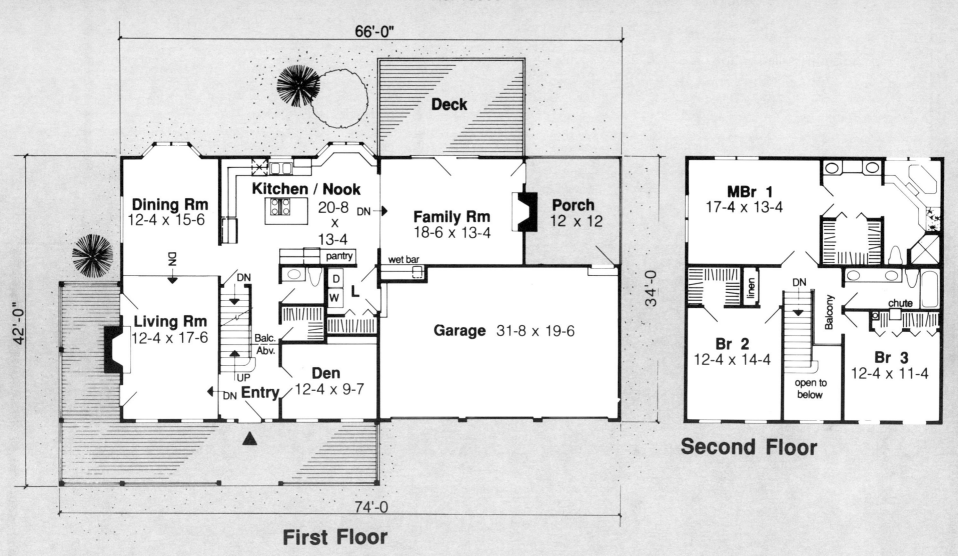

66'-0"

Deck

Dining Rm
12-4 x 15-6

Kitchen / Nook
20-8
x
13-4

DN

Family Rm
18-6 x 13-4

Porch
12 x 12

pantry

wet bar

D
W

L

42'-0"

34'-0

DN

DN

Living Rm
12-4 x 17-6

Balc.
Abv.

UP

DN **Entry**

Den
12-4 x 9-7

Garage   31-8 x 19-6

74'-0

First Floor

MBr 1
17-4 x 13-4

linen

DN

Balcony

chute

Br 2
12-4 x 14-4

open to
below

Br 3
12-4 x 11-4

Second Floor

PLAN NO. 10805

OVERSIZED WINDOWS LET SUN SHINE IN

- Two-story panorama greets guests through double doors into Foyer
- Fireplaced Living Room and formal Dining Room flank impressive entry
- Step up one level into Family Room with bay windows and inviting fireplace
- U-shaped Kitchen with triangular island embraces Family Room for convenient entertaining with friends or late night snacking with family
- Den located down the hall from family areas sports private passage to outdoor deck
- Ascend unique stairway to gain access to three Bedrooms and two Baths
- Included in Master Suite is huge walk-in closet
- Repose leisurely as spa in Master Bath massages aching muscles
- Stroll out to private deck to complete relaxation on warm evenings

- MAIN FLOOR — 1,843 SQ. FT.
- UPPER FLOOR — 1,053 SQ. FT.
- GARAGE — 760 SQ. FT.

TOTAL LIVING AREA — 2,896 SQ. FT.

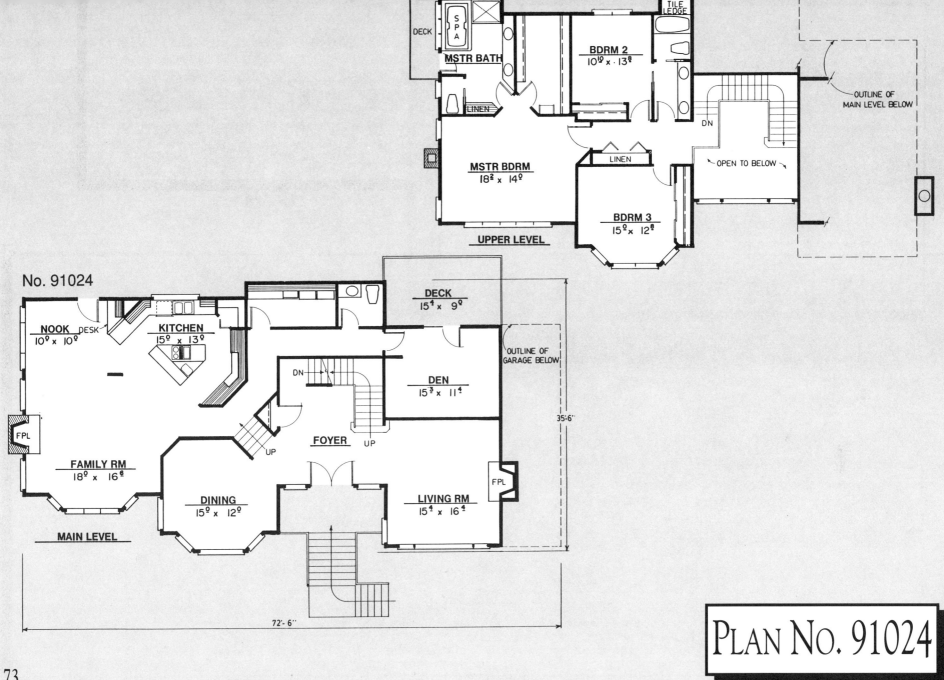

MSTR BATH

DECK

S P A

TILE LEDGE

BDRM 2
10^{10} x 13^{8}

LINEN

DN

OUTLINE OF
MAIN LEVEL BELOW

MSTR BDRM
18^{2} x 14^{0}

LINEN

OPEN TO BELOW

BDRM 3
15^{0} x 12^{8}

UPPER LEVEL

No. 91024

DECK
15^{4} x 9^{0}

NOOK
10^{0} x 10^{0}

DESK

KITCHEN
15^{0} x 13^{0}

OUTLINE OF
GARAGE BELOW

DN

DEN
15^{3} x 11^{4}

35'-6"

FPL

UP

FOYER

UP

FAMILY RM
18^{0} x 16^{8}

FPL

DINING
15^{0} x 12^{0}

LIVING RM
15^{4} x 16^{4}

MAIN LEVEL

72'- 6''

PLAN No. 91024

UNIQUE CONTEMPORARY LIVING

- ☐ Effectively planned corridor Kitchen extends into traffic-free space and exits to deck that makes outdoors part of all social areas

- ☐ Dining and Living/Family Room on space-expanded diagonal enriched with windows gives extra light coupled with beauty

- ☐ Master Bedroom on separate level includes luxurious compartmentalized Bath and opens to Study with private deck

- ☐ Two Bedrooms, full Bath, and Laundry Room share lower level with Recreation Room and storage area

- ☐ Huge Recreation Room provides perfect spot for large groups of guests or safe place for the kids to congregate

- ☐ Framing uses large studs and rafters spaced at wide intervals to cut construction time, reduce the need for lumber and open deeper gaps for thicker insulating batts

- ☐ UPPER LEVEL — 1,423 SQ. FT.
- ☐ LOWER LEVEL — 1,420 SQ. FT.
- ☐ GARAGE — 478 SQ. FT.

TOTAL LIVING AREA — 2,843 SQ. FT.

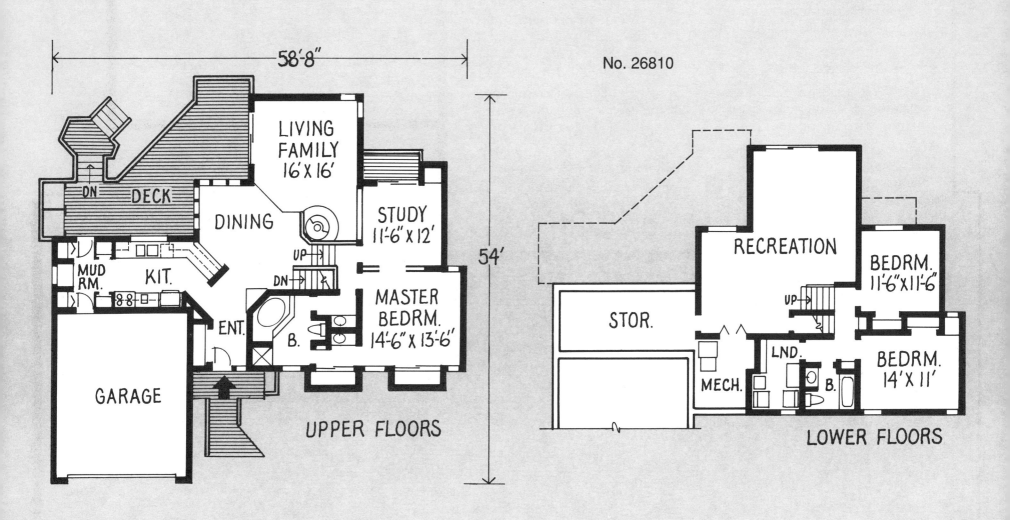

58'-8"

LIVING
FAMILY
16' X 16'

DECK

DN

DINING

STUDY
11'-6" X 12'

MUD
RM.

KIT.

UP

DN

MASTER
BEDRM.
14'-6" X 13'-6"

ENT.

B.

GARAGE

UPPER FLOORS

54'

No. 26810

RECREATION

STOR.

UP

BEDRM.
11'-6" X 11'-6"

LND.

MECH.

B.

BEDRM.
14' X 11'

LOWER FLOORS

PLAN No. 26810

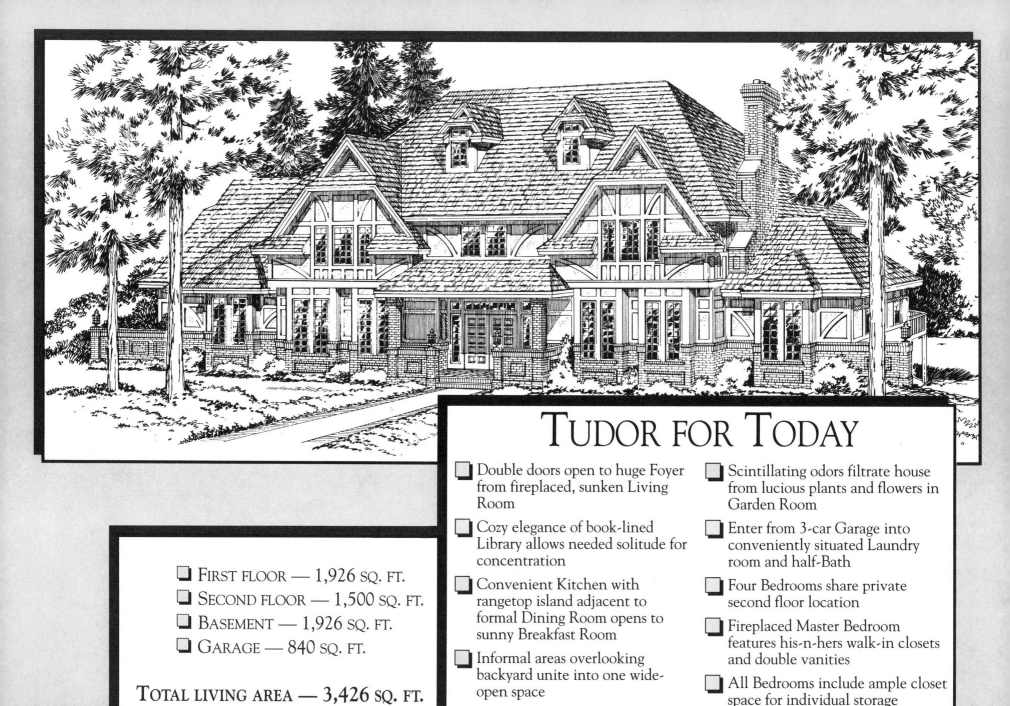

TUDOR FOR TODAY

- Double doors open to huge Foyer from fireplaced, sunken Living Room

- Cozy elegance of book-lined Library allows needed solitude for concentration

- Convenient Kitchen with rangetop island adjacent to formal Dining Room opens to sunny Breakfast Room

- Informal areas overlooking backyard unite into one wide-open space

- Scintillating odors filtrate house from lucious plants and flowers in Garden Room

- Enter from 3-car Garage into conveniently situated Laundry room and half-Bath

- Four Bedrooms share private second floor location

- Fireplaced Master Bedroom features his-n-hers walk-in closets and double vanities

- All Bedrooms include ample closet space for individual storage

- First floor — 1,926 sq. ft.
- Second floor — 1,500 sq. ft.
- Basement — 1,926 sq. ft.
- Garage — 840 sq. ft.

TOTAL LIVING AREA — 3,426 SQ. FT.

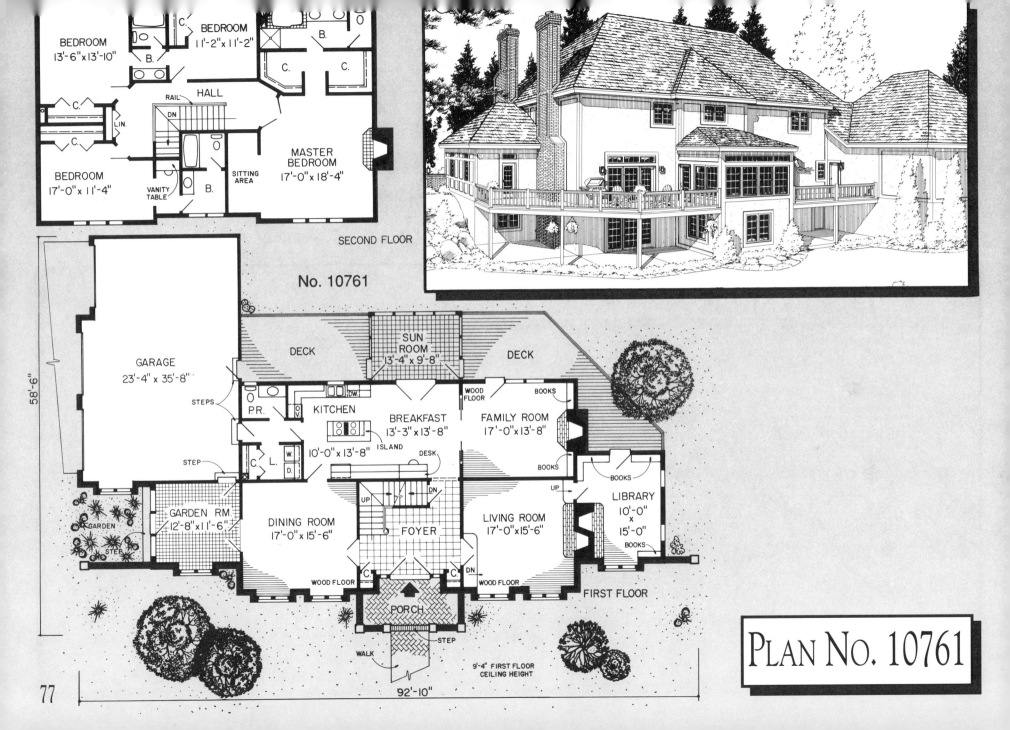

BEDROOM
13'-6" x 13'-10"

BEDROOM
11'-2" x 11'-2"

C.

B.

C.

C.

HALL

RAIL

DN

LIN.

C.

C.

BEDROOM
17'-0" x 11'-4"

VANITY TABLE

B.

SITTING AREA

MASTER BEDROOM
17'-0" x 18'-4"

SECOND FLOOR

No. 10761

GARAGE
23'-4" x 35'-8"

58'-6"

DECK

SUN ROOM
13'-4" x 9'-8"

DECK

STEPS

P.R.

KITCHEN

WOOD FLOOR

BOOKS

FAMILY ROOM
17'-0" x 13'-8"

BREAKFAST
13'-3" x 13'-8"

ISLAND

STEP

C.

L.

W.
D.

10'-0" x 13'-8"

DESK

BOOKS

BOOKS

GARDEN RM.
12'-8" x 11'-6"

GARDEN

STEP

DINING ROOM
17'-0" x 15'-6"

UP

DN

FOYER

LIVING ROOM
17'-0" x 15'-6"

UP

LIBRARY
10'-0"
x
15'-0"

BOOKS

WOOD FLOOR

C.

DN

C.

WOOD FLOOR

FIRST FLOOR

PORCH

WALK

STEP

9'-4" FIRST FLOOR
CEILING HEIGHT

92'-10"

77

PLAN No. 10761

SUNNY AND WARM

- Multi-level plan unfolds as you walk through Foyer
- Den/Study provides quiet area for homework or pleasurable pastimes away from active areas
- Four steps up, active areas revolve around hexagonal hallway giving every room distinctive shape
- Pass-through between island Kitchen and Dining Room render mealtimes effortless
- Fireplaces keep formal and family living areas toasty even on coldest days
- Relax on rear deck when weather is nice
- Staircase off Foyer winds up to four spacious Bedrooms and two full Baths
- Fabulous Master Suite's crowning touch is seen in Bath with raised spa

- FIRST FLOOR — 1,593 SQ. FT.
- SECOND FLOOR — 1,224 SQ. FT.
- BASEMENT — 1,638 SQ. FT.
- GARAGE — 760 SQ. FT.

TOTAL LIVING AREA — 2,817 SQ. FT.

No. 91029

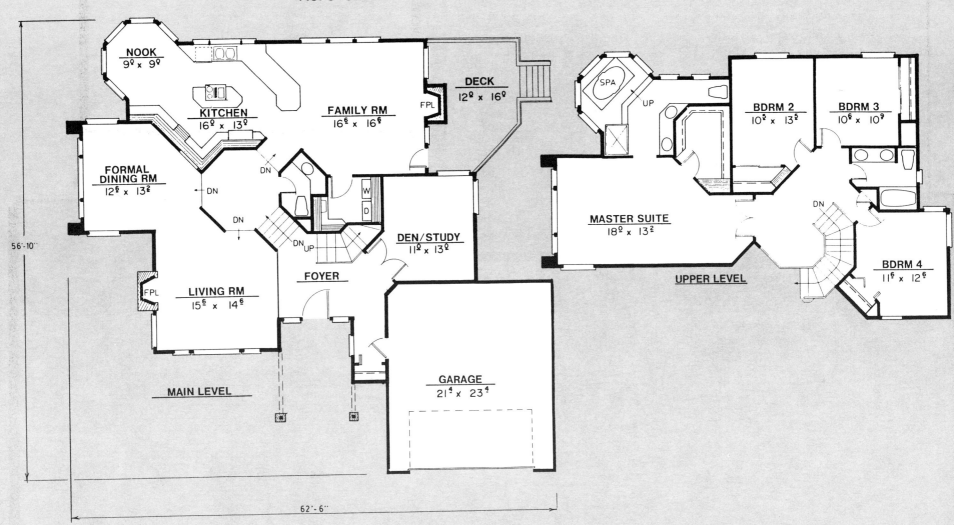

NOOK
9⁰ x 9⁰

KITCHEN
16⁸ x 13⁰

FAMILY RM
16⁶ x 16⁶

FPL

DECK
12⁰ x 16⁰

FORMAL
DINING RM
12⁸ x 13²

DN

DN

DN

W
D

DN UP

DEN/STUDY
11⁰ x 13⁰

FPL

LIVING RM
15⁶ x 14⁶

FOYER

GARAGE
21⁴ x 23⁴

MAIN LEVEL

56'-10"

62'-6"

SPA

UP

MASTER SUITE
18⁰ x 13²

BDRM 2
10² x 13⁵

BDRM 3
10⁶ x 10⁹

DN

BDRM 4
11⁶ x 12⁶

UPPER LEVEL

PLAN NO. 91029

79

ANGLED GARAGE HOUSES BONUS ROOM

- ☐ Double French doors leading to quiet Den add sophisticated touch to tiled Foyer

- ☐ Beautiful bay window, cathedral-type ceiling and fireplace in Living Room provide perfect setting for formal gatherings

- ☐ Dining Room adjacent to Living Room accommodates many dinner guests

- ☐ Expansive Kitchen features room-size Pantry and stove top island with snack bar

- ☐ Informal Nook surrounded by windows offers peaceful corner for early morning tea just off Kitchen

- ☐ Master Suite on second floor includes huge walk-in closet and vaulted ceilings with private Master Bath

- ☐ Bonus Room over 3-car Garage furnishes great place for kids' indoor activities

- ☐ Two additional Bedrooms sharing full Bath with double basin vanity complete second floor amenities

☐ MAIN FLOOR — 1,660 SQ. FT.
☐ UPPER FLOOR — 1,200 SQ. FT.
☐ BONUS ROOM — 356 SQ. FT.
☐ GARAGE — 3-CAR

TOTAL LIVING AREA — 3,216 SQ. FT.

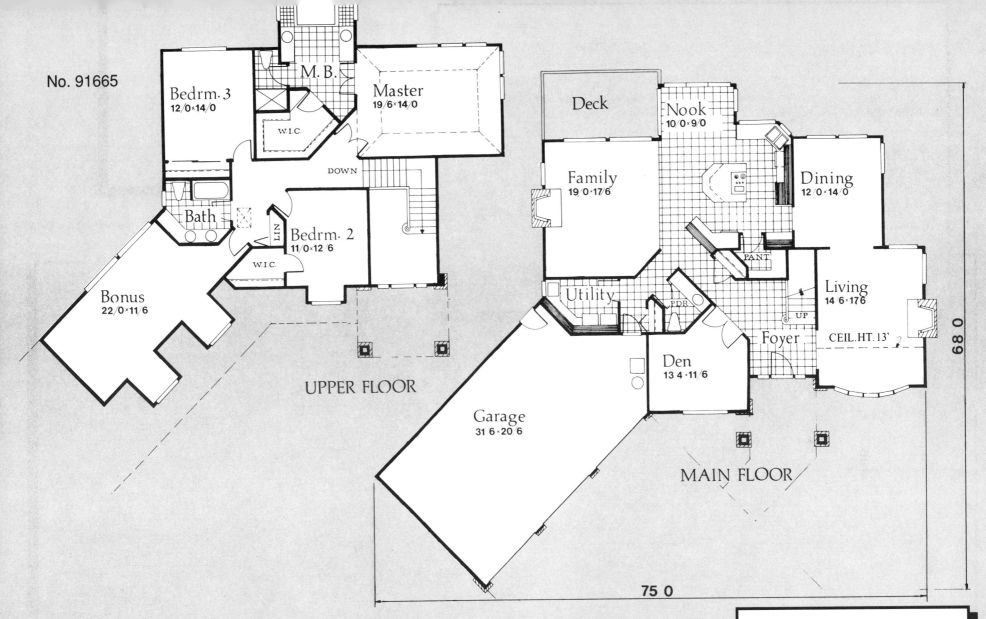

No. 91665

Bedrm. 3
12/0×14/0

M. B.

Master
19/6×14/0

W.I.C.

DOWN

Bath

LIN

Bedrm. 2
11/0×12/6

W.I.C.

Bonus
22/0×11/6

UPPER FLOOR

Deck

Nook
10/0×9/0

Family
19/0×17/6

Dining
12/0×14/0

PANT.

Utility

Living
14/6×17/6

PDR.

UP

Foyer

CEIL. HT. 13'

Den
13 4×11/6

Garage
31 6×20/6

MAIN FLOOR

68 0

75 0

81

PLAN No. 91665

LOFTY TOWER OVERLOOKS ENTRANCE

- ❑ Bump-out windows, hexagonal ceiling, and curving wall of adjacent stairway give Parlor and Dining Room distinctive angles
- ❑ Three first-floor Bedrooms occupy quiet quarters away from busy living areas
- ❑ Master Bedroom features twin walk-in closets with separate doorways to shared Bath facilities
- ❑ Enter house from 3-car Garage through Utility Room doubling as mudroom

- ❑ Fireplaced Living Room with exposed-beam ceiling and built-in wetbar extend welcome to all
- ❑ Fireplaced Hearth Room adjoining island Kitchen is cozy family mealtime spot
- ❑ Ascend curved stairway to tower Loft on second floor overlooking Entry
- ❑ Two additional Bedrooms include individual walk-in closets, and share full Bath

---

- ❑ FIRST FLOOR — 2,887 SQ. FT.
- ❑ SECOND FLOOR — 1,488 SQ. FT.
- ❑ BASEMENT — 2,888 SQ. FT.
- ❑ GARAGE — 843 SQ. FT.

TOTAL LIVING AREA — 4,375 SQ. FT.

No. 10733

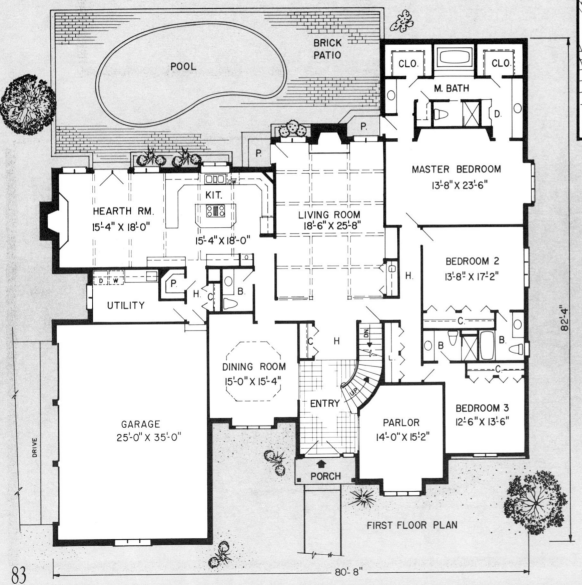

POOL

BRICK PATIO

M. BATH

CLO. CLO.

D.

MASTER BEDROOM
13'-8" X 23'-6"

HEARTH RM.
15'-4" X 18'-0"

KIT.
15'-4" X 18'-0"

LIVING ROOM
18'-6" X 25'-8"

BEDROOM 2
13'-8" X 17'-2"

C.

H.

H.

UTILITY

P.

H. C.

B.

DINING ROOM
15'-0" X 15'-4"

C

H

DN
UP

L.

B

B.

C.

GARAGE
25'-0" X 35'-0"

ENTRY

PARLOR
14'-0" X 15'-2"

BEDROOM 3
12'-6" X 13'-6"

DRIVE

PORCH

FIRST FLOOR PLAN

82'-4"

80'-8"

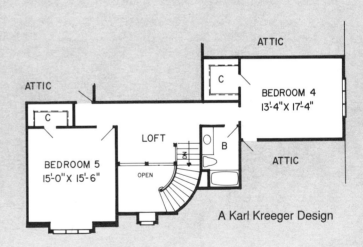

ATTIC

ATTIC

C

BEDROOM 4
13'-4" X 17'-4"

ATTIC

BEDROOM 5
15'-0" X 15'-6"

LOFT

OPEN

DN

B

A Karl Kreeger Design

PLAN NO. 10733

ARCHES DOMINATE FACADE

- Window walls and French doors link inground pool and surrounding brick patio with interior living areas

- Shelving for books frame fireplace in large Living Room

- Island Kitchen situated to be conducive to formal meals taken in Dining Room or relaxed family feasting in Breakfast Room

- Two additional Bedrooms on second level enjoy private dressing area and walk-in closets

- Hallway separating two Bedrooms on first floor allows each room to be quiet retreat

- Master Bedroom includes his-n-hers separate baths and double walk-in closet with built-in storage chest and shoe rack

- Skylit Library on bridge open to Living Room affords housing for extensive collections of books

- Wetbar with wine storage provides convenience and room for large buffet in Family Room

- FIRST FLOOR — 3,625 SQ. FT.
- SECOND FLOOR — 937 SQ. FT.
- GARAGE — 636 SQ. FT.

TOTAL LIVING AREA — 4,562 SQ. FT.

No. 10666

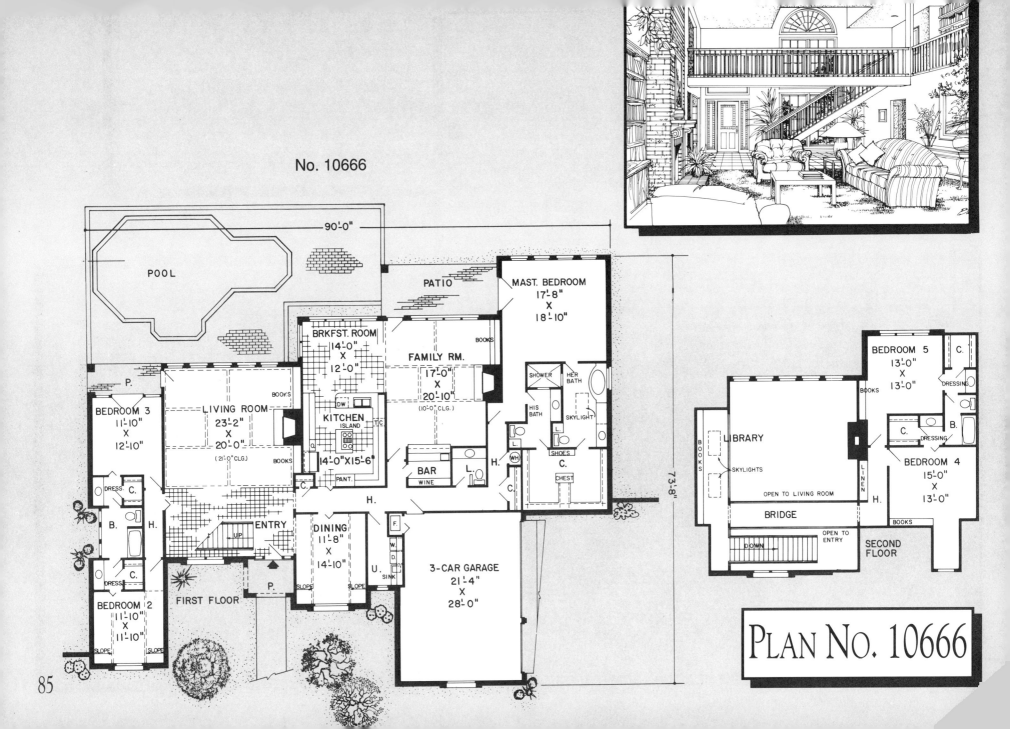

POOL

90'-0"

PATIO

BRKFST. ROOM
14'-0"
X
12'-0"

FAMILY RM.
17'-0"
X
20'-10"
(10'-0" CLG.)

BOOKS

MAST. BEDROOM
17'-8"
X
18'-10"

P.

BEDROOM 3
11'-10"
X
12'-10"

BOOKS

LIVING ROOM
23'-2"
X
20'-0"
(21'-0" CLG.)

BOOKS

DW

KITCHEN
ISLAND
14'-0" X 15'-6"

T.C.

SHOWER

HER BATH

HIS BATH

SKYLIGHT

L.

SHOES

C.

CHEST

DRESS.

C.

B.

H.

C.

PANT.

BAR
WINE

L.

L.

H.

C.

WH

ENTRY

UP

DINING
11'-8"
X
14'-10"

F.

3-CAR GARAGE
21'-4"
X
28'-0"

W.

D.

U.

SINK

C.

BEDROOM 2
11'-10"
X
11'-10"

DRESS.

FIRST FLOOR

P.

SLOPE

SLOPE

SLOPE

SLOPE

H.

LIBRARY

SKYLIGHTS

BOOKS

OPEN TO LIVING ROOM

BRIDGE

DOWN

OPEN TO ENTRY

LINEN

BOOKS

BEDROOM 5
13'-0"
X
13'-0"

C.

DRESSING

C.

DRESSING

B.

BEDROOM 4
15'-0"
X
13'-0"

H.

BOOKS

SECOND FLOOR

73'-8"

PLAN NO. 10666

85

Tudor with Wide-Open Floor Plan

- First floor — 1,662 sq. ft.
- Second floor — 1,247 sq. ft.
- Unfinished Room — 538 sq. ft.
- Basement — 1,662 sq. ft.
- Garage — 700 sq. ft.

Total living area — 2,909 sq. ft.

- Pass through covered entry into vaulted Foyer lit from above by arched window
- Sunny spacious Dining and Living Room combination separated by decorative columns
- Fling open French doors in bay-windowed Den for extra room when entertaining many guests
- Spill out to rear patio accessible from fireplaced Family Room
- Convenient Kitchen includes cheerful Nook for informal meals and rangetop island
- Ascend curved staircase in Foyer to find ample sleeping quarters for large family
- Extravagant Master Suite features private reading alcove and deck
- Substantial spare room over 3-car Garage for storage or recreational room

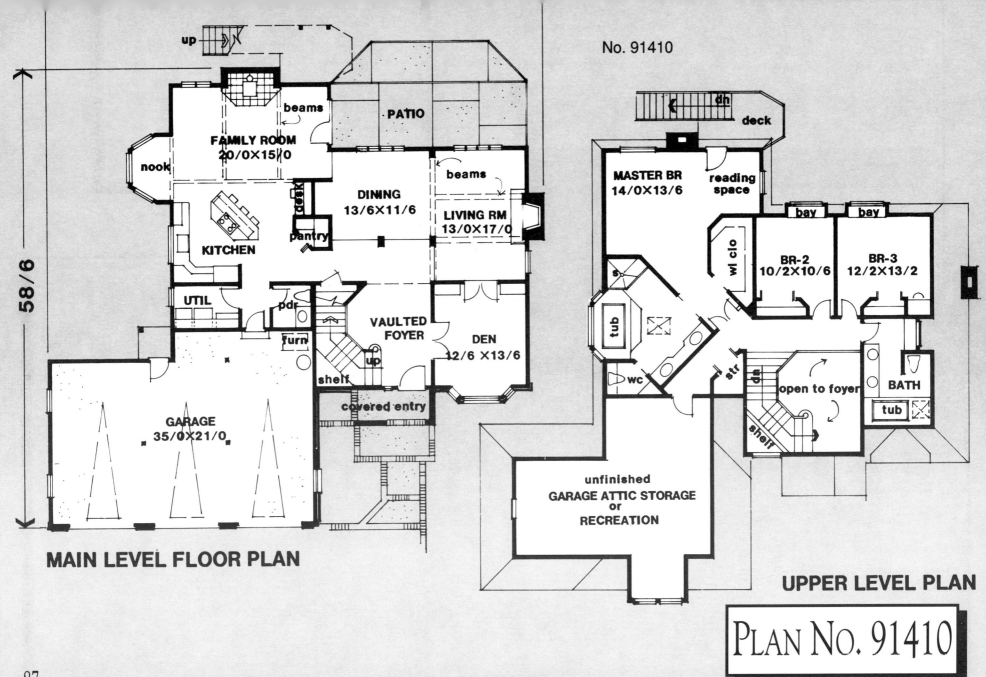

No. 91410

MAIN LEVEL FLOOR PLAN

58/6

up

beams

PATIO

FAMILY ROOM
20/0×15/0

nook

desk

pantry

KITCHEN

DINING
13/6×11/6

beams

LIVING RM
13/0×17/0

UTIL

pdr

furn

VAULTED FOYER

shelf

up

DEN
12/6 ×13/6

GARAGE
35/0×21/0

covered entry

UPPER LEVEL PLAN

dn

deck

MASTER BR
14/0×13/6

reading space

bay   bay

wl clo

s

BR-2
10/2×10/6

BR-3
12/2×13/2

tub

wc

str

dn

open to foyer

BATH

shelf

tub

unfinished
GARAGE ATTIC STORAGE
or
RECREATION

PLAN NO. 91410

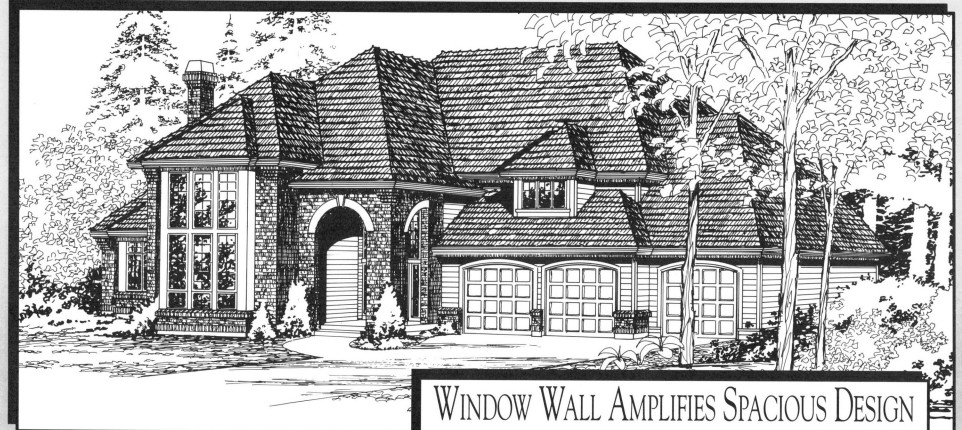

WINDOW WALL AMPLIFIES SPACIOUS DESIGN

- Ornately designed staircase in Entry leads to second-floor landing overlooking Family Room

- Private Study with built-in bookshelves enjoins Master Bedroom featuring extra-sized walk-in closet and spacious Bath with double vanities, linen closet, tub and shower

- Fireplaced Living Room magnified by triple floor-to-ceiling windows opens to formal Dining Area for entertaining ease

- Island Kitchen surrounded by cabinet space framed by pantry and sunlit Nook

- Vast Family Room features fireplace, built-in bookshelves and overlooks wrap-around deck

- Two Bedrooms on second floor share full double-vanitied Bath with Bonus Room

- Three-car Garage enhanced by decorative dormer above provides extra storage space

---

- FIRST FLOOR — 2,043 SQ. FT.
- SECOND FLOOR — 1,236 SQ. FT.
- GARAGE — 921 SQ. FT.

TOTAL LIVING AREA — 3,279 SQ. FT.

No. 92104

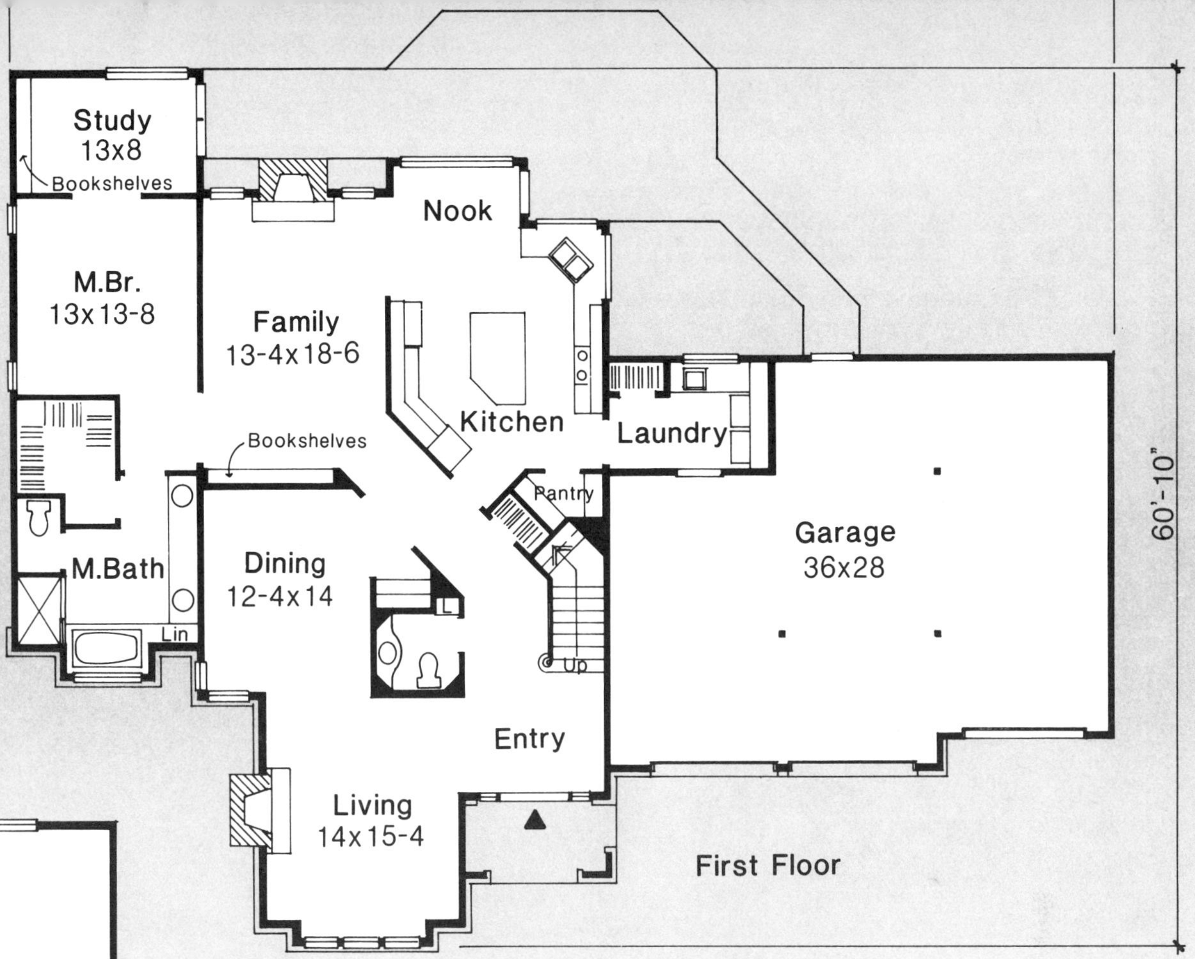

Study
13x8
Bookshelves

M.Br.
13x13-8

Family
13-4x18-6

Nook

Kitchen

Laundry

Bookshelves

M.Bath

Dining
12-4x14

Lin

Pantry

Up

Garage
36x28

Entry

Living
14x15-4

First Floor

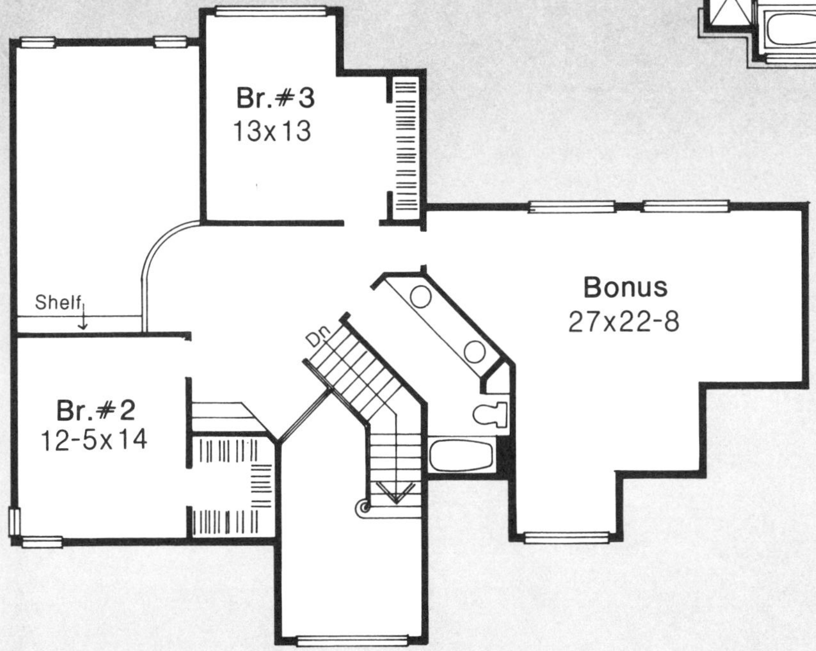

60'-10"

Br.#3
13x13

Bonus
27x22-8

Shelf

Dn

Br.#2
12-5x14

Second Floor

PLAN No. 92104

IMPRESSIVE TWO STORY STUCCO

- ☐ Graceful window arches with keystone detailing soften high hip roofline

- ☐ Three-car Garage with rear entry allows full exterior architectural display

- ☐ Grand Foyer with fully curved staircase enjoins formal sunken fireplaced Living Room and super-sized Dining Room

- ☐ Kitchen presents uniquely different geometric concept to allow full two-sided view

- ☐ Secluded Den away from traffic area affords quiet solitude

- ☐ Fireplaced Family Room has added dimension of tastefully designed double windows allowing extra light and air circulation

- ☐ Sprawling angular shaped Master Bedroom studded with beautiful window works and private fireplace for additional warmth highlighted by full Master Bath featuring double vanity and huge walk-in closet

- ☐ FIRST FLOOR — 2,108 SQ. FT.
- ☐ SECOND FLOOR — 1,884 SQ. FT.
- ☐ GARAGE — 952 SQ. FT.

TOTAL LIVING AREA — 3,992 SQ. FT.

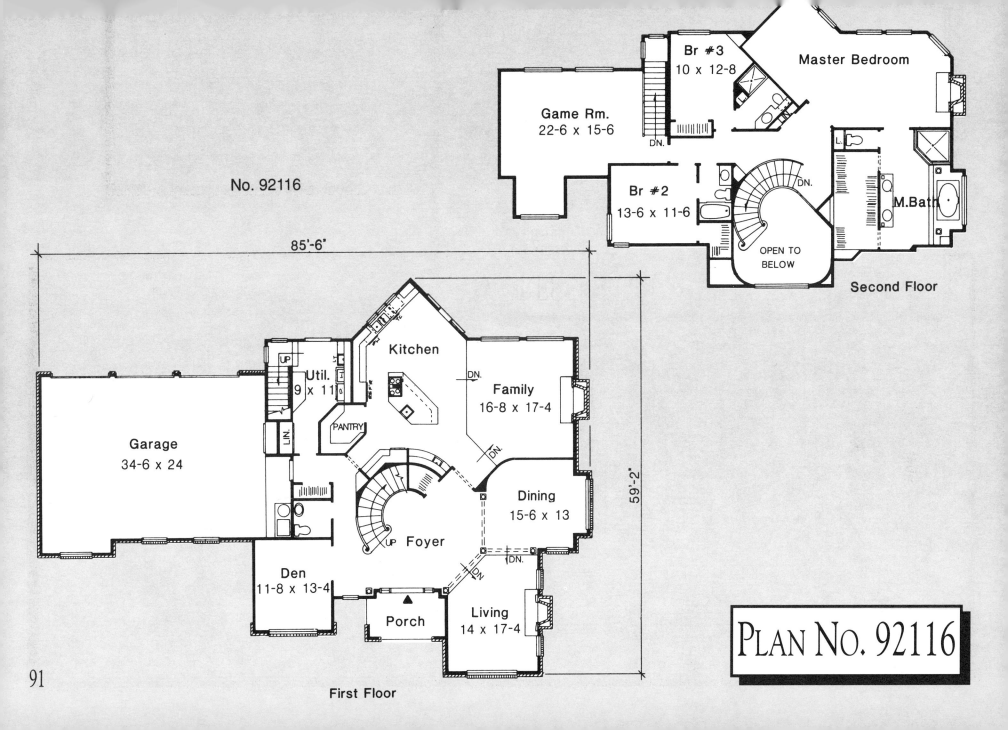

No. 92116

Game Rm.
22-6 x 15-6

Br #3
10 x 12-8

Master Bedroom

Br #2
13-6 x 11-6

DN.

OPEN TO
BELOW

M.Bath

Second Floor

85'-6"

59'-2"

UP

Util.
9 x 11

LIN.

PANTRY

Kitchen

DN.

Family
16-8 x 17-4

DN.

Garage
34-6 x 24

UP   Foyer

Dining
15-6 x 13

DN.

Den
11-8 x 13-4

Porch

DN.

Living
14 x 17-4

PLAN No. 92116

First Floor

MODERN TUDOR HARD TO RESIST

- ☐ Partake of morning coffee in seven-sided Breakfast Room

- ☐ Island Kitchen affords easy access to Dining Room

- ☐ Family Room features exposed wood beams adding atmosphere to impressive home

- ☐ Energy-saving Sun Room and unobtrusive Study flank Family Room for convenience

- ☐ Balcony at top of stairs overlooks grand Entry

- ☐ Master Bedroom with recessed ceiling encompasses entire wing for spacious living

- ☐ Master Bath encourages pampering with double vanity, walk-in closet, sauna, whirlpool bath, and hot tub

- ☐ Graceful curving staircase enhances exciting tiled Entry with two-story ceiling

- ☐ Three additional Bedrooms on second floor feature individual walk-in closets for plenty of personal storage area

- ☐ FIRST FLOOR — 2,457 SQ. FT.
- ☐ SECOND FLOOR — 1,047 SQ. FT.
- ☐ SUN ROOM — 213 SQ. FT.
- ☐ BASEMENT — 2,457 SQ. FT.
- ☐ GARAGE — 837 SQ. FT.

TOTAL LIVING AREA — 3,717 SQ. FT.

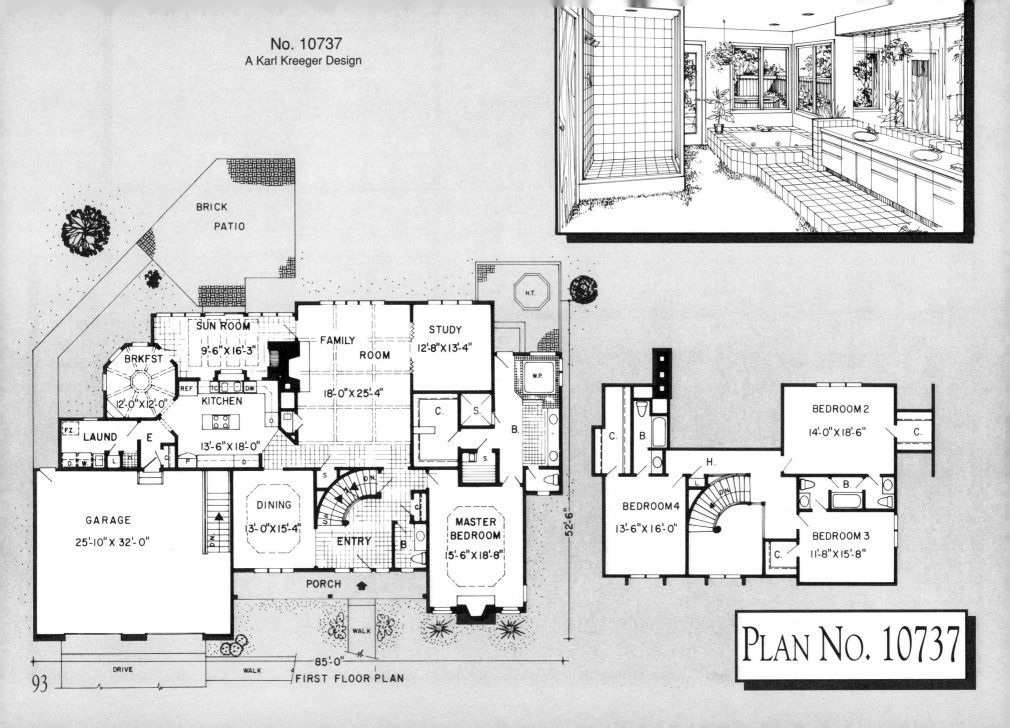

No. 10737

A Karl Kreeger Design

BRICK PATIO

SUN ROOM
9'-6" X 16'-3"

FAMILY ROOM
18'-0" X 25'-4"

STUDY
12'-8" X 13'-4"

H.T.

BRKFST
12'-0" X 12'-0"

REF. TC DW.

KITCHEN
13'-6" X 18'-0"

W.P.

C.

S.

B.

S.

FZ

LAUND

E

D. W. L

P

D

GARAGE
25'-10" X 32'-0"

DINING
13'-0" X 15'-4"

UP DN

S.

C

B

ENTRY

MASTER BEDROOM
15'-6" X 18'-8"

PORCH

WALK

52'-6"

DRIVE

WALK

85'-0"

FIRST FLOOR PLAN

BEDROOM 2
14'-0" X 18'-6"

C.

C.

B.

H.

L DN

B.

BEDROOM 4
13'-6" X 16'-0"

BEDROOM 3
11'-8" X 15'-8"

C.

PLAN NO. 10737

93

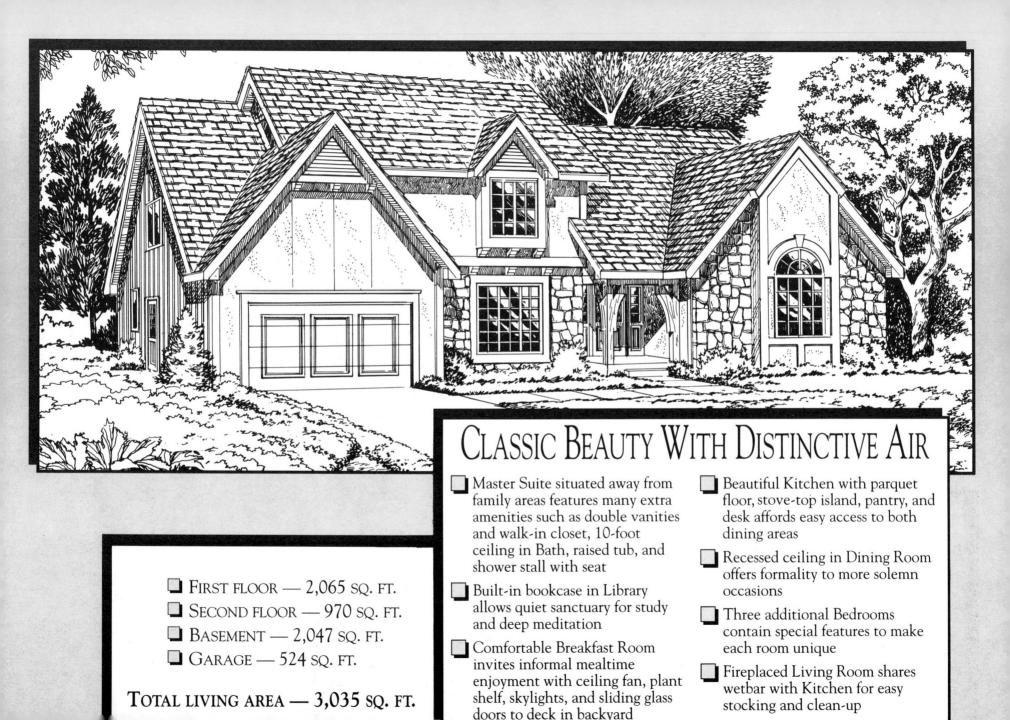

CLASSIC BEAUTY WITH DISTINCTIVE AIR

- ☐ FIRST FLOOR — 2,065 SQ. FT.
- ☐ SECOND FLOOR — 970 SQ. FT.
- ☐ BASEMENT — 2,047 SQ. FT.
- ☐ GARAGE — 524 SQ. FT.

TOTAL LIVING AREA — 3,035 SQ. FT.

- ☐ Master Suite situated away from family areas features many extra amenities such as double vanities and walk-in closet, 10-foot ceiling in Bath, raised tub, and shower stall with seat

- ☐ Built-in bookcase in Library allows quiet sanctuary for study and deep meditation

- ☐ Comfortable Breakfast Room invites informal mealtime enjoyment with ceiling fan, plant shelf, skylights, and sliding glass doors to deck in backyard

- ☐ Beautiful Kitchen with parquet floor, stove-top island, pantry, and desk affords easy access to both dining areas

- ☐ Recessed ceiling in Dining Room offers formality to more solemn occasions

- ☐ Three additional Bedrooms contain special features to make each room unique

- ☐ Fireplaced Living Room shares wetbar with Kitchen for easy stocking and clean-up

No. 20094

A Karl Kreeger Design

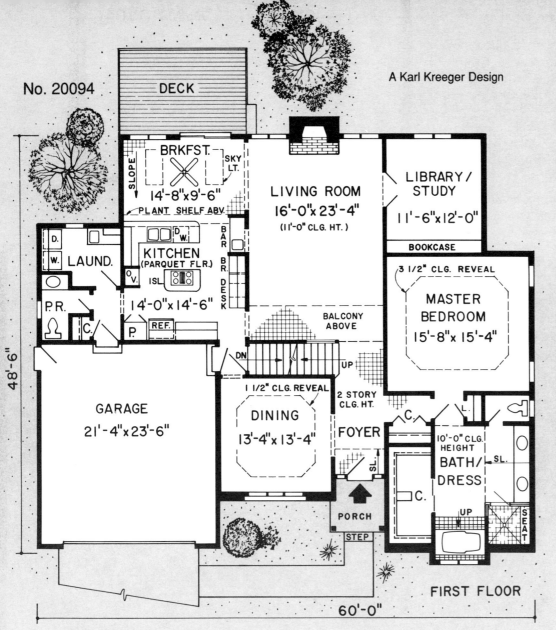

DECK

BRKFST.
14'-8"x9'-6"
SKY LT.
SLOPE
PLANT SHELF ABV.

LIVING ROOM
16'-0"x 23'-4"
(11'-0" CLG. HT.)

LIBRARY/
STUDY
11'-6"x 12'-0"

BOOKCASE

KITCHEN
(PARQUET FLR.)
14'-0"x 14'-6"
D. W. DW.
O.V.
ISL.

LAUND.

BAR
BR
DESK

3 1/2" CLG. REVEAL

P.R.
C.

P.
REF.

MASTER
BEDROOM
15'-8"x 15'-4"

BALCONY
ABOVE

GARAGE
21'-4"x 23'-6"

DN
UP

1 1/2" CLG. REVEAL

2 STORY
CLG. HT.

DINING
13'-4"x 13'-4"

FOYER

C.

10'-0" CLG.
HEIGHT

BATH/
DRESS

SL.
SL.

C.

UP
SEAT

PORCH

STEP

FIRST FLOOR

48'-6"

60'-0"

BATH
1/2 WALL

BEDROOM
12'-0"x 13'-4"
C.

SECOND FLOOR

TO ATTIC

L.

1/2 WALL

BALCONY
RAIL

DN

BEDROOM
13'-0"x 11'-6"
C.

FOYER
BELOW

B.

C.

BEDROOM
13'-4"x 14'-4"

C.

LEDGE

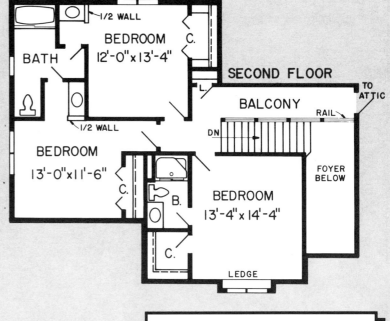

PLAN NO. 20094

95

BEAUTY ON GRAND SCALE

- ☐ Gracious home has look of English manor house with all amenities modern families desire

- ☐ Two-story skylit Foyer dominated by curving staircase

- ☐ Living and Dining Rooms flow together in beautiful symmetry

- ☐ Informal areas in rear of house include large island Kitchen with walk-in pantry, sunny Breakfast Room and sunken Family Room with fireplace and convenient access to backyard patio

- ☐ Two Bathrooms, Laundry Room, and book-lined Study complete first-floor accommodations

- ☐ Master Bedroom has fireplace for chilly nights, his-n-hers closets, window seat, garden spa tub and beautiful pan-vaulted ceiling

- ☐ Other three spacious Bedrooms have multitude of closet space and share two full Baths

- ☐ Cedar closet and Bonus Room over Garage occupy remainder of second level

- ☐ FIRST FLOOR — 2,103 SQ. FT.
- ☐ SECOND FLOOR — 2,133 SQ. FT.
- ☐ BASEMENT — 2,103 SQ. FT.
- ☐ GARAGE — 855 SQ. FT.

TOTAL LIVING AREA — 4,236 SQ. FT.

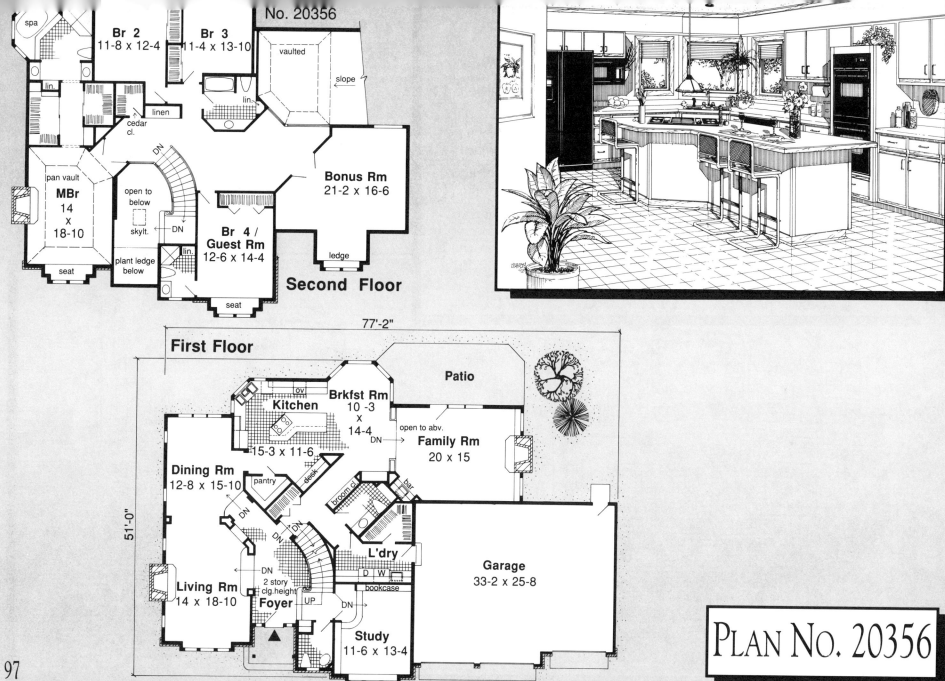

Second Floor

- spa
- Br 2 — 11-8 x 12-4
- Br 3 — 11-4 x 13-10
- No. 20356
- vaulted
- slope
- lin.
- linen
- cedar cl.
- pan vault
- MBr — 14 x 18-10
- open to below
- skylt.
- DN
- DN
- plant ledge below
- lin.
- Br 4 / Guest Rm — 12-6 x 14-4
- Bonus Rm — 21-2 x 16-6
- ledge
- seat
- seat

First Floor

77'-2"

51'-0"

- Kitchen — 15-3 x 11-6
- ov
- Brkfst Rm — 10-3 x 14-4
- Patio
- open to abv.
- DN
- Family Rm — 20 x 15
- Dining Rm — 12-8 x 15-10
- pantry
- desk
- broom cl.
- bar
- DN
- DN
- DN
- L'dry
- Living Rm — 14 x 18-10
- DN
- 2 story clg. height
- Foyer
- UP
- DN
- D W
- bookcase
- Garage — 33-2 x 25-8
- Study — 11-6 x 13-4

PLAN NO. 20356

HEARTH ROOM HIGHLIGHTS PLAN

- Fireplace in Hearth Room surrounded by windows for warm cozy atmosphere
- Unusual ceiling adds distinctive beauty to unique Hearth Room
- Spacious Kitchen features plenty of counter space with central work island
- Step down to the sunken Family Room for refreshments at the built-in bar

- Fireplace in Family Room flanked by bookcases invites informal relaxation
- Sizable Dining Room lends itself for formal entertaining
- Master Bedroom sports his-n-hers walk-in closets plus private Bath
- Bedrooms two and three share Bath but have individual basins
- Bedroom four has personal Bath and ample closet space

- FIRST FLOOR — 1,697 SQ. FT.
- SECOND FLOOR — 1,624 SQ. FT.
- BASEMENT — 1,697 SQ. FT.
- GARAGE — 586 SQ. FT.

TOTAL LIVING AREA — 3,321 SQ. FT.

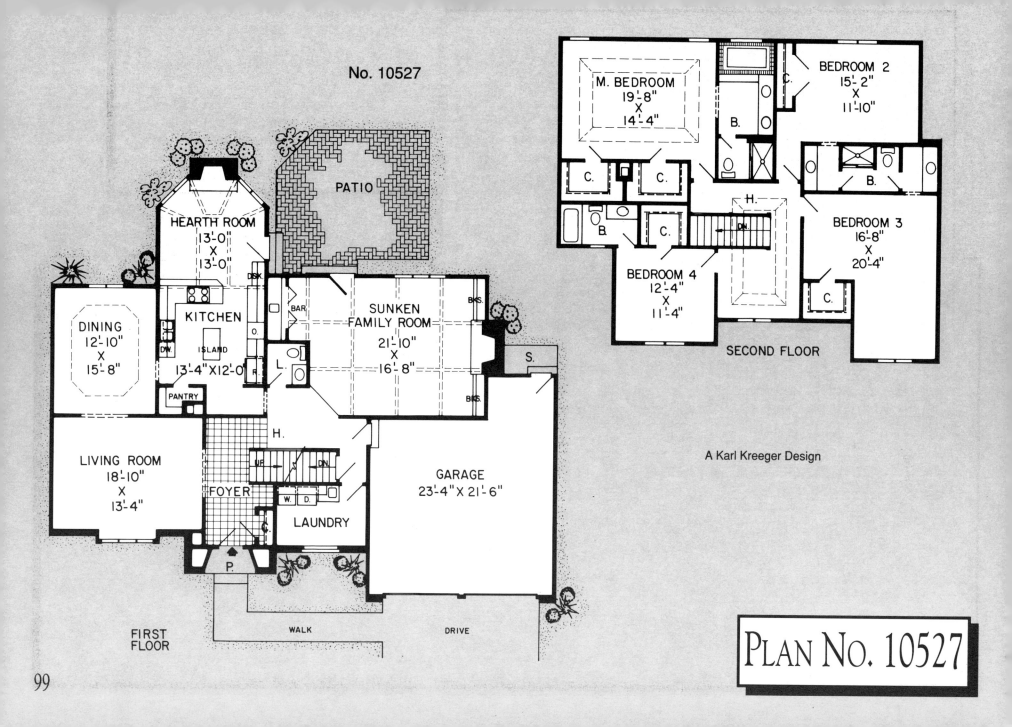

No. 10527

FIRST FLOOR

HEARTH ROOM
13'-0"
X
13'-0"

PATIO

DINING
12'-10"
X
15'-8"

KITCHEN

13'-4" X 12'-0"

ISLAND

DSK.

DW.

O.

R.

BAR

PANTRY

SUNKEN FAMILY ROOM
21'-10"
X
16'-8"

BKS.

BKS.

S.

LIVING ROOM
18'-10"
X
13'-4"

FOYER

H.

L.

W. D.

LAUNDRY

UP DN

C.

P.

GARAGE
23'-4" X 21'-6"

WALK

DRIVE

SECOND FLOOR

M. BEDROOM
19'-8"
X
14'-4"

BEDROOM 2
15'-2"
X
11'-10"

C.

B.

C.

C.

B.

C.

H.

DN

BEDROOM 3
16'-8"
X
20'-4"

BEDROOM 4
12'-4"
X
11'-4"

C.

A Karl Kreeger Design

PLAN No. 10527

L. SHELLENBARGER

SOLID ELEGANCE IN HUMBLE BRICK BEAUTY

- ☐ A bright skylit Entry welcomes guests into this elegant home
- ☐ Family activities occur in central section comprised of expansive array of rooms warmed by a woodstove
- ☐ Large Kitchen features pantry with unique accessibility, cooktop island with grill, long counters, and a backyard view
- ☐ Eating Nook awash in natural light from bay window reflects bright and cheerful atmosphere

- ☐ Woodstove warms both Nook and Family Room large enough for couches, home entertainment center and pool table
- ☐ Fireplaced Living Room, Dining Room, and Office located on front-facing side of living area
- ☐ Master Suite has huge walk-in closet, spa, and double vanities
- ☐ Three additional bedrooms share another skylit, compartmentalized bathroom with double vanities

---

- ☐ LIVING AREA — 3,173 SQ. FT.
- ☐ GARAGE — 636 SQ. FT.

TOTAL LIVING AREA — 3,173 SQ. FT.

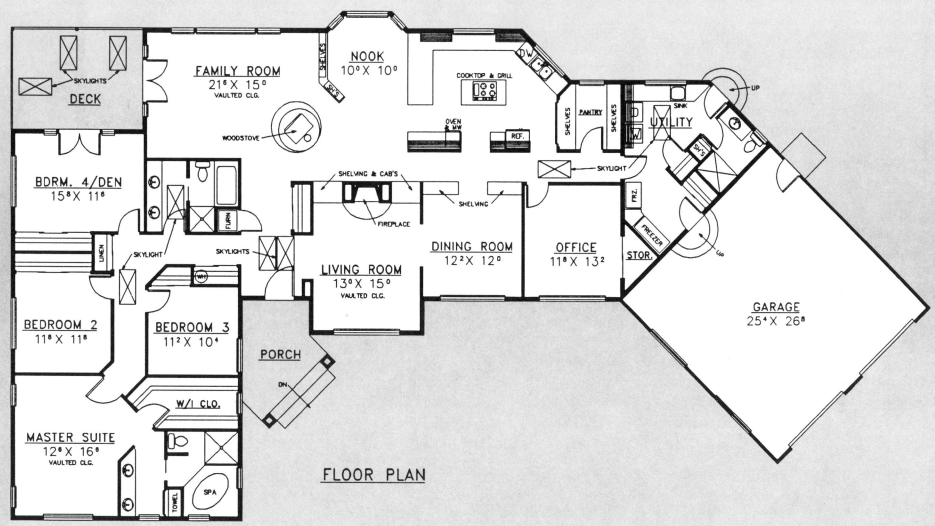

FLOOR PLAN

PLAN NO. 91735

ARCHES ADD CHARM

- Covered porch leads to large Entry with added touch of convenient window seat

- Fireplaced Living Room separated from Entry and Dining area with decorative columns

- Island Kitchen offering cabinets and counter space all around is complemented by eat-in Nook

- Family Room with uniquely shaped fireplace shares space with Den and opens to oversized patio affording perfect view of backyard

- Master Bedroom featuring plenty of windows and closet space opens to luxurious Bath with double vanities, extra-large shower stall, window seat and steps up to modern whirlpool tub

- Bedrooms Two and Three are equal in size, shape and design and share full Bath with double vanity, tub and linen closet

- Bedroom Four offers extra length for easy placement of furniture, large closet, and window seat

- FIRST FLOOR — 1,623 SQ. FT.
- SECOND FLOOR — 1,502 SQ. FT.
- GARAGE — 805 SQ. FT.

TOTAL LIVING AREA — 3,125 SQ. FT.

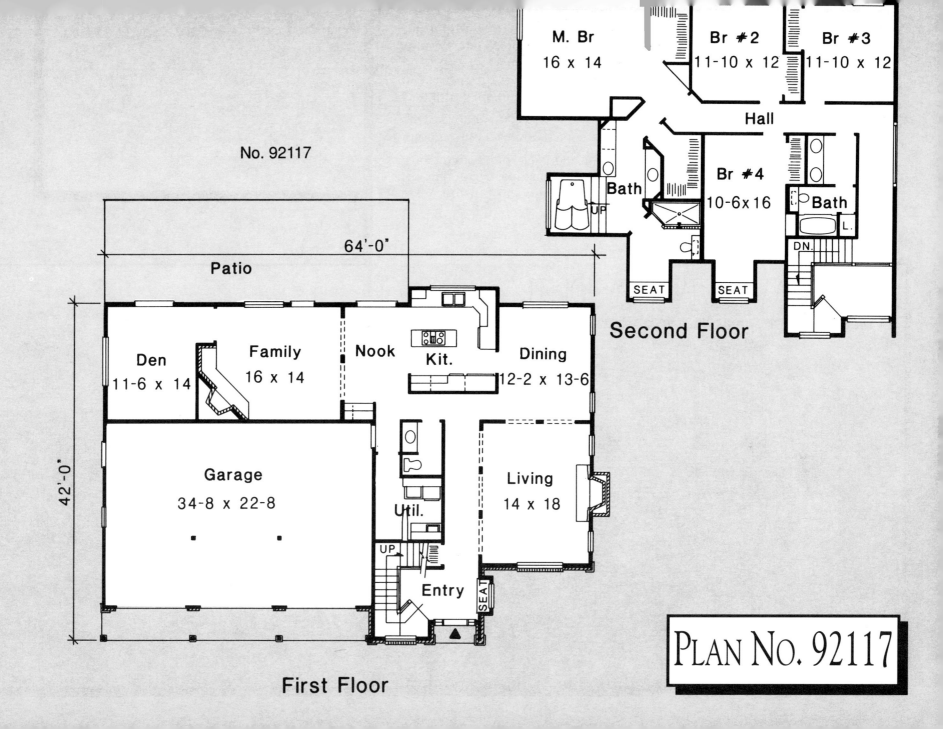

No. 92117

Second Floor

M. Br
16 x 14

Br #2
11-10 x 12

Br #3
11-10 x 12

Hall

Bath

Br #4
10-6 x 16

Bath

UP

L.

DN.

SEAT

SEAT

64'-0"

Patio

42'-0"

Den
11-6 x 14

Family
16 x 14

Nook

Kit.

Dining
12-2 x 13-6

Garage
34-8 x 22-8

Util.

Living
14 x 18

UP

Entry

SEAT

First Floor

PLAN NO. 92117

Country Exterior with Many Amenities

- Curved arches flanked by formal columns mark passages between rooms in family living area
- Semi-formal Parlor with see-through fireplace linked to Family Room reserved for quiet pursuits
- Master Suite is solitary sleeping quarters on main floor
- Columns flank oversized bathtub in Master Bath which contains his-n-hers walk-in closets, double vanities, and compartmentalized toilet

- Family Room accessible from bright, window-lined eating Nook
- Spacious country Kitchen conveniently situated near both Nook and Dining Room
- Graceful open staircase curves up one side of wide, two-story Entry has overlook at upper landing
- Three additional Bedrooms upstairs share Bathroom designed to handle heavy traffic with ease

- First floor — 1,979 sq. ft.
- Second floor — 905 sq. ft.
- Basement — 1,961 sq. ft.
- Garage — 588 sq. ft.

Total living area — 2,884 sq. ft.

No. 91730

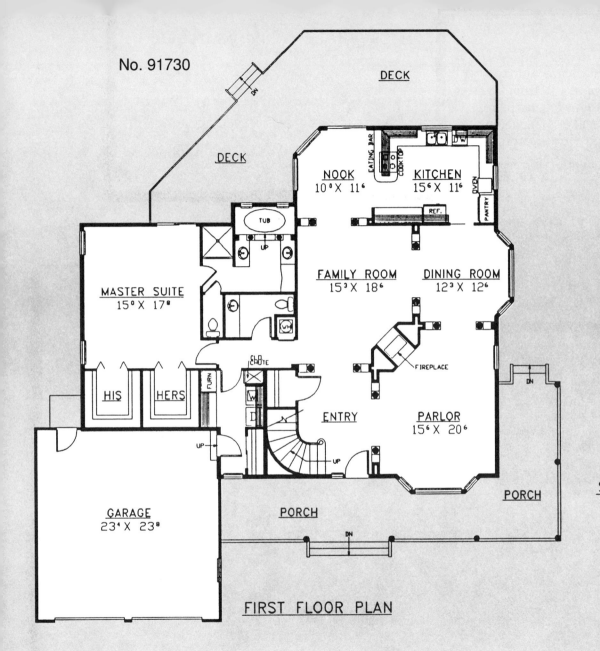

DECK

DECK

NOOK
10⁰ X 11⁶

KITCHEN
15⁶ X 11⁶

EATING BAR

COOKTOP

OVEN

PANTRY

REF.

TUB

UP

MASTER SUITE
15⁰ X 17⁸

FAMILY ROOM
15³ X 18⁶

DINING ROOM
12³ X 12⁶

FIREPLACE

CLO. CHUTE

FURN

HIS   HERS

W

D

UP

ENTRY

PARLOR
15⁶ X 20⁶

DN

UP

PORCH

GARAGE
23' X 23⁸

PORCH

DN

FIRST FLOOR PLAN

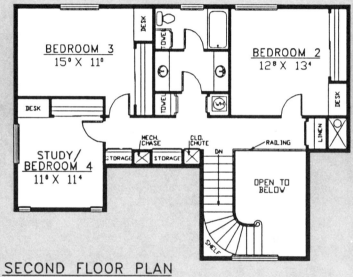

BEDROOM 3
15⁰ X 11⁰

DESK

TOWEL

BEDROOM 2
12⁸ X 13⁴

DESK

DESK

TOWEL

MECH.
CHASE

CLO.
CHUTE

RAILING

LINEN

STUDY/
BEDROOM 4
11⁰ X 11⁴

STORAGE

STORAGE

DN

OPEN TO
BELOW

SHELF

DN

SECOND FLOOR PLAN

PLAN No. 91730

SPACIOUS STUCCO

- ☐ Open Foyer gives sunny, airy atmosphere and leads straight through to rear of home

- ☐ Fireplaced Living Room off Foyer is studded with windows on three sides and has sliders to the deck

- ☐ Magnificent Family Room has efficiency of fireplace, added light from desirable sliding glass doors and plenty of windows, and adds outdoor feeling to wide-open Nook and Kitchen

- ☐ Powder room with shower makes the book-lined Den ideal guest room

- ☐ Wide Dining area has added convenience of multi-purpose luxurious deck

- ☐ Plush Master Bedroom shows sloped ceilings, large walk-in closet and private Bath

- ☐ Four other Bedrooms are all good-sized with extra closet space and are effectively located near two equally beautiful Baths

- ☐ FIRST FLOOR — 1,452 SQ. FT.
- ☐ SECOND FLOOR — 1,431 SQ. FT.
- ☐ BONUS ROOM — 316 SQ. FT.
- ☐ GARAGE — 3-CAR

TOTAL LIVING AREA — 3,199 SQ. FT.

No. 91630

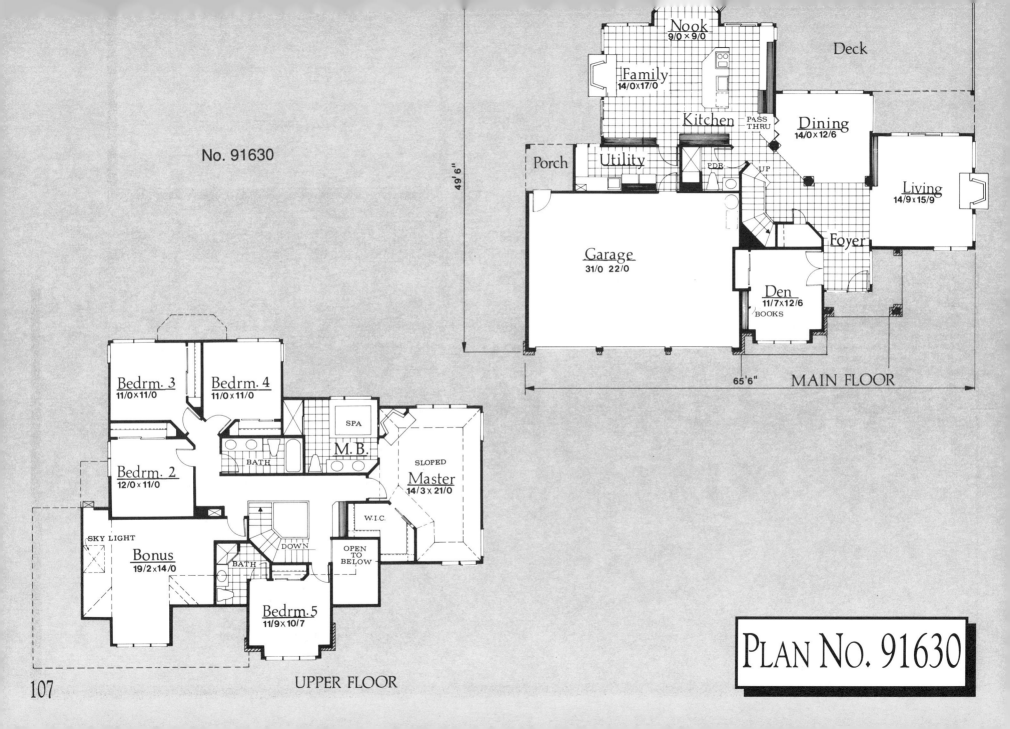

Deck

Nook
9/0 × 9/0

Family
14/0 × 17/0

Kitchen

Dining
14/0 × 12/6

PASS THRU

Living
14/9 × 15/9

Porch

Utility

P.D.R.

UP

Foyer

Garage
31/0 22/0

Den
11/7 × 12/6
BOOKS

49' 6"

65'6" **MAIN FLOOR**

Bedrm. 3
11/0 × 11/0

Bedrm. 4
11/0 × 11/0

SPA

M. B.

BATH

SLOPED
Master
14/3 × 21/0

Bedrm. 2
12/0 × 11/0

W.I.C.

SKY LIGHT

Bonus
19/2 × 14/0

DOWN

BATH

OPEN TO BELOW

Bedrm. 5
11/9 × 10/7

UPPER FLOOR

PLAN No. 91630

BUILT IN TRADITION OF BYGONE ERA

- ☐ Convenient built-in china cabinets in formal Dining Room and wood-beamed Breakfast Room

- ☐ Handy island work center in adjoining Kitchen opens to cheerful Breakfast area

- ☐ Luxurious full Bath with Powder room just off sunny Library enhanced by ample bookshelves

- ☐ Third floor expansion is future option for Playroom, Studio, Study or Sewing room

- ☐ Cabinets line both doorways into fireplaced, oversized Family Room complete with sliding glass doors leading out to jumbo-sized porch

- ☐ Immense Master suite includes huge walk-in closet, dressing room decorated with charming window seats and two-part Bath

- ☐ Front and rear porches complete the Georgian tradition

- ☐ Exceptional closet space in three plush second-floor Bedrooms

- ☐ FIRST FLOOR — 1,884 SQ. FT.
- ☐ SECOND FLOOR — 1,521 SQ. FT.
- ☐ OPTIONAL THIRD FLOOR — 808 SQ. FT.
- ☐ BASEMENT — 984 SQ. FT.
- ☐ GARAGE — 2-CAR

TOTAL LIVING AREA — 3,405 SQ. FT.

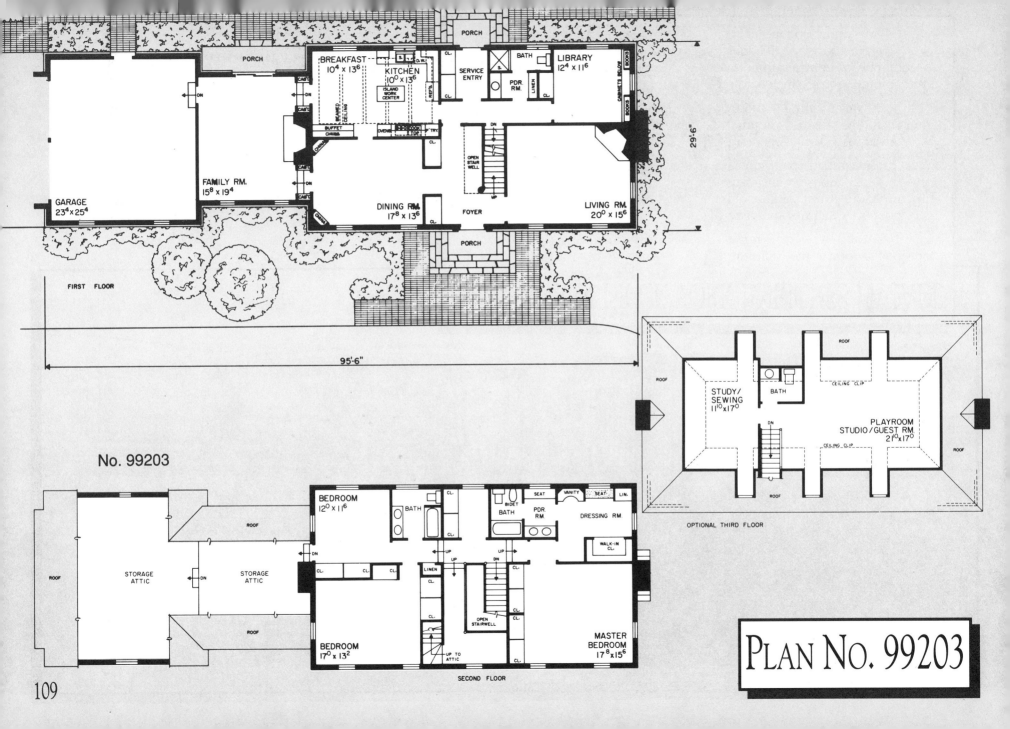

UNCOMMON BRICKWORK ENRICHES FACADE

- Study adjacent to main Entry located in Master Suite wing to insure quiet solitude
- Vaulted Master Suite sports individual his-n-hers walk-in closets and twin basin vanity
- Provocative raised tub with window overlooking side yard and sloping ceiling is focal feature of Master Bath
- Placement of wetbar just off formal Living Room conducive to simplified servicing of guests
- Living Room overlooks poolside vistas
- Spacious Kitchen with food preparation island flows directly into Family Room with exposed beams on cathedral ceiling
- Breakfast Nook with lots of windows provides eating area for informal family meals
- Three additional Bedrooms and two full Baths on second floor supply plenty of room for remainder of family

- FIRST FLOOR — 2,304 SQ. FT.
- SECOND FLOOR — 852 SQ. FT.
- GARAGE — 3-CAR

TOTAL LIVING AREA — 3,156 SQ. FT.

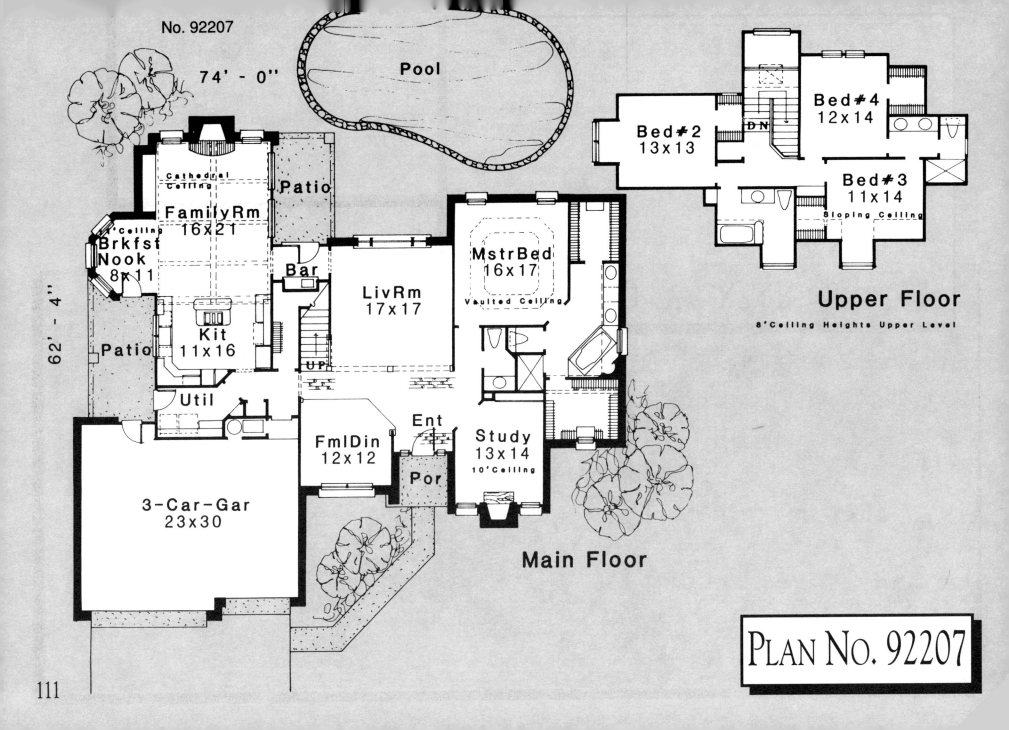

No. 92207

74' - 0"

62' - 4"

Pool

Cathedral Ceiling

FamilyRm
16x21

Patio

Brkfst Nook
8x11

Bar

LivRm
17x17

MstrBed
16x17
Vaulted Ceiling

Kit
11x16

Patio

Util

UP

3-Car-Gar
23x30

FmlDin
12x12

Ent

Por

Study
13x14
10'Ceiling

Main Floor

Bed#2
13x13

DN

Bed#4
12x14

Bed#3
11x14
Sloping Ceiling

Upper Floor

8'Ceiling Heights Upper Level

PLAN No. 92207

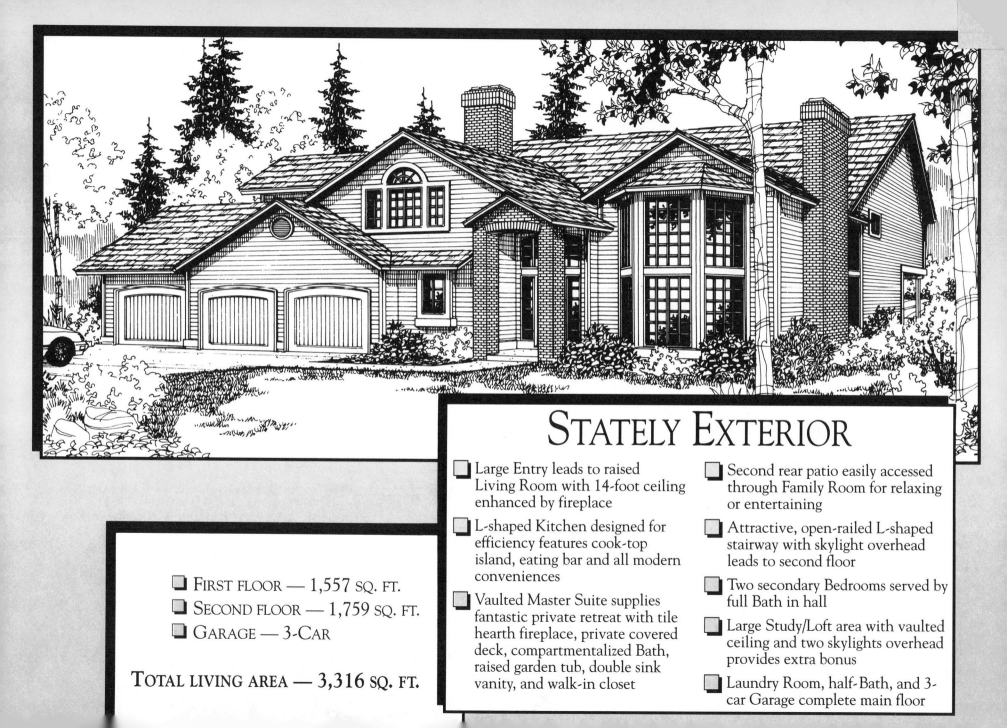

STATELY EXTERIOR

- Large Entry leads to raised Living Room with 14-foot ceiling enhanced by fireplace

- L-shaped Kitchen designed for efficiency features cook-top island, eating bar and all modern conveniences

- Vaulted Master Suite supplies fantastic private retreat with tile hearth fireplace, private covered deck, compartmentalized Bath, raised garden tub, double sink vanity, and walk-in closet

- Second rear patio easily accessed through Family Room for relaxing or entertaining

- Attractive, open-railed L-shaped stairway with skylight overhead leads to second floor

- Two secondary Bedrooms served by full Bath in hall

- Large Study/Loft area with vaulted ceiling and two skylights overhead provides extra bonus

- Laundry Room, half-Bath, and 3-car Garage complete main floor

---

- FIRST FLOOR — 1,557 SQ. FT.
- SECOND FLOOR — 1,759 SQ. FT.
- GARAGE — 3-CAR

TOTAL LIVING AREA — 3,316 SQ. FT.

No. 91337

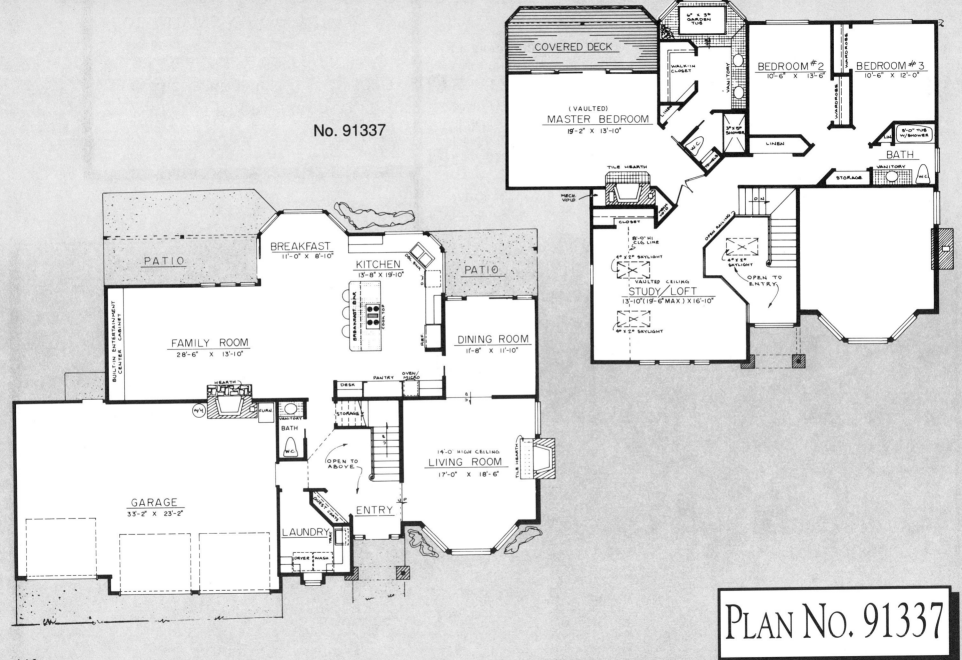

COVERED DECK

(VAULTED)
MASTER BEDROOM
19'-2" X 13'-10"

6" X 5"
GARDEN
TUB

WALK-IN
CLOSET

VANITORY

BEDROOM #2
10'-6" X 13'-6"

BEDROOM #3
10'-6" X 12'-0"

WARDROBE

LINEN

3" X 5"
SHOWER

W.C.

TOWELS

LINEN

BATH

5'-0" TUB
W/SHOWER

STORAGE

VANITORY

W.C.

TILE HEARTH

MECH.
VOID

CLOSET

8'-0" HI
CLG. LINE

4" X 2" SKYLIGHT

VAULTED CEILING

STUDY/LOFT
13'-10" (19'-6" MAX) X 16'-10"

4" X 2" SKYLIGHT

4" X 2"
SKYLIGHT

DN

OPEN RAILING

OPEN TO
ENTRY

BREAKFAST
11'-0" X 8'-10"

KITCHEN
13'-8" X 19'-10"

DBL. SINK

PATIO

PATIO

FAMILY ROOM
28'-6" X 13'-10"

BUILT-IN ENTERTAINMENT CENTER CABINET

BREAKFAST BAR

COOK TOP

REF.

DINING ROOM
11'-8" X 11'-10"

HEARTH

W/H

FURN.

VANITORY

BATH

W.C.

DESK

PANTRY

OVEN/
MICRO

STORAGE

OPEN TO
ABOVE

14'-0" HIGH CEILING
LIVING ROOM
17'-0" X 18'-6"

TILE HEARTH

GARAGE
33'-2" X 23'-2"

GUEST COATS

ENTRY

LAUNDRY

TRAY

DRYER WASH

UP

PLAN NO. 91337

113

SURROUND YOURSELF WITH LUXURY

- Staircase landing splits ascent into separate wings creating aura of seclusion in fourth Bedroom

- Two more Bedrooms on second level retain personal walk-in closets and basins, but share lavatory facilities

- Spacious Family Room enables vast Living Room to be reserved for more formal entertaining

- Master Bedroom complex with huge walk-in closet featuring double shoe storage areas, chests, and plenty of clothes space

- Courtyard area isolates Master Bedroom and second Bedroom from busy living areas

- Kitchen design allows easy access to Breakfast Area and formal Dining Room

- FIRST FLOOR — 4,075 SQ. FT.
- SECOND FLOOR — 1,179 SQ. FT.
- GARAGE — 633 SQ. FT.

TOTAL LIVING AREA — 5,254 SQ. FT.

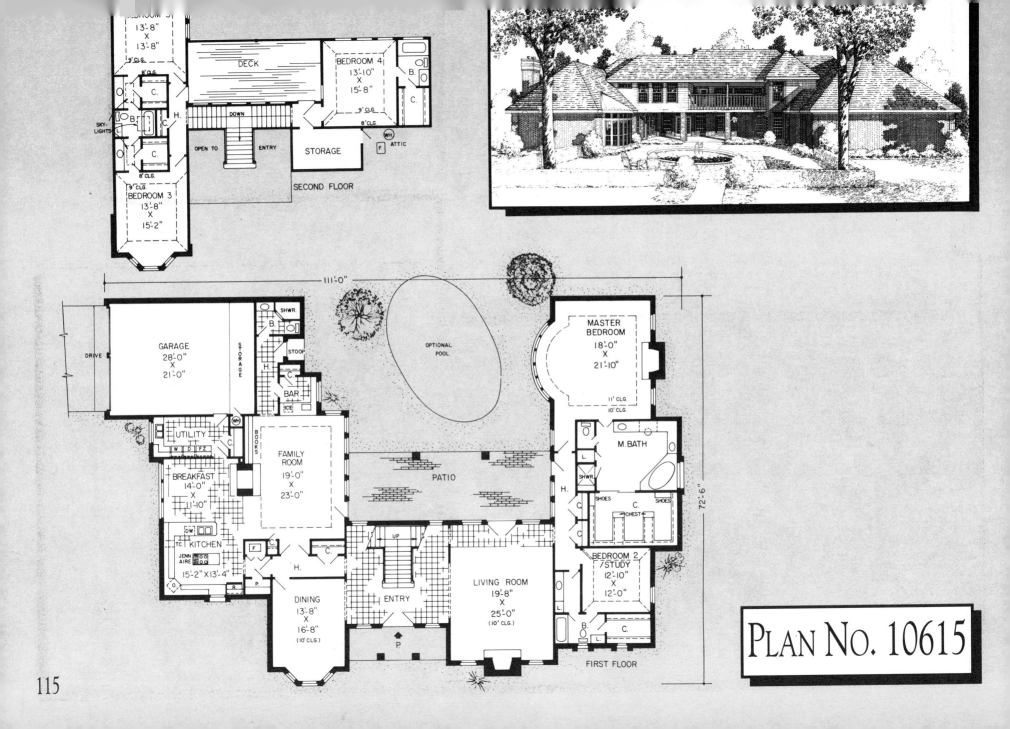

BEDROOM 5
13'-8"
X
13'-8"
9' CLG.

DECK

BEDROOM 4
13'-10"
X
15'-8"

B.

C.

9' CLG.
8' CLG.

SKY-LIGHTS

C.

C.

H.

B.

OPEN TO

DOWN

ENTRY

STORAGE

WH

F

ATTIC

8' CLG.

BEDROOM 3
13'-8"
X
15'-2"

9' CLG.

SECOND FLOOR

111'-0"

OPTIONAL POOL

MASTER BEDROOM
18'-0"
X
21'-10"

11' CLG.
10' CLG.

DRIVE

GARAGE
28'-0"
X
21'-0"

STORAGE

SHWR.

B.

STOOP

H.

C.

BAR

ICE

WH

UTILITY

W D FZ

C.

BOOKS

FAMILY ROOM
19'-0"
X
23'-0"

PATIO

M. BATH

L.

SHWR.

C.

C.

C.

SHOES

C.

SHOES

CHEST

L.

BREAKFAST
14'-0"
X
11'-10"

DW

TC KITCHEN

JENN AIRE

15'-2" X 13'-4"

F

C.

H.

C.

R.

P.

UP

C.

LIVING ROOM
19'-8"
X
25'-0"
(10' CLG.)

L.

BEDROOM 2 / STUDY
12'-10"
X
12'-0"

B.

L.

C.

72'-6"

DINING
13'-8"
X
16'-8"
(10' CLG.)

ENTRY

P.

FIRST FLOOR

PLAN No. 10615

RELAX AND ENJOY!

- L-shaped plan generously studded with windows provides magnificant view of pool area
- Balcony overlooking Entry leads to two Bedrooms sharing full adjoining Bath
- Fireplaced Master Bedroom ushers you to private skylit spa area shielded from road by high retaining wall
- Cabana along backside of 3-car Garage houses two dressing rooms and Baths complete with Sauna
- Kitchen complete with food preparation island contains ample counter space
- Locality of Kitchen allows all active areas to be served easily
- Sunny Breakfast Room grants beautiful poolside view
- Fireplaced Game Room with wetbar accommodates family fun time
- Covered patio near pool offers shady relief from summer sun

- FIRST FLOOR — 3,169 SQ. FT.
- SECOND FLOOR — 678 SQ. FT.
- GARAGE — 678 SQ. FT.

TOTAL LIVING AREA — 3,847 SQ. FT.

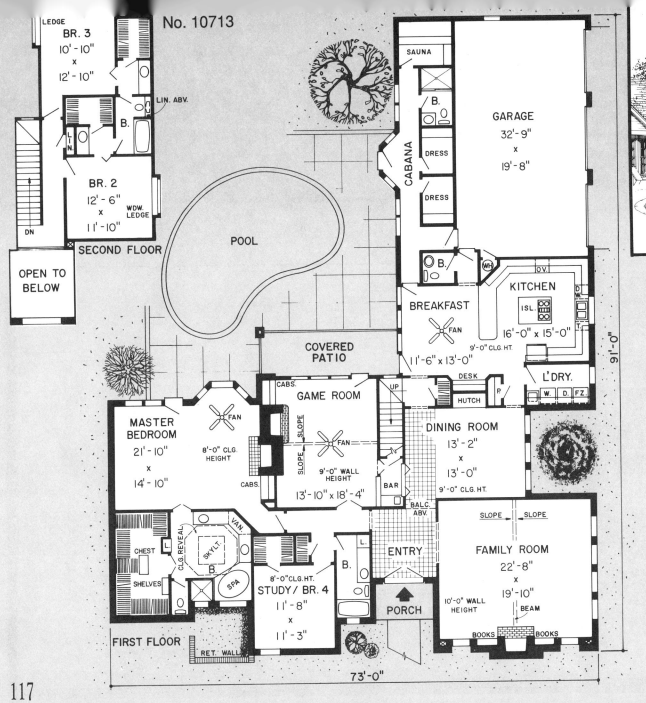

LEDGE

BR. 3
10'-10"
x
12'-10"

LIN. ABV.

B.

LIN.

BR. 2
12'-6"
x
11'-10"

WDW. LEDGE

DN

SECOND FLOOR

OPEN TO BELOW

SAUNA

B.

CABANA

DRESS

DRESS

GARAGE
32'-9"
x
19'-8"

POOL

B.

WH

O.V.

KITCHEN
16'-0" x 15'-0"

ISL.

D.W.

BREAKFAST
11'-6" x 13'-0"

FAN

9'-0" CLG. HT.

COVERED PATIO

DESK

HUTCH

L'DRY.

W. **D.** **FZ.**

CABS.

GAME ROOM

UP

P.

MASTER BEDROOM
21'-10"
x
14'-10"

FAN

8'-0" CLG. HEIGHT

SLOPE **SLOPE**

FAN

9'-0" WALL HEIGHT

13'-10" x 18'-4"

CABS.

BAR

DINING ROOM
13'-2"
x
13'-0"

9'-0" CLG. HT.

BALC. ABV.

CHEST

CLG. REVEAL

SKYLT.

VAN.

B.

SPA

SHELVES

L.

B.

L.

ENTRY

FAMILY ROOM
22'-8"
x
19'-10"

SLOPE **SLOPE**

STUDY / BR. 4
11'-8"
x
11'-3"

8'-0" CLG. HT.

10'-0" WALL HEIGHT

BEAM

PORCH

BOOKS **BOOKS**

FIRST FLOOR

RET. WALL

73'-0"

91'-0"

PLAN NO. 10713

IMPRESSIVE STATELY BRICK MASTERPEICE

- Dramatic staircase creates highly asthetic vision in tiled Foyer

- Three Bedrooms on upper floor each contain personal walk-in closets and private retreats

- Tasteful Library provides safe, accessible keeping for extensive collection of books while sharing view from balcony with hallway

- Family Room sports twelve-foot bar and loads of extra storage space as well as exit to patio

- Spacious Kitchen leads through to Breakfast Room for informal family meals

- Master Suite extends entire length of left side of home making retirement from busy activity pleasurable

- Huge windows accent Sitting Room with fireplace in Master Bedroom

- Master Bath leads into enormous walk-in closet providing abundant space for clothing storage

- FIRST FLOOR — 2,807 SQ. FT.
- SECOND FLOOR — 1,182 SQ. FT.
- GARAGE — 580 SQ. FT.

TOTAL LIVING AREA — 3,989 SQ. FT.

No. 10667

FIRST FLOOR

2-CAR GARAGE
28'-0"
X
22'-0"

DRIVE

F. WH

W. D.

CLO.

FZ U.

SHWR.

BRKFST.
12'-6" X 11'-0"

L.

M.BATH

DW **KITCHEN**

MC.

ISLAND
12'-6" X 14'-2"

DESK

MASTER BEDROOM
15'-10"
X
16'-8"

BOOKS

SITTING
12'-10" X 8'-0"

DINING
12'-4"
X
14'-0"

PANT.

UP

H.

FOYER
LIBRARY ABOVE

P.

PATIO

FAMILY ROOM
14'-4"
X
18'-10"

42" WALL

BAR

H.

C. L.

STORAGE

LIVING RM.
16'-8"
X
19'-10"

74'-0"

65'-8"

119

SECOND FLOOR

BEDROOM 4
15'-2"
X
11'-0"

DECK

ATTIC

C. WH

C.

H.

STOR.

L.

B.

C.

C.

B.

L. H.

OPEN TO FOYER

DOWN

BEDROOM 2
12'-6"
X
12'-4"

BOOKS

LIBRARY
15'-8"
X
11'-4"

BOOKS

H.

BEDROOM 3
13'-2"
X
10'-10"

PLAN NO. 10667

CHARMING CLASSIC STUCCO

- ☐ Exterior offers keystones and corner quoining detail for elegance

- ☐ Staircase in elaborate Entry climbs up to large secluded Loft

- ☐ Extraordinary Master Bedroom with access to private deck includes lavish Bath with corner spa and elegant extra-long double vanity

- ☐ Open Dining Area, separated from Entry by columns, has plenty of space and lighting

- ☐ Uniquely-designed island Kitchen flows into attractive window-surrounded Nook and fireplaced Family Room

- ☐ Step down into Parlor with fireplace and exit to oversized backyard deck

- ☐ Spacious book-lined Den is tucked away in private corner and features access to deck

- ☐ Separate Laundry Room with large capacity enhanced by nearby closet for extra storage

- ☐ FIRST FLOOR — 1,881 SQ. FT.
- ☐ SECOND FLOOR — 1,496 SQ. FT.
- ☐ GARAGE — 963 SQ. FT.

TOTAL LIVING AREA — 3,377 SQ. FT.

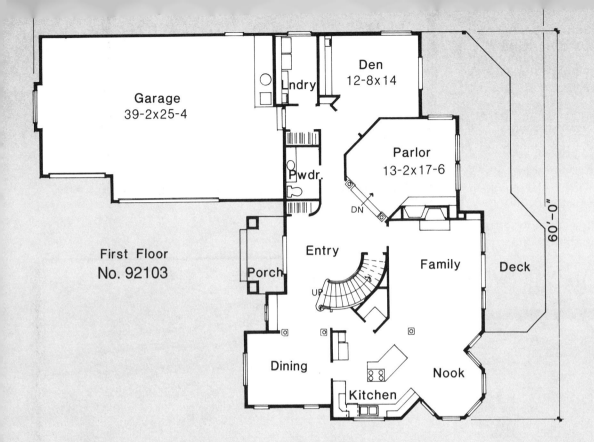

Garage
39-2x25-4

Lndry

Den
12-8x14

Pwdr.

Parlor
13-2x17-6

First Floor
No. 92103

Entry

DN

Porch

UP

Family

Deck

Dining

Nook

Kitchen

60'-0"

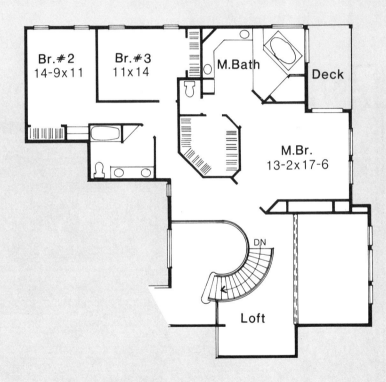

Br.#2
14-9x11

Br.#3
11x14

M.Bath

Deck

M.Br.
13-2x17-6

DN

Loft

Second Floor

PLAN No. 92103

121

FACADE GRACED BY CARRIAGE LIGHTS

- High-ceilinged Master Suite features opulent whirlpool bath
- Walk out to redwood deck through atrium doors in Living Room or Breakfast Area
- Formal Dining Room just steps away from Kitchen for unrestrained service ease
- Sizable Kitchen features food preparation island and plant ledge
- Sunny Breakfast Area opens into Kitchen for informal meals
- Enormous Living Room with wood-beamed ceilings provides ample relaxation room for entire family
- Three additional Bedrooms on second level share full Bath and possess plenty of individual closet space
- Bi-level Study affords quiet place for reading, homework, or just peaceful seclusion
- Bookcase-lined balcony overlooks Dining Room and Foyer below

- FIRST FLOOR — 2,049 SQ. FT.
- SECOND FLOOR — 1,253 SQ. FT.
- BASEMENT — 2,049 SQ. FT.
- GARAGE — 544 SQ. FT.

TOTAL LIVING AREA — 3,302 SQ. FT.

No. 10650

REDWOOD DECK

SEATING

DN

LEDGE
KITCHEN
C   DW
16'-2" x 14'-4"

BREAKFAST
10'-0" x 11'-4"

D   W
LAUNDRY

OV
PAN-TRY
P.R.
C.

LIVING ROOM
11'-0"
CEILING
18'-0"
x
27'-4"

SEAT
SHWR
WHIRL-POOL
BATH
C.
VANITY

HALL

DINING ROOM
12'-10" x 13'-4"

OPEN ABOVE
DN
UP

FOYER

9'-0" CEILING

MASTER BEDROOM
14'-0" x 21'-4"

A Karl Kreeger Design

GARAGE
22'-4" x 23'-8"

PORCH

WALK

FIRST FLOOR

DRIVEWAY

60'-4"

60'-0"

123

LIVING ROOM BELOW

BEDROOM 3
11'-10"
x
12'-4"

BEDROOM 4
10'-8" x 15'-2"

C.

LIN.

HALL

C.

BATH

BOOKCASE

BOOKCASE

RAIL   RAIL

UP

DN

BALCONY

RAILING

DN

STUDY
13'-10 x 24'-8"

DESK

C.

BEDROOM 2
12'-10" x 13'-0"

SLOPED CEILING

STORAGE

SLOPED CL'G

SECOND FLOOR

PLAN No. 10650

MASTER SUITE CROWNS OUTSTANDING PLAN

- Luxurious Master Suite includes private Study and walk-in closet
- Master Bath sports double vanities, shower and whirlpool for total relaxation in privacy
- Two additional Bedrooms situated away from living areas provide ample space for children
- Fourth Bedroom adjoins the Family Room on lower level
- Spacious Kitchen boasts pantry and snack island
- Family Room joins backyard patio via sliding glass doors
- 25-foot oak floors and bow window in Great Room portray magnificant appreciation of finer things in life
- Slate floors add elegance to formal Dining area
- Plan features numerous decks for added enjoyment of outdoor living
- Extra storage space provided on second floor

- MAIN LEVEL — 1,742 SQ. FT.
- UPPER LEVEL — 809 SQ. FT.
- LOWER LEVEL — 443 SQ. FT.
- BASEMENT — 1,270 SQ. FT.
- GARAGE — 558 SQ. FT.

TOTAL LIVING AREA — 2,994 SQ. FT.

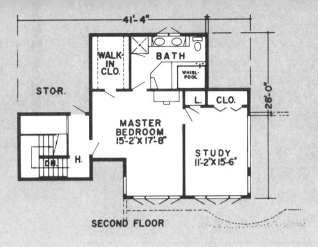

41'-4"

WALK-IN CLO.

BATH

STOR.

WHIRL-POOL

L. CLO.

28'-0"

MASTER BEDROOM
15'-2" X 17'-8"

H.

STUDY
11'-2" X 15'-6"

SECOND FLOOR

No. 10334

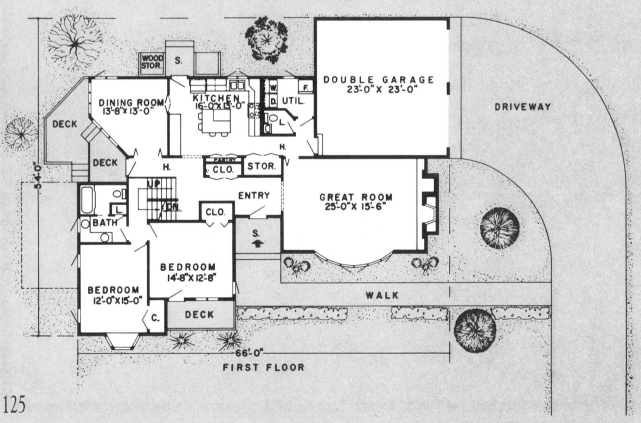

WOOD STOR.

S.

DINING ROOM
13'-8" X 13'-0"

KITCHEN
16'-0" X 15'-0"

W.

F.

D.

UTIL.

L.

DOUBLE GARAGE
23'-0" X 23'-0"

DRIVEWAY

DECK

DECK

H.

PANTRY

CLO.

STOR.

H.

BATH

L.

UP

DN.

CLO.

ENTRY

GREAT ROOM
25'-0" X 15'-6"

54'-0"

S.

BEDROOM
14'-8" X 12'-8"

BEDROOM
12'-0" X 15'-0"

C.

DECK

WALK

66'-0"

FIRST FLOOR

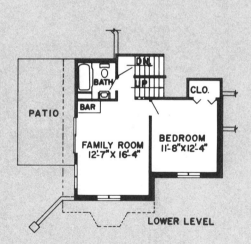

PATIO

BAR

BATH

DN.

CLO.

FAMILY ROOM
12'-7" X 16'-4"

BEDROOM
11'-8" X 12'-4"

LOWER LEVEL

PLAN No. 10334

125

SKYLIGHTS BRIGHTEN ROOMS

- Rounded covered porch leads to aesthetically pleasing Entry with skylight for extra brightness and elegant circular staircase

- Kitchen features skylight, plenty of cabinet space, eat-in Nook and exits to extra-long double deck

- Sunken fireplaced Living Room flooded with light from two large windows has access to deck

- Convenient first-floor Laundry Room has built-in shelving and ample space for appliances

- Master Bedroom has added luxury of private high-walled deck

- Master Bath offers skylight, double vanity, elegant window seat, his and hers showers, and enormous walk-in closet

- Recreation Room with fireplace has interesting window works and includes easy access to top deck

- Three-car Garage has decorative window allowing added light and attractiveness

- First floor — 2,314 sq. ft.
- Basement — 1,302 sq. ft.
- Garage — 1,017 sq. ft.

Total living area — 3,616 sq. ft.

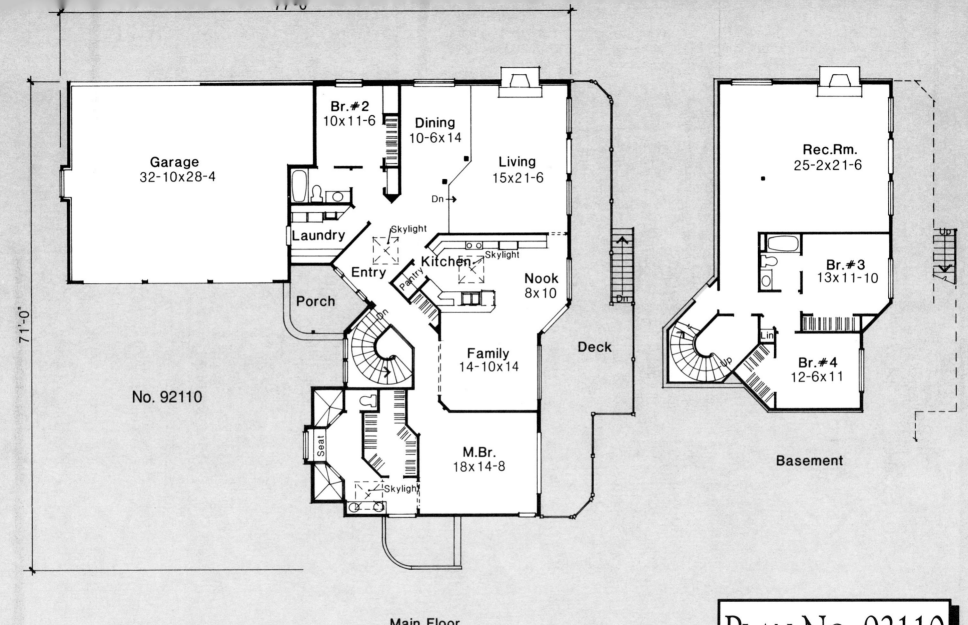

77'-6

71'-0"

Garage
32-10x28-4

Br.#2
10x11-6

Dining
10-6x14

Living
15x21-6

Dn →

Laundry

Skylight

Entry

Kitchen

Skylight

Nook
8x10

Pantry

Porch

Dn

No. 92110

Family
14-10x14

Deck

Dn

Seat

Skylight

M.Br.
18x14-8

Main Floor

Basement

Rec.Rm.
25-2x21-6

Up

Br.#3
13x11-10

Lin

Up

Br.#4
12-6x11

PLAN No. 92110

FIREPLACES ADD WARMTH

- Vaulted ceiling, gently curving staircase and high, arched windows in Entry create airy celebration of light and space

- Formal Dining Room with built-in hutch and Living Room with appealing ceiling lines frame impressive Entry

- Large island Kitchen opens into cheery Eating Nook

- Oversized pantry outside Kitchen lends extra room for day-to-day necessities

- Family Room includes fireplace, paddle fan, built-in, room-size wetbar, and direct access to backyard patio

- Superb Master Bedroom warmed by its own fireplace has French doors leading to personal patio

- Three additional Bedrooms on second level with walk-in closets assure ample storage space

- Enjoy sunny afternoons on deck off Library on second floor

- FIRST FLOOR — 2,803 SQ. FT.
- SECOND FLOOR — 1,076 SQ. FT.
- GARAGE — 721 SQ. FT.

TOTAL LIVING AREA — 3,879 SQ. FT.

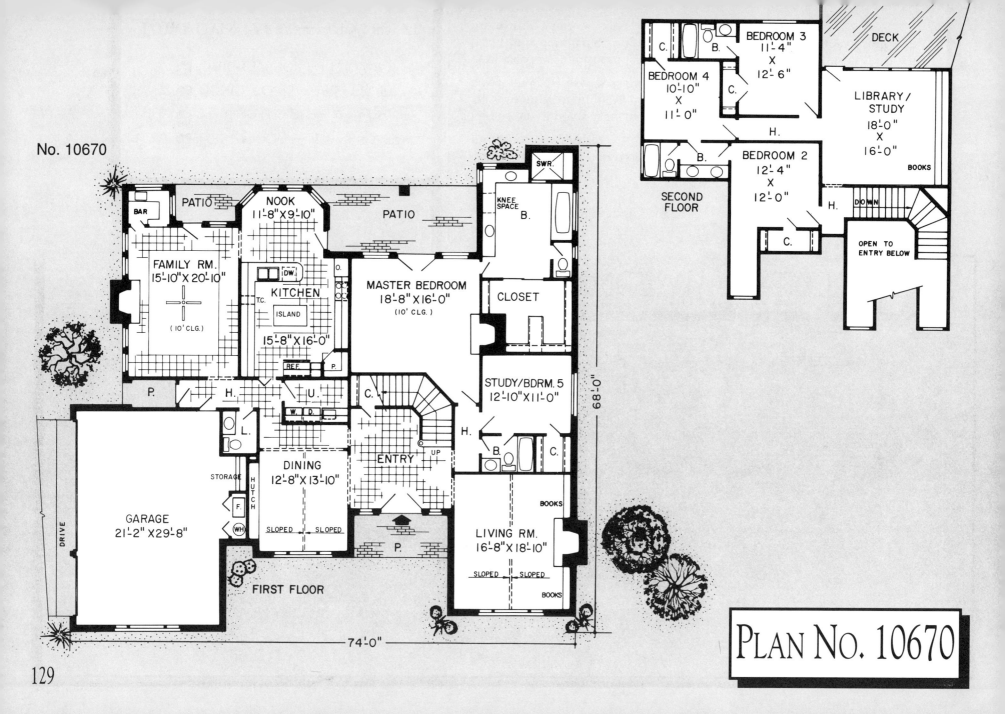

No. 10670

SECOND FLOOR

BEDROOM 3
11'-4"
X
12'-6"

BEDROOM 4
10'-10"
X
11'-0"

C.

B.

C.

B.

DECK

LIBRARY/
STUDY
18'-0"
X
16'-0"

BOOKS

H.

BEDROOM 2
12'-4"
X
12'-0"

B.

H.

DOWN

C.

OPEN TO
ENTRY BELOW

FIRST FLOOR

BAR

PATIO

NOOK
11'-8"X9'-10"

PATIO

SWR.

KNEE
SPACE

B.

FAMILY RM.
15'-10"X 20'-10"

(10' CLG.)

DW

KITCHEN

ISLAND

TC.

15'-8"X16'-0"

O.

REF.

P.

MASTER BEDROOM
18'-8"X16'-0"
(10' CLG.)

CLOSET

P.

H.

U.

W.D.

C.

STUDY/BDRM. 5
12'-10"X11'-0"

H.

B.

C.

L.

STORAGE

HUTCH

F.

WH

DINING
12'-8"X13'-10"

SLOPED   SLOPED

ENTRY

UP

LIVING RM.
16'-8"X18'-10"

BOOKS

SLOPED   SLOPED

BOOKS

GARAGE
21'-2" X29'-8"

DRIVE

P.

68'-0"

74'-0"

129

PLAN No. 10670

ELEGANCE WITH EXTRAS

- ❑ Three-car side-entry Garage opens to exceptional Shop perfect for housing tools or garden equipment
- ❑ Generous covered porch opens into impressive Entry
- ❑ Large Den doubles as main floor guest room with ample walk-in closet and easy access to full Bath
- ❑ Fireplaced Living Room features beautifully detailed ceiling and interesting window works

- ❑ Formal Dining Area more than adequate for meeting entertainment needs
- ❑ Family Room fully contained for privacy flows into large windowed Nook to bring in light
- ❑ Island Kitchen with added pantry is united with Family Room
- ❑ King-sized Master Bedroom leads to extravagant Master Bath with double vanity, shower stall, tub, and linen closet

---

- ❑ FIRST FLOOR — 1,615 SQ. FT.
- ❑ SECOND FLOOR — 2,537 SQ. FT.
- ❑ BONUS ROOM — 481 SQ. FT.
- ❑ GARAGE/SHOP — 1,242 SQ. FT.

TOTAL LIVING AREA — 4,152 SQ. FT.

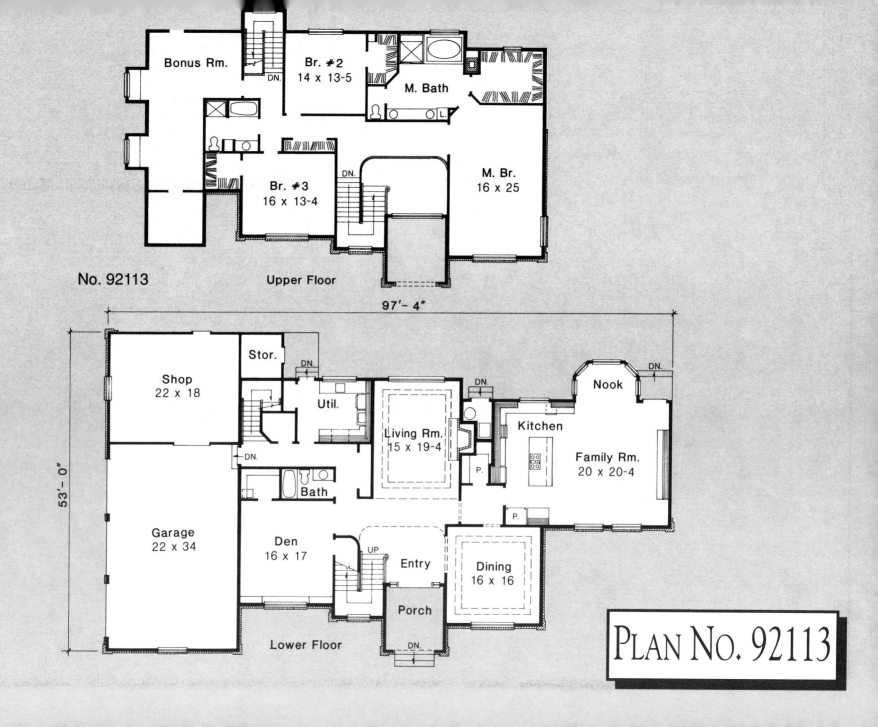

Bonus Rm.

Br. #2
14 x 13-5

DN.

M. Bath

Br. #3
16 x 13-4

DN.

M. Br.
16 x 25

No. 92113

Upper Floor

97'- 4"

Shop
22 x 18

Stor.

DN.

Util.

Nook

DN.

Living Rm.
15 x 19-4

Kitchen

DN.

P.

Family Rm.
20 x 20-4

53'- 0"

DN.

Bath

P.

Garage
22 x 34

Den
16 x 17

UP

Entry

Dining
16 x 16

Porch

DN.

Lower Floor

PLAN NO. 92113

VAULTED CEILINGS MAKE HOME SPECIAL

- Survey two-story Morning Room and yard beyond from vantage point upstairs
- Stately Dining Room displays special ceiling works
- Island Kitchen separated from Morning Room by counter bar
- Delight in pool vistas from covered patio
- Two Bedrooms adjoining full Bath and covered deck share upper level with Loft

- Master Suite opens into spacious king-size Bedroom flowing into awesome Sitting Room with built-in bar and fireplace
- Skylit Master Bath features his-n-hers basins and leads directly into double walk-in closet
- Additional Bedroom adjacent to Master Suite doubles as Study
- Both Family Room and Living Room include beamed, ten-foot ceilings, massive fireplaces, and share wetbar and access to patio

- FIRST FLOOR — 4,014 SQ. FT.
- SECOND FLOOR — 727 SQ. FT.
- GARAGE — 657 SQ. FT.

TOTAL LIVING AREA — 4,741 SQ. FT.

No. 10698

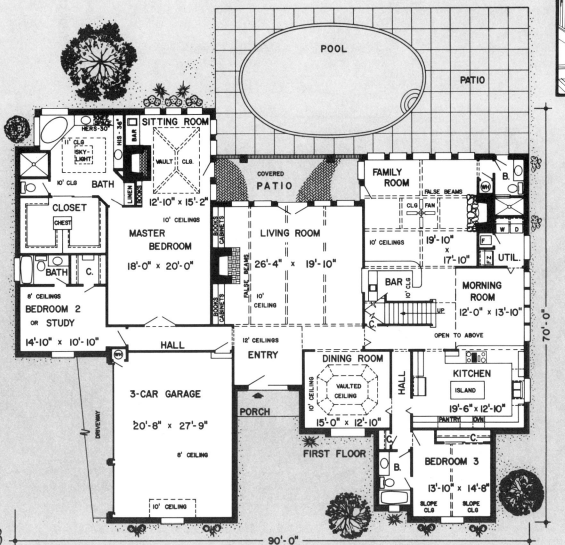

SITTING ROOM
VAULT CLG.
12'-10" x 15'-2"
10' ceilings

HERS-30"
BAR
HIS - 36"
LINEN
BOOKS

CLG
SKYLIGHT
10' CLG
BATH

CLOSET
CHEST
BATH
C.
8' ceilings

BEDROOM 2
OR STUDY
14'-10" x 10'-10"

MASTER BEDROOM
18'-0" x 20'-0"

BOOKS CABINETS
FALSE BEAMS
BOOKS CABINETS

LIVING ROOM
26'-4" x 19'-10"
10' CEILING

COVERED PATIO

FAMILY ROOM
CLG FAN
FALSE BEAMS
10' ceilings
19'-10" x 17'-10"

B.
WH
W D
F
FZ
UTIL.

POOL

PATIO

HALL

ENTRY
12' ceilings

PORCH
10' CEILING

DINING ROOM
VAULTED CEILING
15'-0" x 12'-10"
10' CEILING

BAR
10' CLG

MORNING ROOM
12'-0" x 13'-10"
OPEN TO ABOVE

UP

KITCHEN
ISLAND
19'-6" x 12'-10"
PANTRY OVN

3-CAR GARAGE
20'-8" x 27'-9"
8' CEILING
10' CEILING

DRIVEWAY

FIRST FLOOR

HALL

B.
C. C.

BEDROOM 3
13'-10" x 14'-8"
SLOPE CLG   SLOPE CLG

70'-0"

90'-0"

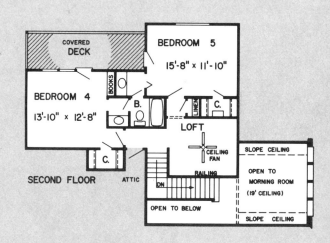

COVERED DECK

BEDROOM 5
15'-8" x 11'-10"

BEDROOM 4
13'-10" x 12'-8"

BOOKS
B.
LINEN
C.
C.
C.

LOFT
CEILING FAN
RAILING
DN
OPEN TO BELOW

SLOPE CEILING
OPEN TO MORNING ROOM (19' CEILING)
SLOPE CEILING

SECOND FLOOR   ATTIC

PLAN No. 10698

- FIRST FLOOR — 1,469 SQ. FT.
- SECOND FLOOR — 1,241 SQ. FT.
- BASEMENT — 1,469 SQ. FT.
- GARAGE — 667 SQ. FT.

TOTAL LIVING AREA — 2,710 SQ. FT.

HOME HAS TRADITIONAL WARMTH

- Abundant windows and covered porch exudes cordial welcome to all
- Escort guests into sunken Living Room just off Foyer
- Functional Kitchen embraces island with stove top, pantry, and bay window
- Fireplaced Great Room features access to both screened porch and outdoor deck for great family barbeques

- Gracious staircase leads to Bedrooms each including individual walk-in closets
- Optional Sitting Room can be used as spare bedroom or nursery
- Sizable Master Bedroom suite boasts two large walk-in closets
- Allow aches and pains to dissolve in gentle massage from jacuzzi exclusive to Master Bath

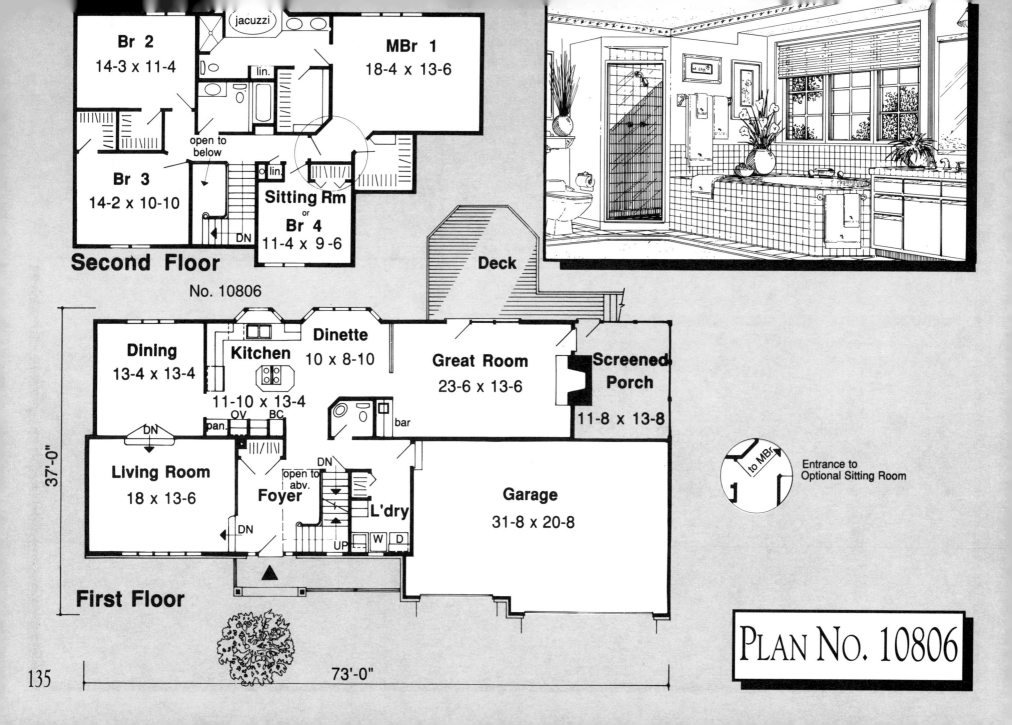

Br 2
14-3 x 11-4

jacuzzi

MBr 1
18-4 x 13-6

lin.

open to below

lin

Br 3
14-2 x 10-10

Sitting Rm
or
Br 4
11-4 x 9-6

DN

Second Floor

No. 10806

Dining
13-4 x 13-4

Kitchen
11-10 x 13-4

Dinette
10 x 8-10

Great Room
23-6 x 13-6

Deck

Screened Porch
11-8 x 13-8

DN

OV BC

pan.

Living Room
18 x 13-6

DN

open to abv.

Foyer

DN

bar

DN

L'dry

UP W D

Garage
31-8 x 20-8

to MBr

Entrance to
Optional Sitting Room

37'-0"

First Floor

73'-0"

135

PLAN NO. 10806

LUXURY PLUS

- Extra roomy secluded Master Bedroom features double-door entry from wide hallway
- Spacious Master Bath has double vanity, enjoyable spa tub, and unique carousel closet for added convenience
- Enormous Family Room is complemented by vaulted ceilings, double skylights and fireplace
- Specifically designed to be handicapped accessible

- Fireplaced Living Room with cathedral ceiling and protruding arched windows give regal effect
- Formal well-lighted Dining Room continues theme with tray ceiling and jutting windows
- Upstairs hall with elegant Balcony overlooking Family Room below affords extra traffic space
- Additional Bedrooms located off Balcony have super-sized closets, decorative dormers letting in additional light and share full Bath

- FIRST FLOOR — 1,967 SQ. FT.
- SECOND FLOOR — 1,087 SQ. FT.
- GARAGE — 650 SQ. FT.

TOTAL LIVING AREA — 3,054 SQ. FT.

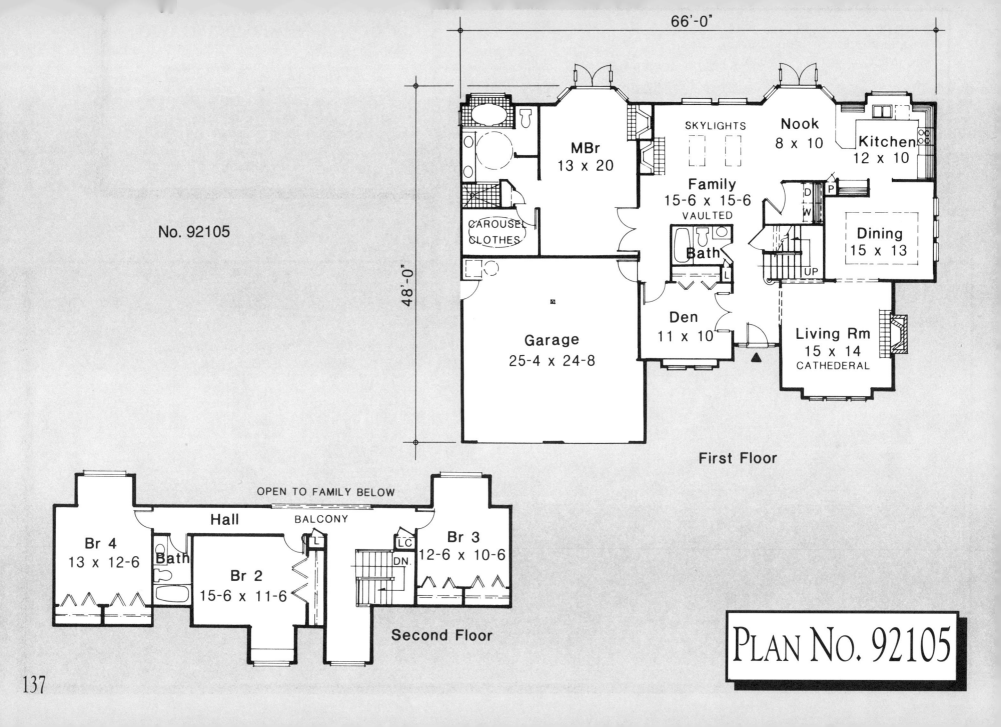

66'-0"

48'-0"

No. 92105

SKYLIGHTS

MBr
13 x 20

Nook
8 x 10

Kitchen
12 x 10

Family
15-6 x 15-6
VAULTED

CAROUSEL
CLOTHES

Bath

D
W
P

Dining
15 x 13

Garage
25-4 x 24-8

Den
11 x 10

UP

Living Rm
15 x 14
CATHEDERAL

First Floor

OPEN TO FAMILY BELOW

Hall

BALCONY

Br 4
13 x 12-6

Bath

L

LC

Br 3
12-6 x 10-6

Br 2
15-6 x 11-6

DN.

Second Floor

PLAN No. 92105

137

DREAM HOUSE AT HOME ON HILLTOP

- ☐ Escort guests into Parlor bordering Foyer for comfortable chats

- ☐ Ample island Kitchen positioned for simple service of formal banquets in adjacent Dining Room as well as intimate family meals in Breakfast Nook

- ☐ Unusual contour with bay windows of Breakfast Nook allows sunny enjoyment of morning refreshment

- ☐ Step down to sunken Family Room with fireplace and plenty of windows for overview of backyard

- ☐ Master Suite becomes luxurious retreat for occupants with his-n-hers walk-in closets, vanities and private spa

- ☐ Second Bedroom on first floor includes personal access to full Bath

- ☐ Descend to lower level for ulitmate relaxation in Execise Room, Rec Room with full wetbar and Sauna

- ☐ MAIN FLOOR — 2,580 SQ. FT.
- ☐ BASEMENT FLOOR — 2,235 SQ. FT.
- ☐ GARAGE — 571 SQ. FT.

TOTAL LIVING AREA — 4,815 SQ. FT.

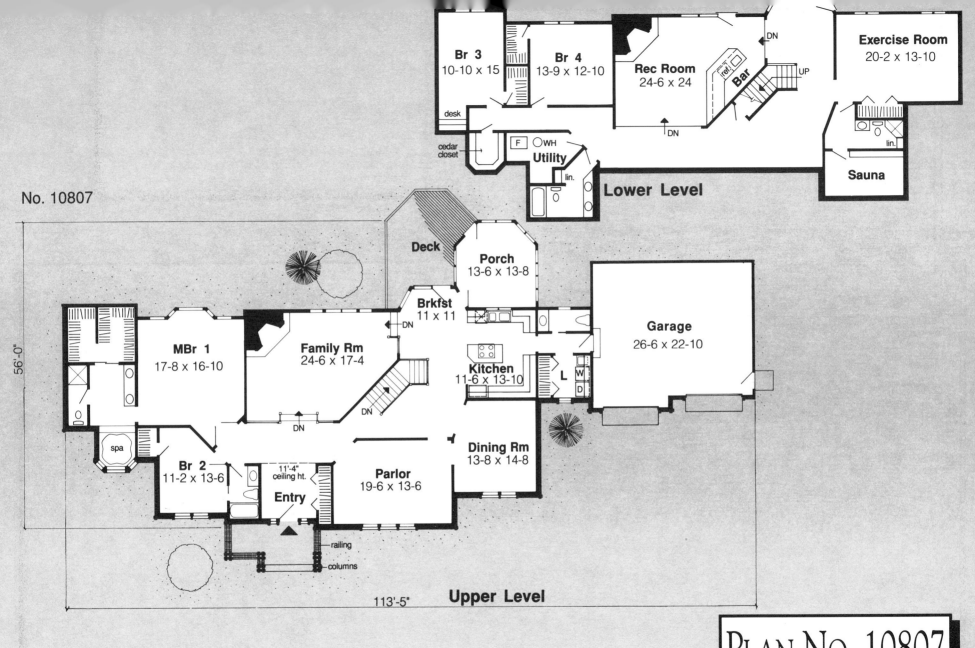

No. 10807

Br 3
10-10 x 15

Br 4
13-9 x 12-10

Rec Room
24-6 x 24

Bar

Exercise Room
20-2 x 13-10

DN
UP
DN

desk

cedar closet

Utility

F WH

lin.

Sauna

lin.

Lower Level

Deck

Porch
13-6 x 13-8

Brkfst
11 x 11

DN

Garage
26-6 x 22-10

MBr 1
17-8 x 16-10

Family Rm
24-6 x 17-4

DN

DN

DN

Kitchen
11-6 x 13-10

L

W
D

spa

Br 2
11-2 x 13-6

11'-4"
ceiling ht.

Entry

Parlor
19-6 x 13-6

Dining Rm
13-8 x 14-8

railing

columns

56'-0"

113'-5"

Upper Level

PLAN No. 10807

139

PERFECT FOR PARTIES

- ☐ Greet guests in fabulous Foyer adorned with impressive two-story gallery behind beautiful curving stairway
- ☐ Leisurely unwind with family and friends in Family Room with vaulted ceiling, large windows, built-in bar, and lots of space
- ☐ Entertain guests in Dining Room for more formal occasions
- ☐ Lovely Sitting Room between two second-floor Bedrooms overlooks Gallery below

- ☐ Master Bedroom with paddle fan offers cool comfort for a good night's rest
- ☐ Lavish Bath in Master Suite features sunken tub to soak away the day's cares
- ☐ Two Bedrooms on upper floor include individual Baths and walk-in closets
- ☐ Cheerful Eating Nook has easy approach to efficient Kitchen
- ☐ Wood beams on ceiling of Living Room exudes warm welcome

☐ FIRST FLOOR — 2,459 SQ. FT.
☐ SECOND FLOOR — 810 SQ. FT.
☐ GARAGE — 660 SQ. FT.

TOTAL LIVING AREA — 3,269 SQ. FT.

FIRST FLOOR

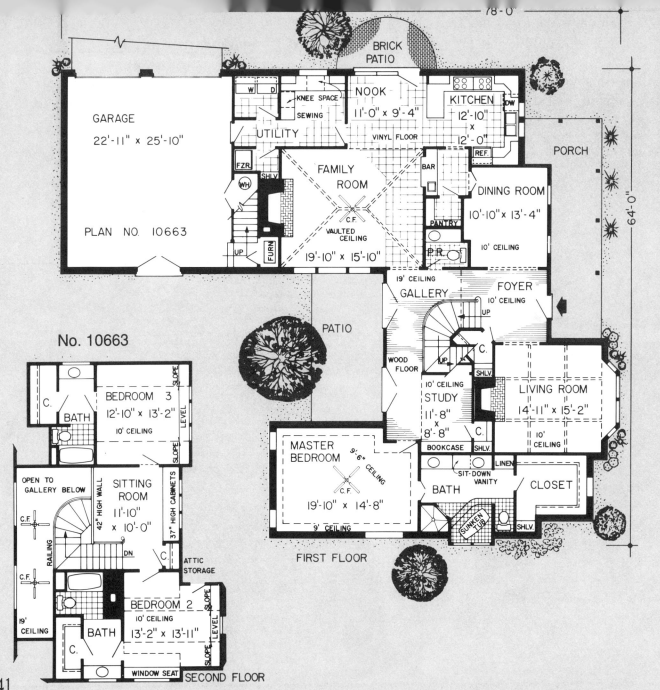

78'-0"

64'-0"

GARAGE
22'-11" x 25'-10"

PLAN NO. 10663

W D
KNEE SPACE
SEWING
UTILITY

NOOK
11'-0" x 9'-4"
VINYL FLOOR

KITCHEN
12'-10"
x
12'-0"

DW

REF.

PORCH

FZR

SHLV.

WH

FAMILY
ROOM

C.F.

VAULTED CEILING

19'-10" x 15'-10"

FURN

UP

BAR

PANTRY

P.R.

DINING ROOM
10'-10" x 13'-4"

10' CEILING

19' CEILING

GALLERY

WOOD
FLOOR

10' CEILING

UP

C.

SHLV.

10' CEILING

FOYER

10' CEILING

BRICK
PATIO

PATIO

STUDY
11'-8"
x
8'-8"

LIVING ROOM
14'-11" x 15'-2"

SHLV.

C.

10'
CEILING

MASTER
BEDROOM

C.F.

9'-6"± CEILING

19'-10" x 14'-8"
9' CEILING

BOOKCASE

SHLV.

SIT-DOWN
VANITY

BATH

LINEN

CLOSET

SUNKEN
TUB

SHLV.

FIRST FLOOR

No. 10663

SECOND FLOOR

C.

BATH

BEDROOM 3
12'-10" x 13'-2"
10' CEILING

SLOPE

SLOPE

LEVEL

OPEN TO
GALLERY BELOW

C.F.

C.F.

RAILING

SITTING
ROOM
11'-10"
x 10'-0"

42" HIGH WALL

37" HIGH CABINETS

DN

C.

ATTIC
STORAGE

19'
CEILING

BATH

C.

BEDROOM 2
13'-2" x 13'-11"
10' CEILING

SLOPE

SLOPE

LEVEL

WINDOW SEAT   SECOND FLOOR

PLAN No. 10663

BRIGGLEBOW

First floor — 2,036 sq. ft.
Second floor — 1,554 sq. ft.
Basement — 2,036 sq. ft.
Garage — 533 sq. ft.
Total living area — 3,590 sq. ft.

Curved Stairway Highlights Design

☐ Sweeping staircase and skylit sloped ceiling in Foyer create elegant sophistication

☐ Step down to fireplaced Living Room off grand Foyer

☐ Large Kitchen features centralized food preparation island and desk for meal planning

☐ Enjoy informal meals in bright Breakfast Nook overlooking backyard deck

☐ Dining Room affords exquisite environment for formal dining

☐ Vaulted ceiling in Family Room and expansive fireplace extend warm welcome

☐ Spacious Master Bedroom includes private bath with double walk-in closets, basins, and raised tub

☐ Enjoy summer evenings on private deck outside Master Bedroom

☐ Two addtional Bedrooms on second floor share full Bath

☐ Cedar closet provides exclusive storage area for valuable items

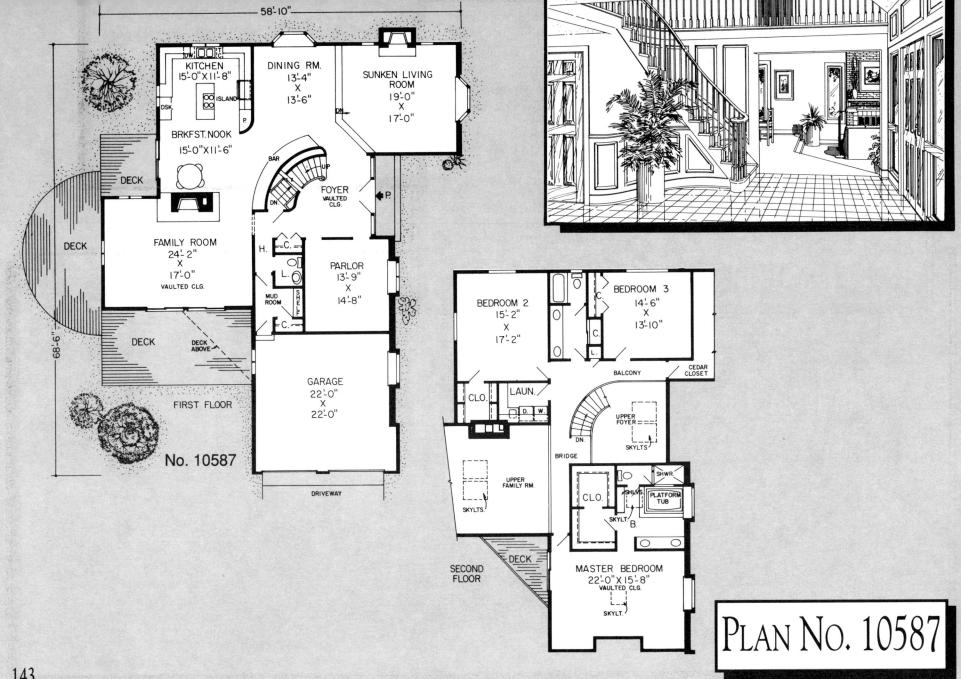

58'-10"

68'-6"

KITCHEN
15'-0" X 11'-8"

DW

DSK.

ISLAND

P.

BRKFST. NOOK
15'-0" X 11'-6"

DECK

DECK

DECK

FAMILY ROOM
24'-2"
X
17'-0"
VAULTED CLG.

DECK

DECK
ABOVE

FIRST FLOOR

No. 10587

DRIVEWAY

DINING RM.
13'-4"
X
13'-6"

BAR

DN

UP

DN

FOYER
VAULTED
CLG.

H.

C.

L.

MUD
ROOM

SHELF

C.

SUNKEN LIVING
ROOM
19'-0"
X
17'-0"

P.

P.

PARLOR
13'-9"
X
14'-8"

GARAGE
22'-0"
X
22'-0"

BEDROOM 2
15'-2"
X
17'-2"

C.

BEDROOM 3
14'-6"
X
13'-10"

C.

L.

BALCONY

CEDAR
CLOSET

CLO.

LAUN.

D. W.

BRIDGE

DN

UPPER FOYER

SKYLTS.

UPPER
FAMILY RM.

SKYLTS.

SECOND
FLOOR

DECK

CLO.

SHLVS.

SKYLT.

SHWR.

SHLVS

PLATFORM
TUB

B.

MASTER BEDROOM
22'-0" X 15'-8"
VAULTED CLG.

SKYLT.

PLAN NO. 10587

143

DORMERED DELIGHT

- [ ] Classic brick masterpiece combines elegance of manor home with convenient features
- [ ] Step down from arched Entry to either formal Living or Dining Rooms divided by columns yet projecting open feeling
- [ ] Relax and enjoy placid atmosphere of Library
- [ ] Master Bedroom features sloped ceiling, relaxing garden spa, oversized walk-in closet and entry to backyard veranda

- [ ] Family Room highlighted by fireplace, sloped ceiling and fabulous glass wall
- [ ] Generously appointed Kitchen includes pantry, loads of cabinets and counter space
- [ ] Second floor contains three Bedrooms each with adjoining Bath and large closets
- [ ] Upstairs also find Gameroom with picturesque window seat and optional fifth Bedroom with adjoining Bath

- [ ] FIRST FLOOR —2,423 SQ. FT.
- [ ] SECOND FLOOR — 1,235 SQ. FT.
- [ ] GARAGE — 507 SQ. FT.

TOTAL LIVING AREA — 3,658 SQ. FT.

No. 20405

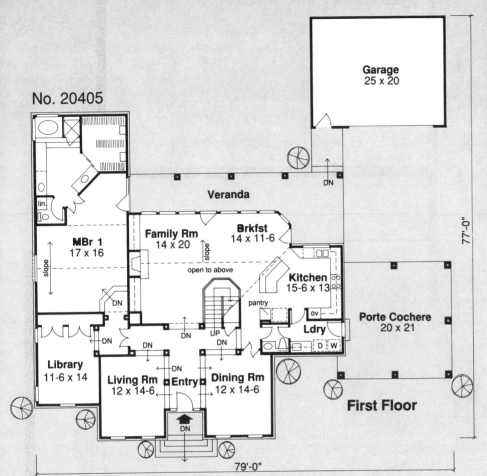

Garage
25 x 20

Veranda

MBr 1
17 x 16

Family Rm
14 x 20

Brkfst
14 x 11-6

open to above

Kitchen
15-6 x 13

pantry

Porte Cochere
20 x 21

Ldry

D W

Library
11-6 x 14

Living Rm
12 x 14-6

Entry

Dining Rm
12 x 14-6

77'-0"

79'-0"

First Floor

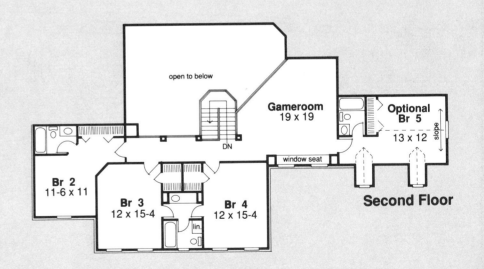

open to below

Gameroom
19 x 19

Optional
Br 5
13 x 12

window seat

Br 2
11-6 x 11

Br 3
12 x 15-4

Br 4
12 x 15-4

Second Floor

PLAN NO. 20405

FIRST-CLASS RECREATION CENTER

- Swimming pool and spa located in daylight basement offers visual enjoyment on all three levels

- Basement is recreational center of entire house with kitchenette, fireplace, bathroom, exercise room, sauna, and more

- Glass surrounds double doors in lofty vaulted Entry

- Both Living Room and Dining Room also feature partially vaulted ceilings

- Take your choice of view when lunching in sunny Nook — poolside, rear vista or back into huge Kitchen

- Guest suite complete with Bathroom, Living Room, and fireplace provides cushy quarters for guests

- Enjoy late night movies while soaking in spa, enjoy refreshments from small kitchen galley, or fall asleep in flickering firelight in Master Suite embodied on entire second floor

- FIRST FLOOR — 3,171 SQ. FT.
- SECOND FLOOR — 1,541 SQ. FT.
- FINISHED BASEMENT — 3,402 SQ. FT.
- GARAGE — 1,281 SQ. FT.

TOTAL LIVING AREA — 8,114 SQ. FT.

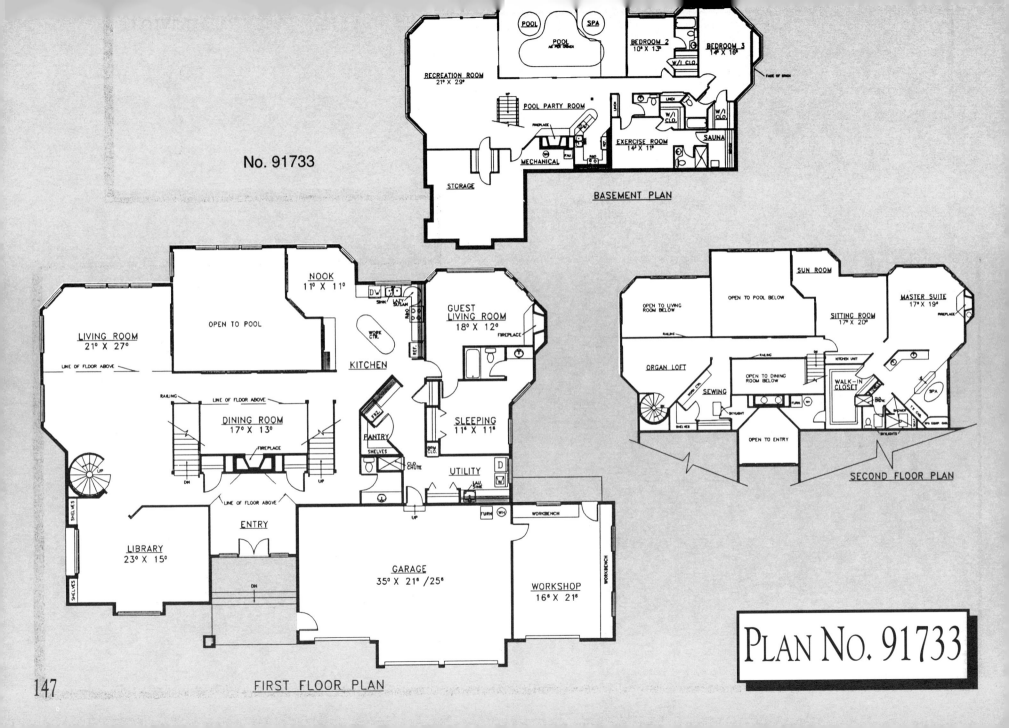

No. 91733

BASEMENT PLAN

POOL

SPA

POOL AS PER OWNER

BEDROOM 2
10° X 13°

BEDROOM 3
14° X 18°

RECREATION ROOM
21° X 29°

W/I CLO.

FACE OF BRICK

POOL PARTY ROOM

LINEN

FIREPLACE

W/I
CLO.

W/I
CLO.

EXERCISE ROOM
14° X 11°

MECHANICAL

SAUNA

STORAGE

FIRST FLOOR PLAN

NOOK
11° X 11°

DW

SINK

LAZY
SUSAN

BBQ

GUEST
LIVING ROOM
18° X 12°

FIREPLACE

OPEN TO POOL

LIVING ROOM
21° X 27°

WORK
CTR.

REF.

LINE OF FLOOR ABOVE

KITCHEN

RAILING

LINE OF FLOOR ABOVE

DINING ROOM
17° X 13°

FIREPLACE

SLEEPING
11° X 11°

FRZ.

PANTRY

SHELVES

CLO.
CHUTE

DRY.
CLO.

UTILITY

D

UP

DN

UP

LINE OF FLOOR ABOVE

SHELVES

LAU.
SINK

W

FURN

WH

WORKBENCH

LIBRARY
23° X 15°

ENTRY

DN

GARAGE
35° X 21°/25°

WORKSHOP
16° X 21°

WORKBENCH

SHELVES

SECOND FLOOR PLAN

SUN ROOM

OPEN TO LIVING
ROOM BELOW

OPEN TO POOL BELOW

MASTER SUITE
17° X 19°

SITTING ROOM
17° X 20°

FIREPLACE

RAILING

RAILING

ORGAN LOFT

KITCHEN UNIT

WORK CTR.

SEWING

OPEN TO DINING
ROOM BELOW

WALK-IN
CLOSET

SPA

SKYLIGHT

SHELVES

SHOWER

T.V. CAB.

SPA EQUIP. BELOW

OPEN TO ENTRY

SKYLIGHTS

PLAN NO. 91733

EXCITING ENERGY-SAVER

- ☐ Tiled Foyer with two-story ceiling flows directly into fireplaced Living Room for impressive welcome to family and friends

- ☐ French doors lead into skylit Sun Room with lots of windows and unobstructed view of backyard

- ☐ Island Kitchen with profusion of counter space and pantry opens to bright Breakfast Room

- ☐ Recessed ceiling in Dining Room adjacent to Kitchen renders formal atmosphere

- ☐ Highlight of Master Bedroom is extravagant Bath featuring double vanities, walk-in closet, Dressing Area, and raised whirlpool tub

- ☐ Overlook Foyer and Living Room from Balcony on second floor

- ☐ Three additional Bedrooms upstairs each include large closet space for ample storage

- ☐ Two Bedrooms share Bathroom facilities but have personal basins and Dressing Area while third Bedroom has private Bath

---

- ☐ FIRST FLOOR — 2,186 SQ. FT.
- ☐ SECOND FLOOR — 983 SQ. FT.
- ☐ BASEMENT — 2,186 SQ. FT.
- ☐ GARAGE — 704 SQ. FT.

TOTAL LIVING AREA — 3,169 SQ. FT.

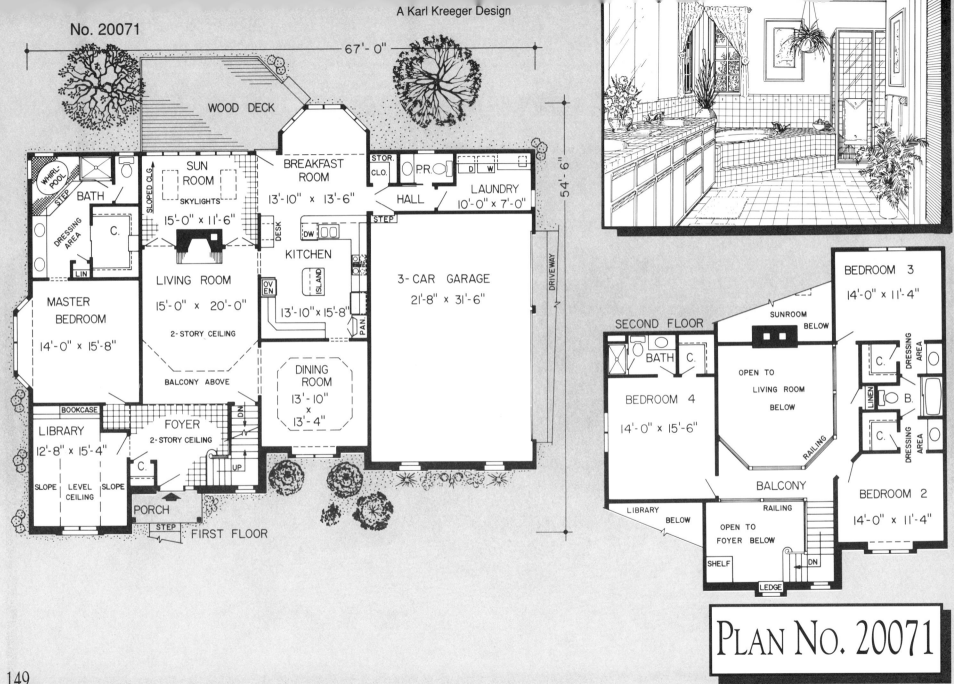

No. 20071

67'- 0"

54'- 6"

WOOD DECK

WHIRL-POOL
STEP
BATH
DRESSING AREA
C.
LIN

SUN ROOM
SLOPED CLG.
SKYLIGHTS
15'-0" x 11'-6"

BREAKFAST ROOM
13'-10" x 13'-6"

STOR.
CLO.
P.R.
D   W

LAUNDRY
10'-0" x 7'-0"

HALL

STEP

DESK

KITCHEN
DW
OVEN
ISLAND
13'-10" x 15'-8"
PAN.

3- CAR GARAGE
21'-8" x 31'-6"

DRIVEWAY

MASTER BEDROOM
14'-0" x 15'-8"

LIVING ROOM
15'-0" x 20'-0"
2- STORY CEILING

BALCONY ABOVE

DINING ROOM
13'-10" x 13'-4"

BOOKCASE

LIBRARY
12'-8" x 15'-4"
SLOPE   LEVEL CEILING   SLOPE

C.

FOYER
2- STORY CEILING

DN
UP

PORCH
STEP
FIRST FLOOR

149

SECOND FLOOR

SUNROOM BELOW

OPEN TO LIVING ROOM BELOW

BEDROOM 3
14'-0" x 11'-4"

BATH   C.

BEDROOM 4
14'-0" x 15'-6"

C.
LINEN
B.
C.
DRESSING AREA
DRESSING AREA

RAILING

BALCONY

BEDROOM 2
14'-0" x 11'-4"

LIBRARY BELOW

RAILING
OPEN TO FOYER BELOW

SHELF
DN
LEDGE

PLAN No. 20071

EXQUISITE ELEGANCE

- Stately exterior reflects careful planning evident thoughout fabulous home
- Entertain guests in elegant yet comfortable style in formal Dining and Living Rooms
- Hearth Room in rear of house is conveniently situated near island Kitchen with built-in pantry
- Laundry Room conveniently located with chute from upstairs
- Enjoy outdoor entertaining on rear deck

- Upstairs Master Bedroom is exquisitely detailed with decorated ceiling
- Adjoining skylit Master Bath leads to enormous walk-in closet
- Three additional huge Bedrooms all with ample closet space located down hall from Master Bedroom
- Second floor has cedar closet for safe out-of-season storage
- Office doubles as fifth bedroom or perfect retreat for quiet study, homework or reading room

- First floor — 1,422 sq. ft.
- Second floor — 1,602 sq. ft.
- Basement — 1,422 sq. ft.
- Garage — 588 sq. ft.

Total living area — 3,024 sq. ft.

Second Floor

Office
11-8 x 10-4

Br 3
11-4 x 11

Br 4
11-8 x 10-8

cedar closet

Br 2
11-4 x 11-4

chute

lin.

lin.

lin.

DN

MBr 1
13-4 x 17-4

decor. ceiling

First Floor

70'-0"

40'-0"

A Karl Kreeger Design

Deck

slope   slope

Brkfst
11 x 9-6

Hearth Rm
18 x 11-4

Garage
23-4 x 23-4

Kit
12 x 13

D   F
W   **Ldry**
chute

pantry

Dining Rm
13-4 x 11-4

decor. ceiling

DN   UP

Living Rm
13-4 x 17-4

Foyer

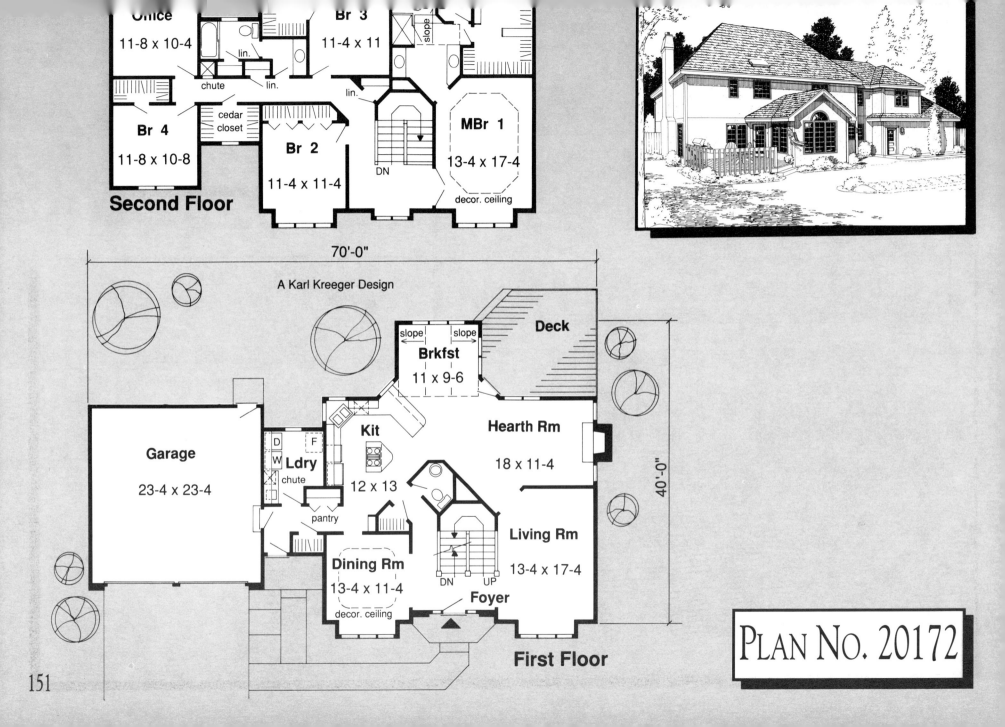

PLAN No. 20172

TRULY PALATIAL MASTER SUITE

- ☐ FIRST FLOOR — 1,875 SQ. FT.
- ☐ SECOND FLOOR — 2,003 SQ. FT.
- ☐ GARAGE — 3-CAR

TOTAL LIVING AREA — 3,878 SQ. FT.

- ☐ Elaborate brick detailing, steeply pitched roof and generous windows accent exterior

- ☐ Inviting covered porch leads to grand Entry with circular staircase and overhead view

- ☐ Fireplaced sunken Living Room adjoins Dining Room with bay windows and coved ceiling

- ☐ Island Kitchen steps into Nook with economically efficient skywall and graduates to fireplaced Family Room

- ☐ Three-car Garage houses furnace and hot water heater allowing more space in Utility Room

- ☐ Master Bedroom features fireplace, elegant cathedral ceiling, plush bay-windowed Sitting Room

- ☐ Master Bath offers overabundant walk-in closet, shower stall, and luxurious corner spa

- ☐ Bonus Play Room over Garage has guest room option and decorative effect of double dormers

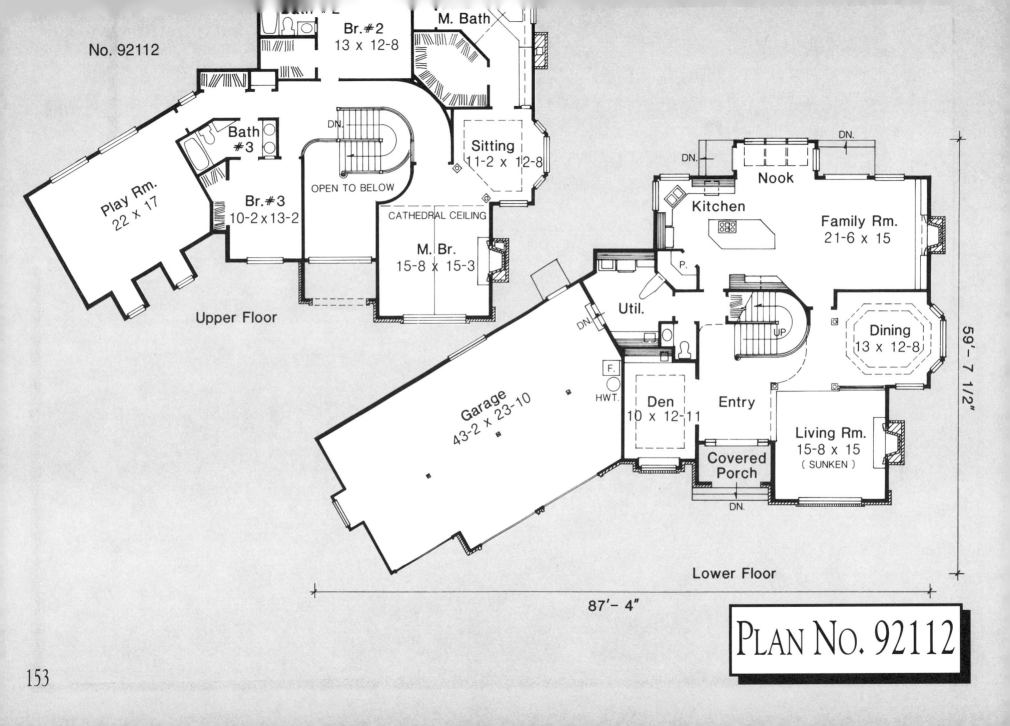

No. 92112

Br.#2
13 x 12-8

M. Bath

Bath #3

Play Rm.
22 x 17

DN.

OPEN TO BELOW

Sitting
11-2 x 12-8

Br.#3
10-2 x 13-2

CATHEDRAL CEILING

M. Br.
15-8 x 15-3

Upper Floor

DN.

DN.

Nook

Kitchen

Family Rm.
21-6 x 15

P.

Util.

UP

Dining
13 x 12-8

Garage
43-2 x 23-10

F.

HWT.

Den
10 x 12-11

Entry

Covered Porch

Living Rm.
15-8 x 15
(SUNKEN)

DN.

Lower Floor

59'- 7 1/2"

87'- 4"

PLAN NO. 92112

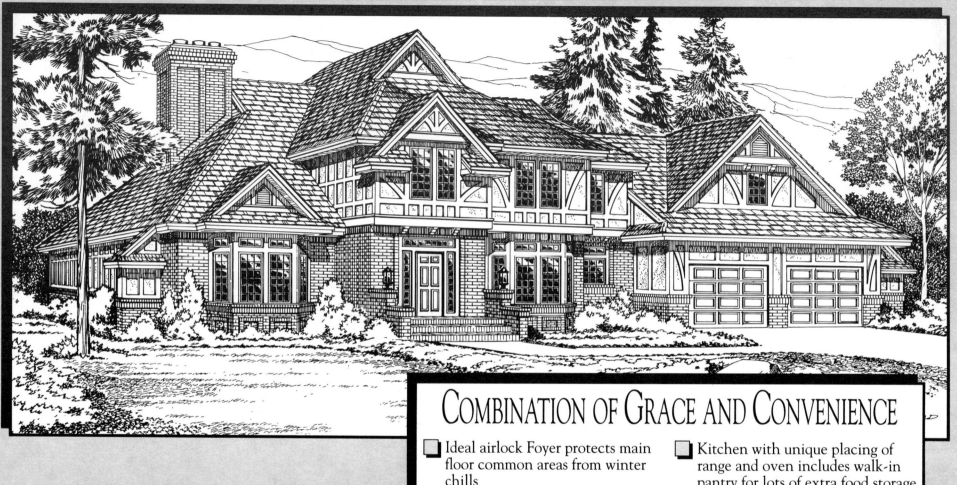

COMBINATION OF GRACE AND CONVENIENCE

- ❑ Ideal airlock Foyer protects main floor common areas from winter chills

- ❑ Pan-vaulted formal Living Room has back-to-back fireplace, intriguing bay window for added sunlight, and added luxury of built-in bookshelves

- ❑ Extra large Dining Room gives atmosphere of luxury and comfort

- ❑ Cheerful Breakfast Room surrounded by huge rear deck features built-in wetbar

- ❑ Kitchen with unique placing of range and oven includes walk-in pantry for lots of extra food storage

- ❑ Spacious Laundry Room includes built-in shelving for added convenience

- ❑ Sprawling Family Room with tray ceiling and bookshelves also leads to uniquely shaped rear deck

- ❑ Vaulted Master Bedroom includes whirlpool bath, double vanity, and over-sized walk-in closet

- ❑ FIRST FLOOR — 1,647 SQ. FT.
- ❑ SECOND FLOOR — 1,191 SQ. FT.
- ❑ BASEMENT — 1,647 SQ. FT.
- ❑ GARAGE — 576 SQ. FT.

TOTAL LIVING AREA — 2,838 SQ. FT.

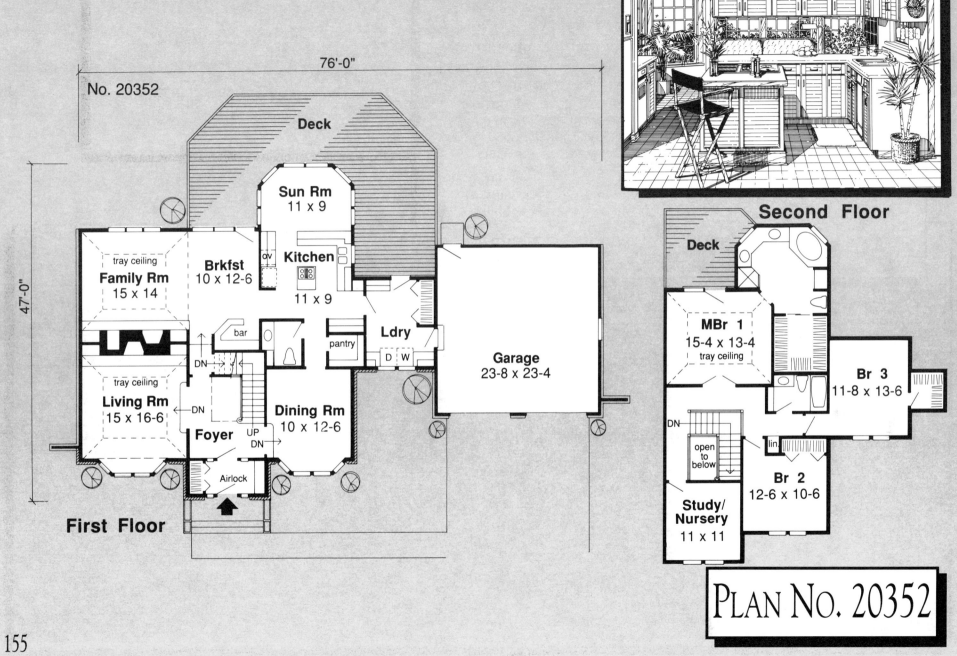

No. 20352

76'-0"

47'-0"

Deck

Sun Rm
11 x 9

Kitchen
11 x 9

ov

Brkfst
10 x 12-6

tray ceiling
Family Rm
15 x 14

bar

Ldry

pantry

D W

Garage
23-8 x 23-4

tray ceiling
Living Rm
15 x 16-6

DN

DN

Foyer

UP
DN

Dining Rm
10 x 12-6

Airlock

First Floor

Second Floor

Deck

MBr 1
15-4 x 13-4
tray ceiling

Br 3
11-8 x 13-6

DN

open
to
below

lin

**Study/
Nursery**
11 x 11

Br 2
12-6 x 10-6

PLAN No. 20352

FRONT BEDROOM FEATURES WINDOW SEAT

- ☐ Sloping roofline creates unusual decorating possibilities in Master Bedroom

- ☐ Feel the day's cares ease away while relaxing on private deck in Master Suite after reposing in Roman tub in skylit Bath

- ☐ Two additional Bedrooms on second floor have ample closet space, and share full Bath

- ☐ Kitchen framed by formal Dining Room and cheery Eating Nook

- ☐ Soaring ceilings generate airy atmosphere throughout design

- ☐ Open railings and single steps separate fireplaced Family and Living Rooms from Entry and Dining Areas

- ☐ Sliders in Family Room and both Dining Rooms open to rear deck and patio to maximize spacious feeling

- ☐ Fourth bedroom complete with full Bath tucked behind garage

☐ FIRST FLOOR — 2,027 SQ. FT.
☐ SECOND FLOOR — 1,476 SQ. FT.
☐ GARAGE — 650 SQ. FT.

TOTAL LIVING AREA — 3,503 SQ. FT.

No. 10758

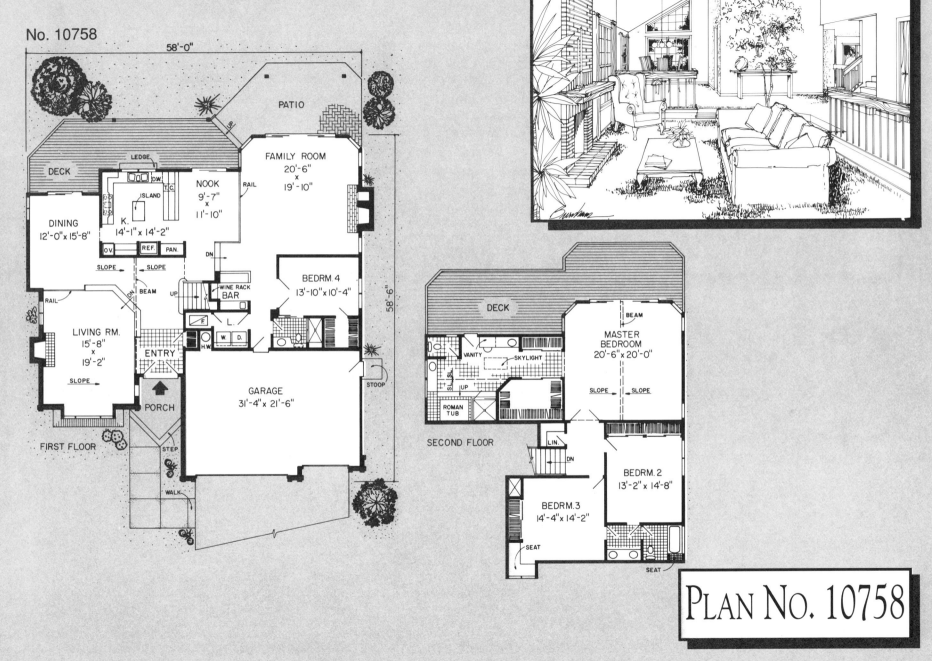

58'-0"

DECK

LEDGE

DW.

T.C.

ISLAND

NOOK
9'-7"
x
11'-10"

RAIL

PATIO

FAMILY ROOM
20'-6"
x
19'-10"

DINING
12'-0" x 15'-8"

K.
14'-1" x 14'-2"

O.V. REF. PAN.

slope   slope

DN

BEAM

RAIL

UP

WINE RACK
BAR

DN

58'-6"

LIVING RM.
15'-8"
x
19'-2"

slope

F.

L.

BEDRM. 4
13'-10" x 10'-4"

ENTRY

W. D.

H.W.

PORCH

GARAGE
31'-4" x 21'-6"

STOOP

STEP

WALK

FIRST FLOOR

DECK

MASTER
BEDROOM
20'-6" x 20'-0"

BEAM

VANITY

SKYLIGHT

SL. SL.

slope   slope

ROMAN
TUB

UP

LIN.

DN

BEDRM. 2
13'-2" x 14'-8"

SECOND FLOOR

BEDRM. 3
14'-4" x 14'-2"

SEAT

SEAT

PLAN No. 10758

BALCONY OFFERS SWEEPING VIEWS

- ☐ Greet arriving guests in impressive Foyer enhanced by two-story ceiling and attractive staircase
- ☐ Large Living Room adjacent to Foyer offers ample accommodations for entertaining many guests
- ☐ Roomy Kitchen opening to Breakfast Room features stove-top island, built-in shelving, desk, china cabinet, eating bar, and much more
- ☐ Step out from Three-Season Porch to enjoy breath of fresh air on deck in backyard
- ☐ Master Suite on second floor provides ideal retreat with raised spa, walk-in closet, sunny Sitting Room, and private deck
- ☐ Overlook beauty of Great Room from Balcony connecting three additional Bedrooms
- ☐ Each Bedroom features built-in window seats or desk and loads of closet space

- ☐ FIRST FLOOR — 1,978 SQ. FT.
- ☐ SECOND FLOOR — 1,768 SQ. FT.
- ☐ BASEMENT — 1,978 SQ. FT.
- ☐ GARAGE — 1,156 SQ. FT.

TOTAL LIVING AREA — 3,746 SQ. FT.

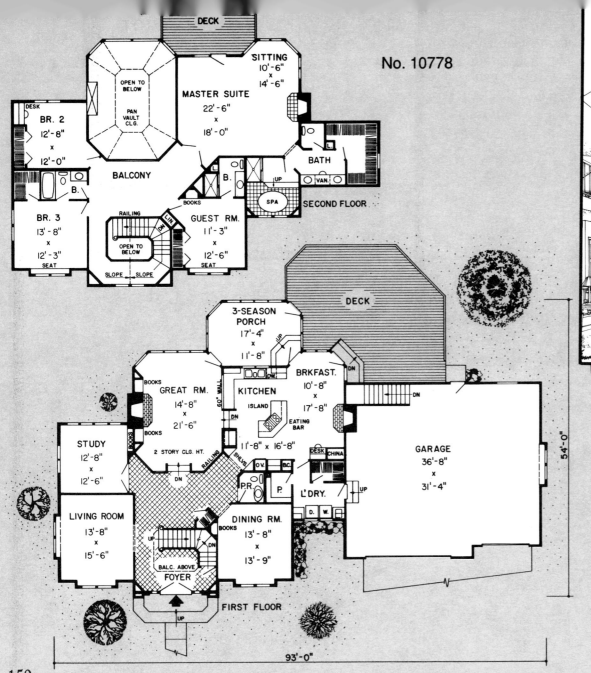

No. 10778

SECOND FLOOR

DECK

SITTING
10'-6"
x
14'-6"

MASTER SUITE
22'-6"
x
18'-0"

OPEN TO BELOW

PAN VAULT CLG.

DESK

BR. 2
12'-8"
x
12'-0"

BALCONY

B.

BR. 3
13'-8"
x
12'-3"
SEAT

RAILING

OPEN TO BELOW

SLOPE   SLOPE

LIN.

BOOKS

B.

BATH

UP

VAN.

SPA

GUEST RM.
11'-3"
x
12'-6"
SEAT

FIRST FLOOR

DECK

3-SEASON PORCH
17'-4"
x
11'-8"

UP

BRKFAST.
10'-8"
x
17'-8"

DN

DN

GREAT RM.
14'-8"
x
21'-6"

2 STORY CLG. HT.

BOOKS

BOOKS

60" WALL

KITCHEN

ISLAND

EATING BAR

11'-8" x 16'-8"

DN

RAILING

SHLVS.

O.V.

B.C.

DESK   CHINA

GARAGE
36'-8"
x
31'-4"

DN

STUDY
12'-8"
x
12'-6"

LIVING ROOM
13'-8"
x
15'-6"

BOOKS

P.R.

P.

L'DRY.

UP

D. W.

DINING RM.
13'-8"
x
13'-9"

UP

DN

BALC. ABOVE

FOYER

UP

54'-0"

93'-0"

159

PLAN No. 10778

ACCENT ON CURVED STAIRCASE

- Overlook impressive tiled Foyer with gracefully curving staircase from Balcony on second floor
- Enter spacious Great Room featuring wood ceiling beams, bar, and welcoming fireplace
- Expansive Kitchen includes lots of counter space, cook center island, pantry, and desk
- Formal Dining Room with interesting ceiling lies just steps away from Kitchen

- Large fireplace and entry onto patio for year round enjoyment complement unique Morning Room
- Luxurious Master Bedroom boasts his-n-hers basins and roomy walk-in closets
- Three additional Bedrooms each have walk-in closets and personal Baths
- Generous Laundry Room leads to 3-car Garage

- FIRST FLOOR — 3,114 SQ. FT.
- SECOND FLOOR — 924 SQ. FT.
- BASEMENT — 3,092 SQ. FT.
- GARAGE — 917 SQ. FT.

TOTAL LIVING AREA — 4,038 SQ. FT.

No. 10537

PATIO

MORNING RM.
12'-4"
X
15'-4"

KITCHEN
18'-4" X 15'-4"
ISLAND
DW
TC

GREAT ROOM
18'-0"
X
25'-4"
(12' CEIL)

M BATH
C.
C.

A Karl Kreeger Design

BEDROOM 3
17'-2"
X
13'-0"
C.

DESK

D W
SINK
PANT.
LAUNDRY
L.
H.
C.
LIN.

BAR

MAST. BEDROOM
21'-2"
X
15'-8"

C.
B.
LIN.

BEDROOM 4
15'-6"
X
15'-4"

BALCONY

FOYER BELOW

H.
B.

SECOND FLOOR

ATTIC

GARAGE
25'-0"
X
35'-4"

DINING
15'-2"
X
15'-4"

C.
BALCONY
ABOVE
DN

FOYER

DN
LINEN
H.

B.
C.

BEDROOM 2
13'-6"
X
14'-10"

PARLOR
14'-0"
X
15'-4"

P.

FIRST FLOOR

WALK

DRIVEWAY

66'-9"

80'-8"

PLAN No. 10537

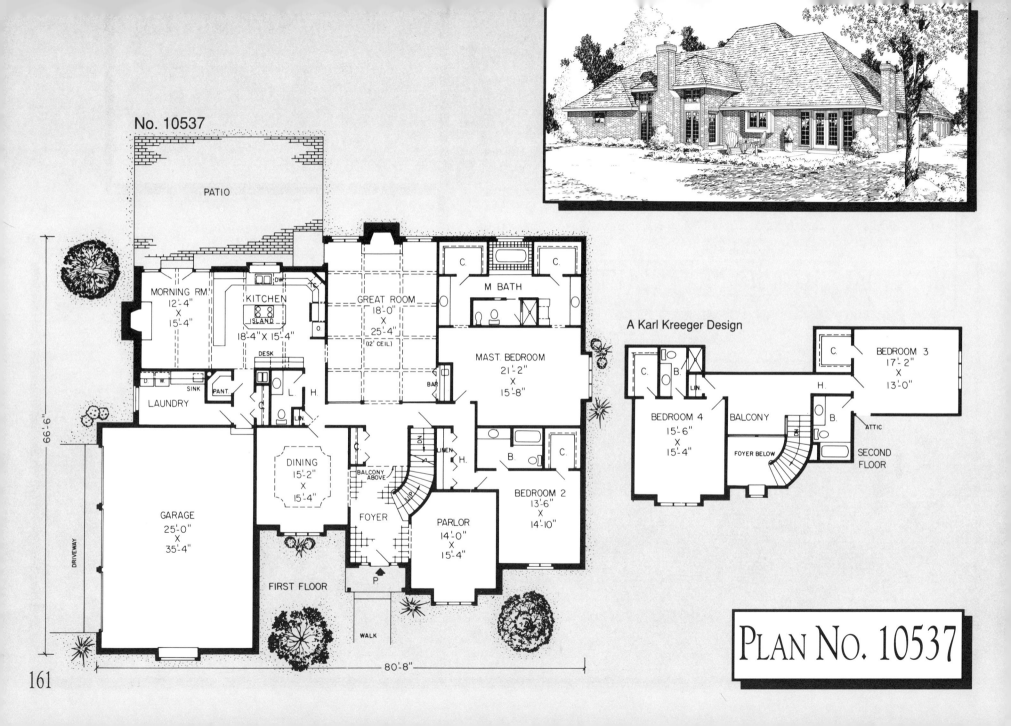

GRACIOUS LIVING IN GOTHIC MANOR

- ☐ Massive Living Room overlooking backyard features fireplace, built-in entertainment center, and decorative columns

- ☐ Spa leads to private deck bordering Master Suite

- ☐ Step into skylit Master Bath from Spa Room for his-n-hers walk-in closets, double vanities, and raised bathtub

- ☐ Efficient island Kitchen located just around corner from room-sized pantry and Dining Room

- ☐ Two staircases lead upstairs to three Bedrooms featuring walk-in closets, full Baths, and personal linen closets

- ☐ Airy Loft and Balcony with view of Foyer links Bedrooms together

- ☐ Curl up with good literature in Library just off Foyer

- ☐ Enjoy breakfast or lunch in skylit garden Breakfast Room

- ☐ Enter home from 3-car Garage through hallway housing Laundry Room and half-Bath

☐ FIRST FLOOR — 3,267 SQ. FT.
☐ SECOND FLOOR — 1,660 SQ. FT.
☐ BASEMENT — 3,267 SQ. FT.
☐ GARAGE — 864 SQ. FT.

TOTAL LIVING AREA — 4,927 SQ. FT.

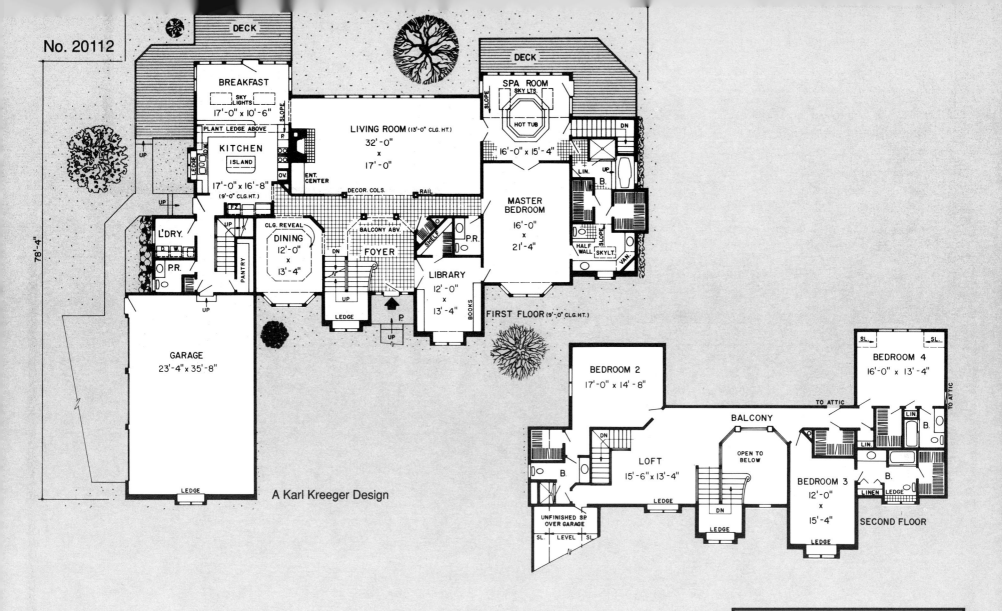

No. 20112

DECK

DECK

BREAKFAST
SKY LIGHTS
17'-0" x 10'-6"
SLOPE

SPA ROOM
SKY LTS.
HOT TUB
SLOPE

LIVING ROOM (13'-0" CLG. HT.)
32'-0"
x
17'-0"

PLANT LEDGE ABOVE

KITCHEN
ISLAND
17'-0" x 16'-8"
(9'-0" CLG.HT.)

16'-0" x 15'-4"

DN

LEDGE

OV.

ENT. CENTER

DECOR. COLS.

RAIL

LIN.

UP

B.

MASTER BEDROOM
16'-0"
x
21'-4"

UP

L'DRY.

D.W.

P.R.

CLG. REVEAL

DINING
12'-0"
x
13'-4"

UP

DN

FOYER

BALCONY ABV.

SHELF

P.R.

HALF WALL

SLOPE

SKYLT.

VAN.

78'-4"

PANTRY

UP

LEDGE

UP

P.

LIBRARY
12'-0"
x
13'-4"

BOOKS

FIRST FLOOR (9'-0" CLG. HT.)

GARAGE
23'-4" x 35'-8"

UP

BEDROOM 2
17'-0" x 14'-8"

SL. SL.

BEDROOM 4
16'-0" x 13'-4"

TO ATTIC

TO ATTIC

LIN.

B.

BALCONY

DN

B.

LOFT
15'-6" x 13'-4"

OPEN TO BELOW

LIN.

LEDGE

A Karl Kreeger Design

LEDGE

DN

BEDROOM 3
12'-0"
x
15'-4"

B.

LINEN

LEDGE

UNFINISHED SP OVER GARAGE

LEDGE

DN

LEDGE

SECOND FLOOR

SL. LEVEL SL.

LEDGE

LEDGE

PLAN NO. 20112

THREE FIREPLACES ADD ELEGANT WARMTH

- ❏ Enjoy sweeping view of vaulted Great Room and two-story Foyer from second floor Balcony

- ❏ Bi-level Master Suite features unique ceiling lines, personal fireplace, and two walk-in closets

- ❏ Snuggle into billions of bubbles designed to tantilize the senses in raised tub in Master Bath

- ❏ Each remaining Bedroom off skylit hall adjoins full Bath and possesses plenty of individual closet space

- ❏ Country Kitchen features cooktop island and greenhouse window ledge ideal for growing herbs

- ❏ Four-season Porch adjoins Breakfast Room and Great Room, and exits onto deck in backyard

- ❏ Impressive Great Room features built-in seats, fireplace, entertainment center, and vaulted two-story ceiling

- ❏ Retreat to book-lined Study next to Living Room for quiet spot to get away from it all

- ❏ FIRST FLOOR — 2,962 SQ. FT.
- ❏ SECOND FLOOR — 1,883 SQ. FT.
- ❏ BASEMENT — 2,962 SQ. FT.
- ❏ GARAGE — 890 SQ. FT

TOTAL LIVING AREA — 4,845 SQ. FT.

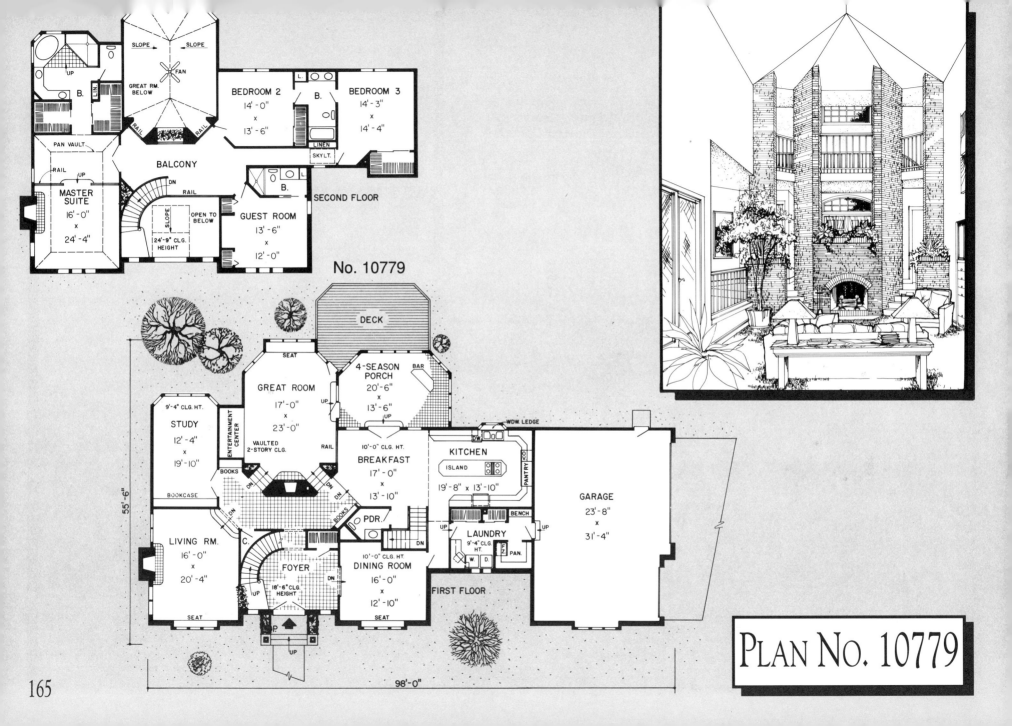

SECOND FLOOR

GREAT RM. BELOW

FAN

BEDROOM 2
14'-0"
x
13'-6"

BEDROOM 3
14'-3"
x
14'-4"

SLOPE   SLOPE

UP

B.
LIN

B.

LINEN

SKYLT.

L

PAN VAULT

RAIL

RAIL

RAIL

BALCONY

DN

L

B.

MASTER SUITE
16'-0"
x
24'-4"

RAIL

UP

SLOPE

OPEN TO BELOW

24'-9" CLG. HEIGHT

GUEST ROOM
13'-6"
x
12'-0"

No. 10779

DECK

SEAT

GREAT ROOM
17'-0"
x
23'-0"

4-SEASON PORCH
20'-6"
x
13'-6"

BAR

UP

UP

9'-4" CLG. HT.

STUDY
12'-4"
x
19'-10"

ENTERTAINMENT CENTER

BOOKS

BOOKCASE

VAULTED 2-STORY CLG.

DN

DN

DN

RAIL

WDW LEDGE

DW

10'-0" CLG. HT.

BREAKFAST
17'-0"
x
13'-10"

KITCHEN

ISLAND

19'-8" x 13'-10"

PANTRY

CO

GARAGE
23'-8"
x
31'-4"

55'-6"

LIVING RM.
16'-0"
x
20'-4"

C.

BOOKS

PDR.

DN

UP

UP

LAUNDRY
9'-4" CLG. HT.

W. D.

PAN.

BENCH

FOYER

DN

18'-6" CLG. HEIGHT

UP

DINING ROOM
16'-0"
x
12'-10"

10'-0" CLG. HT.

FIRST FLOOR

SEAT

SEAT

SEAT

UP

98'-0"

PLAN NO. 10779

165

HOME EXHIBITS SUNNY ATMOSPHERE

- ☐ Sunken bay-windowed Dining Room and Parlor flank gracious Foyer
- ☐ Well-appointed island Kitchen with vaulted ceiling located at rear of house
- ☐ Partake of morning coffee in bright sunny Breakfast Room near Kitchen
- ☐ Step down to quaint Family Room with book-lined walls and cozy fireplace

- ☐ Retire to four-season porch perfect for informal gatherings
- ☐ Tucked behind the Garage find a fourth Bedroom with full Bath
- ☐ Elegant Master Bedroom complete with skylit Bath featuring garden tub and double vanities
- ☐ Ascend central staircase to find two more Bedrooms adorned with individual large walk-in closets
- ☐ Other amenities upstairs include full Bath and cedar closet for out-of-season storage

☐ FIRST FLOOR — 2,424 SQ. FT.
☐ SECOND FLOOR — 638 SQ. FT.
☐ BASEMENT — 2,207 SQ. FT.
☐ GARAGE — 768 SQ. FT.

TOTAL LIVING AREA — 3,062 SQ. FT.

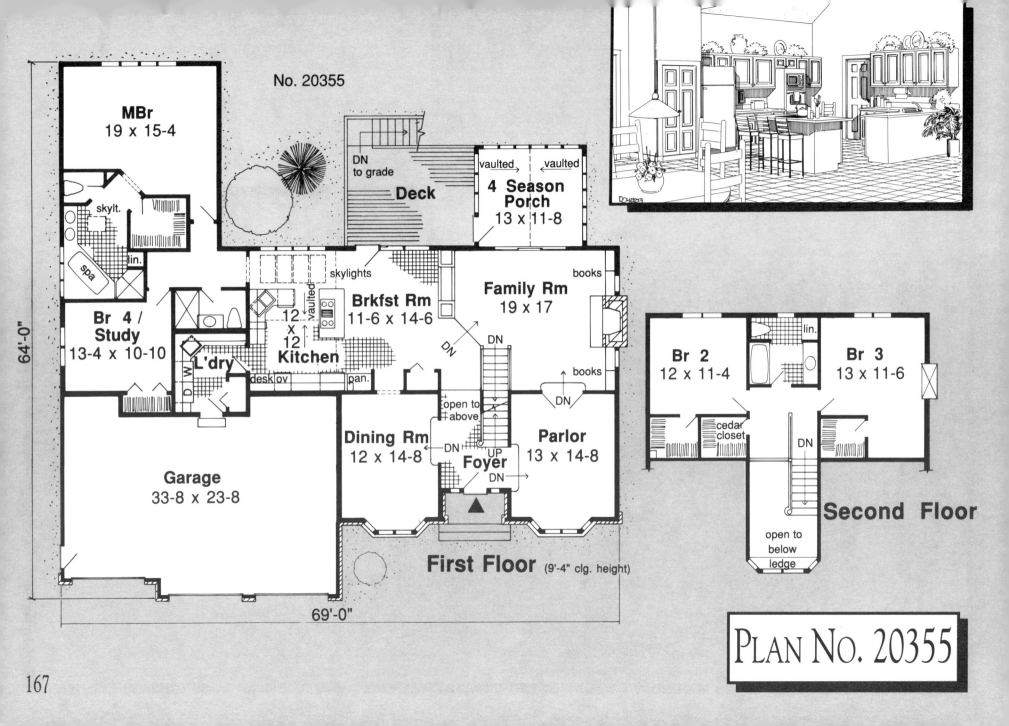

No. 20355

MBr
19 x 15-4

skylt.

spa

lin.

**Br 4 /
Study**
13-4 x 10-10

L'dry

D W

Garage
33-8 x 23-8

Kitchen
12 x 12
vaulted

desk ov

pan.

DN
to grade

Deck

vaulted   vaulted

**4 Season
Porch**
13 x 11-8

skylights

Brkfst Rm
11-6 x 14-6

Family Rm
19 x 17

books

books

DN

DN

open to
above

UP

DN

DN

DN

Dining Rm
12 x 14-8

Foyer

Parlor
13 x 14-8

64'-0"

69'-0"

First Floor (9'-4" clg. height)

Br 2
12 x 11-4

lin.

Br 3
13 x 11-6

cedar
closet

DN

Second Floor

open to
below
ledge

DOHERTY

PLAN NO. 20355

167

SPA-LOVER'S DREAM

- Stepping into Entry, glassed-in Spa Room grabs attention of all who enter

- Spa Room reached from Bathroom, Nook, or through two sets of triple sliding glass doors from deck

- Master Suite has plenty of room for sleeping area and sitting and/or exercise area

- Unique clover-leaf spa nestled in glass block-lined corner nook of Master Suite

- Other features of Master Suite include huge walk-in closet and double vanities

- Room serving as Office, Den, hobby room, or artist's studio conveniently situated close to Master Suite and front entry

- Country Kitchen with island and pantry fills one corner of large Family Room

- Three additional bedrooms have walk-in closets and adjoining Baths

- LIVING AREA — 3,453 SQ. FT.
- GARAGE — 637 SQ. FT.

TOTAL LIVING AREA — 3,453 SQ. FT.

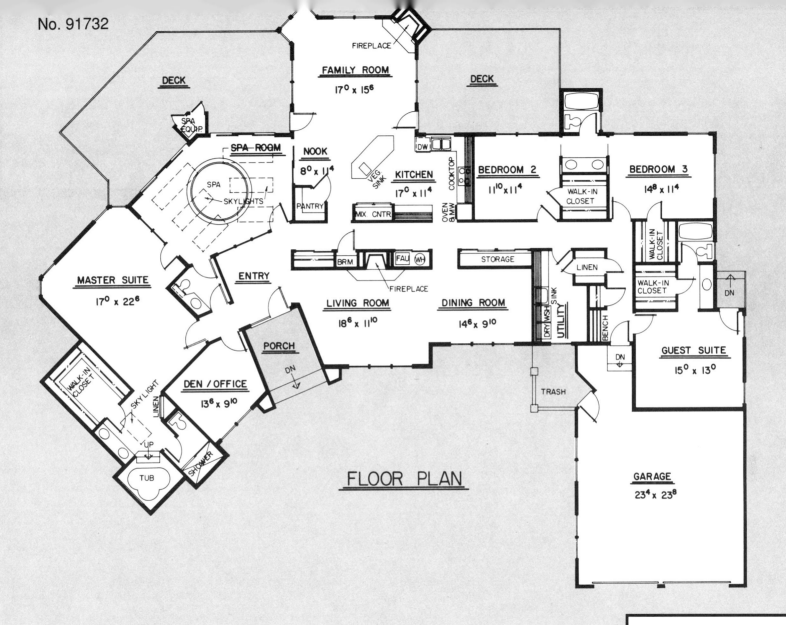

DECK

FIREPLACE

FAMILY ROOM
17⁰ x 15⁶

DECK

SPA EQUIP.

SPA ROOM

NOOK
8⁰ x 11⁴

SPA

SKYLIGHTS

PANTRY

KITCHEN
17⁰ x 11⁴

VEG SINK

COOKTOP

DW

OVEN B.MW

MIX CNTR

BEDROOM 2
11¹⁰ x 11⁴

WALK-IN CLOSET

BEDROOM 3
14⁸ x 11⁴

WALK-IN CLOSET

MASTER SUITE
17⁰ x 22⁶

ENTRY

BRM

FAU WH

FIREPLACE

LIVING ROOM
18⁶ x 11¹⁰

DINING ROOM
14⁶ x 9¹⁰

STORAGE

LINEN

WALK-IN CLOSET

DRY WSH

SINK

UTILITY

BENCH

DN

GUEST SUITE
15⁰ x 13⁰

DN

WALK-IN CLOSET

SKY LIGHT

LINEN

PORCH

DN

DEN / OFFICE
13⁶ x 9¹⁰

TRASH

UP

SHOWER

TUB

FLOOR PLAN

GARAGE
23⁴ x 23⁸

PLAN No. 91732

GEORGIAN DRAMA AT ITS BEST

- Impressive columned facade leads to dramatic two-story Receiving Hall with magnificent stairway as centerpiece
- Vast Gathering Room promotes sunny views of backyard via abundant glass works overlooking beautiful outdoor terrace
- Sizable Living Room with fireplace invites appreciation of hospitality from important guests
- Study with personal entrance to terrace encourages quiet time
- Efficient island Kitchen opens into convenient Breakfast Room
- Contemplate resplendent vision of Receiving Hall from different angle from second-floor Balcony
- Expansive Master Bedroom with fireplace leads to exquisite Master Bath with raised garden tub, double vanities, built-in vanity, and huge walk-in closet
- Three additional Bedrooms and two full Baths occupy remainder of second floor

- FIRST FLOOR — 2,529 SQ. FT.
- SECOND FLOOR — 1,872 SQ. FT.
- BASEMENT — 3,232 SQ. FT.
- GARAGE — 4-CAR

TOTAL LIVING AREA — 4,401 SQ. FT.

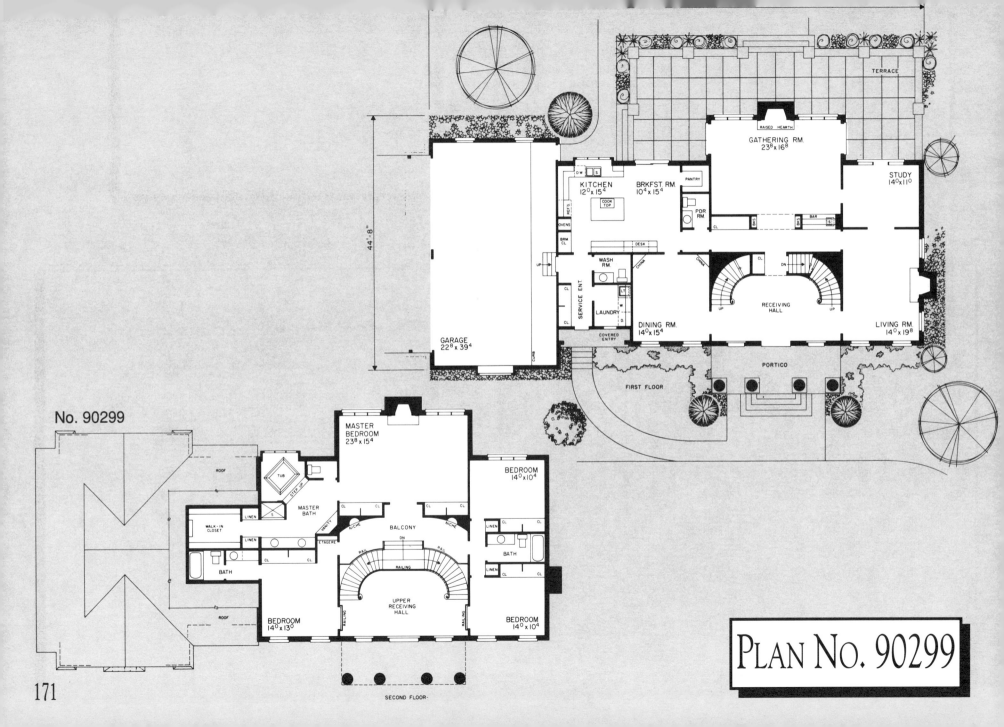

No. 90299

PLAN NO. 90299

TERRACE

GATHERING RM.
23⁸ x 16⁸

RAISED HEARTH

STUDY
14⁰ x 11⁰

KITCHEN
12⁰ x 15⁴

BRKFST. RM.
10⁴ x 15⁴

PANTRY

DW   S

REF'G.

COOK TOP

OVENS

PDR. RM.

CL

BKS.

BKS.

BAR

S

BRM CL

DESK

WASH RM.

CHINA

CHINA

UP

SERVICE ENT.

CL

LAUNDRY

W

D

DN

CL

UP

RECEIVING HALL

UP

LIVING RM.
14⁰ x 19⁸

DINING RM.
14⁰ x 15⁴

COVERED ENTRY

GARAGE
22⁸ x 39⁴

CURB

44'-8"

PORTICO

FIRST FLOOR

MASTER BEDROOM
23⁸ x 15⁴

BEDROOM
14⁰ x 10⁴

ROOF

TUB

STEP UP

MASTER BATH

VANITY

LINEN

S

WALK-IN CLOSET

LINEN

ETAGERE

NICHE

BALCONY

NICHE

CL

CL

CL

CL

LINEN

CL

CL

CL

BATH

CL

CL

BATH

CL

CL

DN

RAILING

RAIL

RAIL

ROOF

RAILING

RAILING

UPPER RECEIVING HALL

BEDROOM
14⁰ x 13⁰

BEDROOM
14⁰ x 10⁴

SECOND FLOOR

IMPRESSIVE AND ELEGANT

- Traditionally-styled classic has timeless appeal with impressive Entry accented with brick pillars

- Sunken formal Living Room with large bay provides abundance of natural light

- Living Room opens to formal Dining Room accessing rear patio

- L-shaped Kitchen features cooktop island, eating bar, pantry, desk and bayed Breakfast Nook all arranged for maximum efficiency

- Kitchen, Nook, and Family Room open to each other presenting "great room" effect

- Den with bay windows, Laundry Room, Bath with shower, and 3-car Garage complete main level

- Luxurious Master Bath features raised whirlpool tub, double sink vanities, and walk-in wardrobe

- Two generously sized secondary Bedrooms share full Bath with raised garden tub and separate shower

- FIRST FLOOR — 1,849 SQ. FT.
- SECOND FLOOR — 1,457 SQ. FT.
- GARAGE — 3-CAR

TOTAL LIVING AREA — 3,306 SQ. FT.

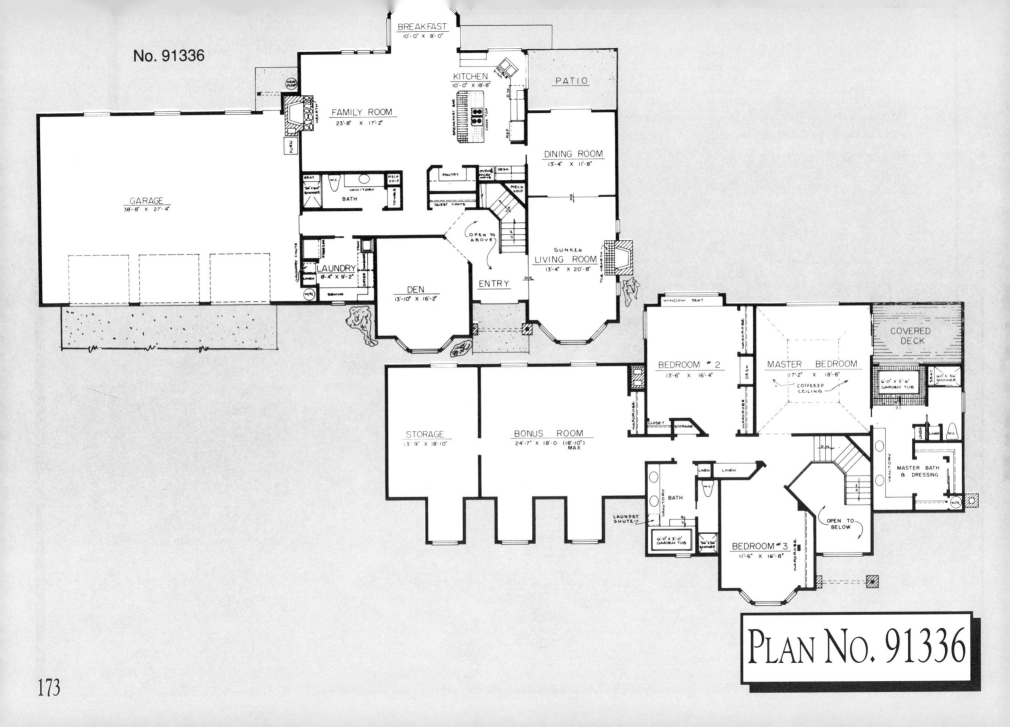

No. 91336

BREAKFAST
10'-0" X 8'-0"

KITCHEN
10'-0" X 18'-8"

PATIO

FAMILY ROOM
23'-8" X 17'-2"

DINING ROOM
13'-4" X 11'-8"

GARAGE
38'-8" X 27'-4"

SEAT
36"X60"
SHOWER
W.C.
VANITORY
BATH
MECH VOID

PANTRY

MECH VOID

OVEN-MICRO WAVE
DESK

GUEST COATS

OPEN TO ABOVE

SUNKEN
LIVING ROOM
13'-4" X 20'-8"

TILE HEARTH

LAUNDRY
8'-4" X 9'-2"

DEN
13'-10" X 16'-2"

ENTRY

WINDOW SEAT

COVERED
DECK

BEDROOM # 2
13'-6" X 16'-4"

MASTER BEDROOM
17'-2" X 18'-8"

COFFERED
CEILING

6'-0" X 3'-6"
GARDEN TUB

SEAT
60"X36"
SHOWER

WARDROBE

CLOSET
STORAGE

WARDROBE

DESK

STORAGE
13'-9" X 18'-10"

BONUS ROOM
24'-7" X 18'-0 (18'-10")
MAX

LINEN
LINEN
W.C.

VANITORY

MASTER BATH
& DRESSING

BATH

LINEN   LINEN

W.C.

VANITORY

OPEN TO
BELOW

LAUNDRY
SHUTE

6'-0" X 3'-0"
GARDEN TUB

36"X36"
SHOWER

BEDROOM # 3
11'-6" X 16'-8"

WARDROBE

PLAN No. 91336

173

TRADITIONAL SPIRIT — CONTEMPORARY LOOK

- Dining Areas easily managed from centrally-located Kitchen

- Enjoy morning quietness overlooking beautiful front yard from Breakfast Room

- Vaulted Family Room with side deck bordering Kitchen for convenient late night snacking

- Pass built-in bar in skylit hallway to step down into sunken Great Room with vaulted ceiling and direct access to backyard patio

- Adult's private wing accentuated with vaulted Master Bedroom with his-n-hers walk-in closets

- Snuggle up with good book in front of fireplace in vaulted Library located in Master Suite wing

- Two additional Bedrooms on opposite side of house provide ample room for remainder of family

- Enter home through 2-car Garage via Utility Room housing laundry facilities

- LIVING AREA — 3,412 SQ. FT.
- BASEMENT — 3,412 SQ. FT.
- GARAGE — 2-CAR

TOTAL LIVING AREA — 3,412 SQ. FT.

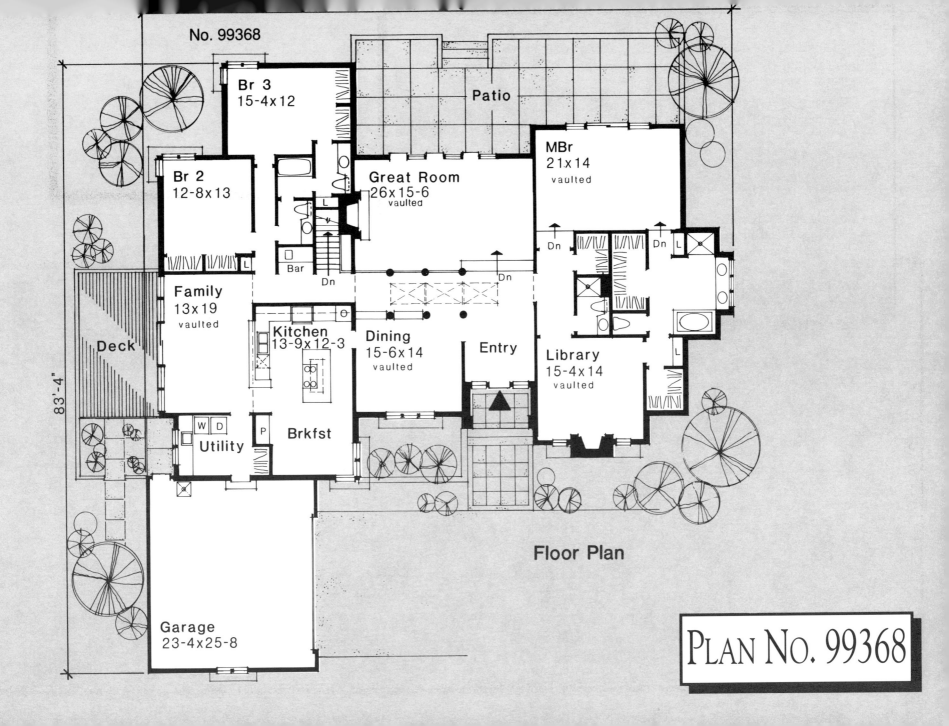

No. 99368

Br 3
15-4x12

Patio

Br 2
12-8x13

MBr
21x14
vaulted

Great Room
26x15-6
vaulted

Bar

Dn

Dn

Dn

Dn

L

L

L

Family
13x19
vaulted

Deck

Kitchen
13-9x12-3

Dining
15-6x14
vaulted

Entry

Library
15-4x14
vaulted

83'-4"

W D

P

Utility

Brkfst

Floor Plan

Garage
23-4x25-8

PLAN No. 99368

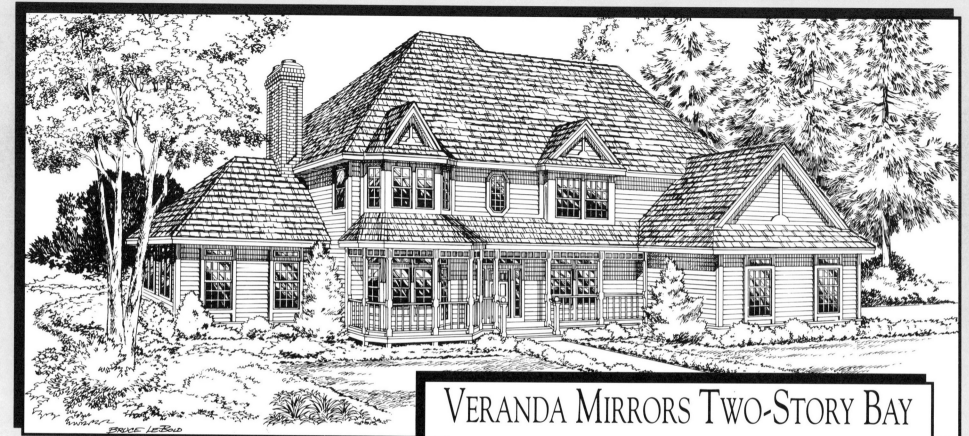

BRUCE LeBOLD

VERANDA MIRRORS TWO-STORY BAY

- ☐ Elegant Victorian with modern twist celebrates classic beauty of turn-of-the-century architecture

- ☐ Eloquent Great Hall flanked by formal Dining Room and Parlor expresses gracious welcome to all who enter

- ☐ Island Kitchen with adjoining full-sized pantry reveal plenty of cupboards and counter space

- ☐ Genial Breakfast corner opens into large Alcove with alternate route leading upstairs

- ☐ Step down into sunken Gathering Room with fireplace, pan vault ceiling, and direct passage to wrap-around porch

- ☐ Double doors open to Master Suite and book-lined Master Retreat with Dormer Sitting Area

- ☐ Elegant Master Bath features raised tub and adjoining cedar closet

- ☐ Other upstairs Bedrooms feature distinctive shapes, huge closets, and access to full Bath with double vanities

- ☐ FIRST FLOOR — 2,108 SQ. FT.
- ☐ SECOND FLOOR — 2,109 SQ. FT.
- ☐ BASEMENT — 1,946 SQ. FT.
- ☐ GARAGE — 764 SQ. FT.

TOTAL LIVING AREA — 4,217 SQ. FT.

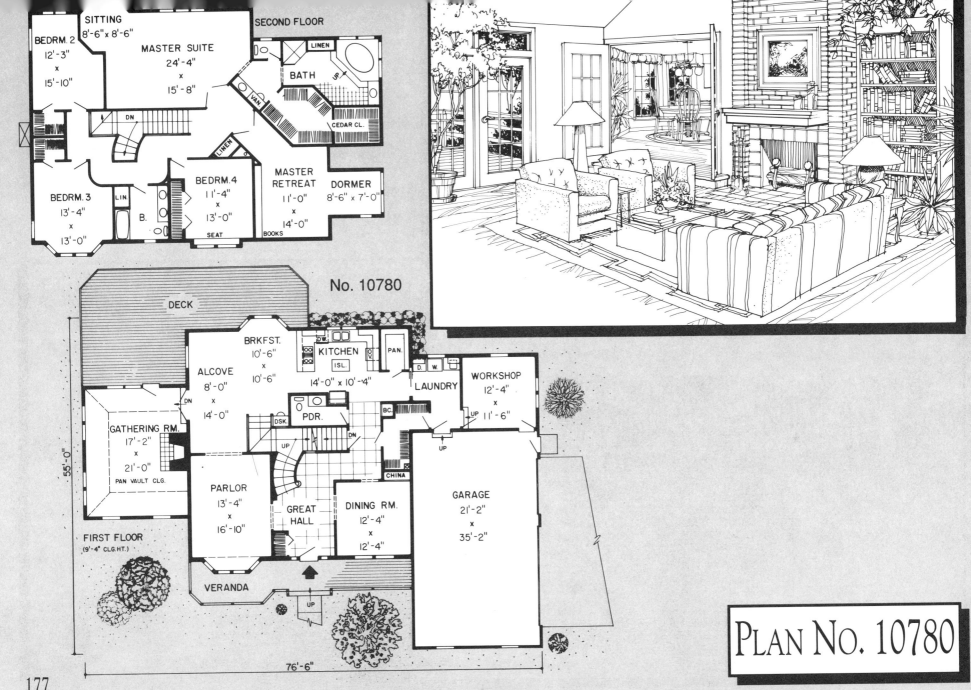

SECOND FLOOR

BEDRM. 2
12'-3" x 15'-10"

SITTING
8'-6" x 8'-6"

MASTER SUITE
24'-4" x 15'-8"

BATH

LINEN

VAN.

CEDAR CL.

DN

BEDRM. 3
13'-4" x 13'-0"

LIN.

B.

LINEN

BEDRM. 4
11'-4" x 13'-0"

SEAT

MASTER RETREAT
11'-0" x 14'-0"

BOOKS

DORMER
8'-6" x 7'-0"

No. 10780

DECK

BRKFST.
10'-6" x 10'-6"

KITCHEN
14'-0" x 10'-4"

DW

ISL.

PAN.

D. W.

ALCOVE
8'-0" x 14'-0"

LAUNDRY

WORKSHOP
12'-4" x 11'-6"

DN

DSK.

PDR.

BC.

UP

GATHERING RM.
17'-2" x 21'-0"

PAN VAULT CLG.

UP

DN

CHINA

UP

PARLOR
13'-4" x 16'-10"

GREAT HALL

DINING RM.
12'-4" x 12'-4"

GARAGE
21'-2" x 35'-2"

FIRST FLOOR
(9'-4" CLG. HT.)

55'-0"

VERANDA

UP

76'-6"

PLAN NO. 10780

LIVING AREA — 3,292 SQ. FT.
GARAGE — 3-CAR

TOTAL LIVING AREA — 3,292 SQ. FT.

EXQUISITE ARCHITECTURAL DETAIL

- Walk through formal Entry to impressive Living Room with fireplace wall framed by unusual window display

- Central hallway with 10-foot ceiling escorts one through Gallery to quiet sleeping wing

- Master Bedroom with vaulted ceiling enjoys comfortable Sitting Area with bay window

- Expansive split walk-in closet in Master Suite connects to Bath with twin basin vanity

- Two additional Bedrooms with walk-in closets share full Bath

- Just steps away from Kitchen is Dining Room formalized with 10-foot octagon ceiling

- Large island Kitchen flows into Dinnette with bay windows for informal family meals

- Family Room sports many amenities such as wetbar, exclusive access to backyard patio and uncommon windows framing fireplace

101' - 1"

73' - 10"

Sitting

MstrBed
16x22

Vaulted
Ceiling

Master

LivRm
17x23

Vaulted Ceiling

Patio

Kit
10'Ceiling
12x13

Din
11x15
10'Ceiling

Patio

Bed#4
12x14

B#3

FamilyRm
16x22

Vaulted Ceiling

Bed#3
11x16

Util

10'Ceiling

Gallery

10'Ceiling

B#2

Bar

FmlDin
12x13
10'Octagon
Ceiling

Ent

Bed#2
12x14
10'Ceiling

3-Car-Gar
20x23

Por

Main Floor

10x21

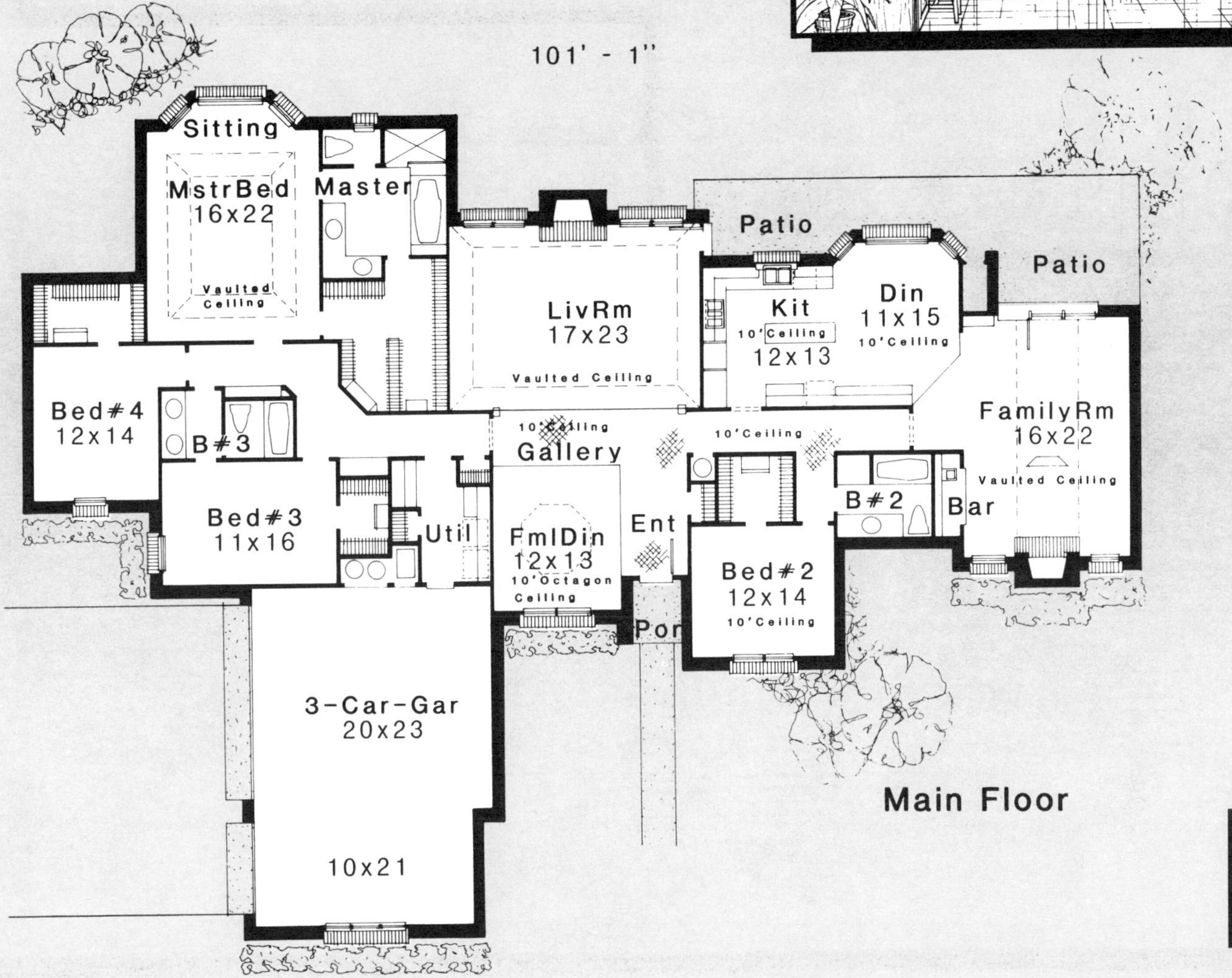

PLAN No. 92209

GRACED BY ARCHWAYS

- Exterior brick detail, columns and archways complete this talk-of-the-town beauty

- Spacious daylight Basement has built-in Bar, and leads to private patio

- Overabundance of space in gigantic lower-level Storage Room

- Master Bedroom features large window seat and gas fireplace visible from bedroom and compartmentalized Bath

- Enjoyment abounds in Dining Room with direct access to rear deck

- Sizeable sunken Family Room features corner fireplace, comfortable window seat and leads to both backyard decks

- Ample Kitchen has walk-in pantry for added storage and bright sunny Nook with access to deck

- Enter convenient Utility Room from 3-car Garage

- MAIN FLOOR — 2,003 SQ. FT.
- BASEMENT — 1,383 SQ. FT.
- GARAGE — 651 SQ. FT.

TOTAL LIVING AREA — 3,386 SQ. FT.

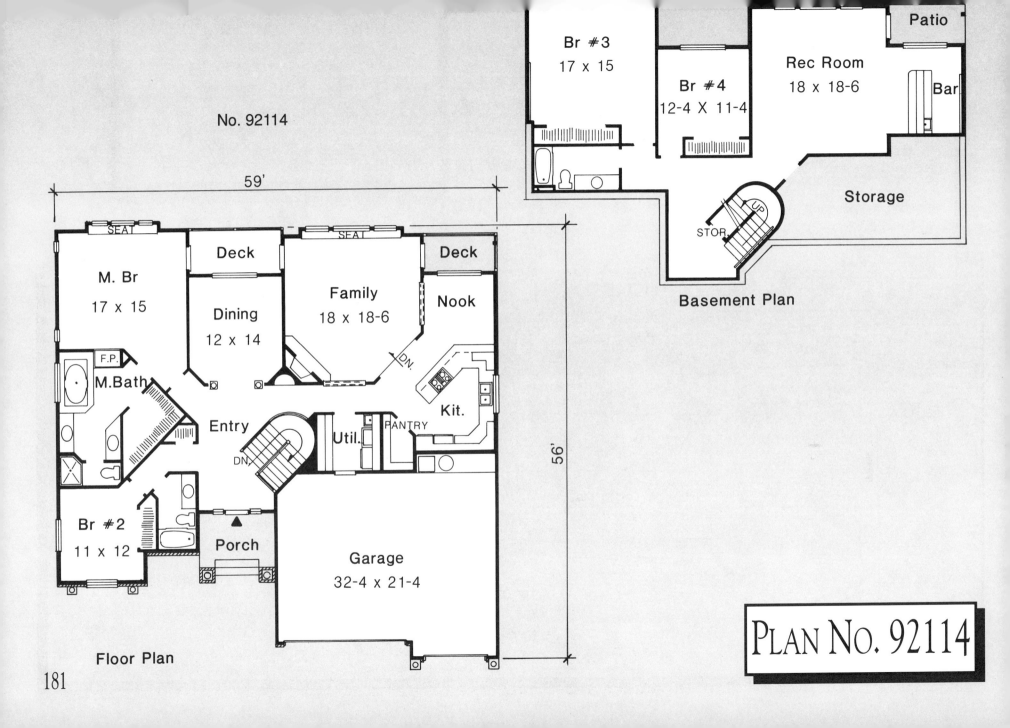

No. 92114

Br #3
17 x 15

Br #4
12-4 X 11-4

Rec Room
18 x 18-6

Patio

Bar

Storage

STOR.

UP

Basement Plan

59'

56'

SEAT

SEAT

M. Br
17 x 15

Deck

Dining
12 x 14

Family
18 x 18-6

Deck

Nook

F.P.

M.Bath

Entry

DN.

DN.

Util.

PANTRY

Kit.

Br #2
11 x 12

Porch

Garage
32-4 x 21-4

Floor Plan

PLAN NO. 92114

SHEER ELEGANCE

- ❑ Stunning entry porch has elegantly detailed wood columns
- ❑ Spacious Foyer provides easy access to all rooms
- ❑ Living Room has heat-circulating fireplace, tray ceiling, and bay window overlooking terrace
- ❑ Two-story Great Room, connected by decorative circular stairway, has imposing brick fireplace surrounded by glass, and lofty ceilings detailed with skylights

- ❑ Master Suite is beautified by walk-in closet and luxurious Bath with 7-foot whirlpool tub and separate shower stall
- ❑ Balcony overlooking Great Room leads to extra large Bedrooms and second Bath with two basins
- ❑ 2-car Garage opens to convenient Mudroom with laundry hook-ups and handy service porch
- ❑ Well-planned Kitchen including snack bar extends to Dinette with eye-appealing bay window

- ❑ FIRST FLOOR — 1,920 SQ. FT.
- ❑ SECOND FLOOR — 1,429 SQ. FT.
- ❑ BASEMENT — 1,734 SQ. FT.
- ❑ GARAGE — 430 SQ. FT.

TOTAL LIVING AREA — 3,349 SQ. FT.

No. 99600

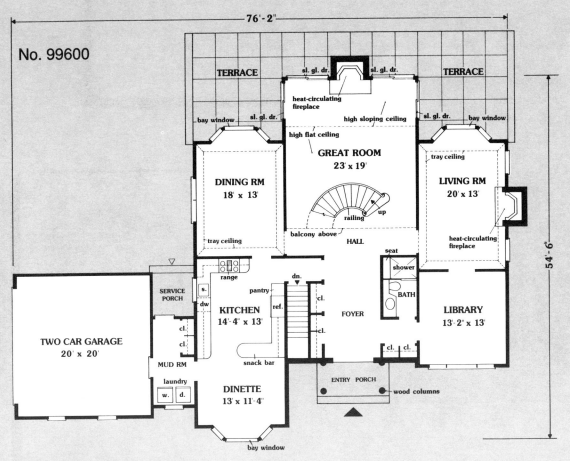

FIRST FLOOR PLAN

76'-2"

54'-6"

TERRACE

TERRACE

sl. gl. dr.   sl. gl. dr.

heat-circulating fireplace

high sloping ceiling

high flat ceiling

bay window   sl. gl. dr.   sl. gl. dr.   bay window

GREAT ROOM
23' x 19'

DINING RM
18' x 13'

LIVING RM
20' x 13'

tray ceiling

tray ceiling

up

railing

balcony above

heat-circulating fireplace

HALL

seat

shower

BATH

range

pantry

dn.

cl.

KITCHEN
14'-4" x 13'

ref.

FOYER

LIBRARY
13'-2" x 13'

s.

SERVICE PORCH

dw

cl.

TWO CAR GARAGE
20' x 20'

MUD RM

cl.

snack bar

cl.   cl.

laundry

w.   d.

DINETTE
13' x 11'-4"

ENTRY PORCH

wood columns

bay window

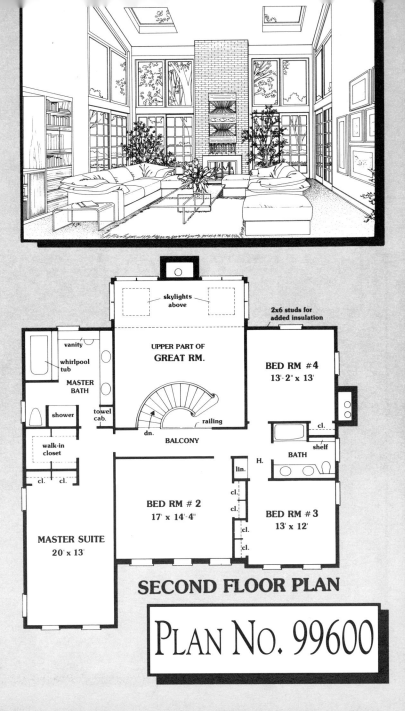

SECOND FLOOR PLAN

skylights above

2x6 studs for added insulation

vanity

whirlpool tub

MASTER BATH

UPPER PART OF GREAT RM.

BED RM #4
13'-2" x 13'

towel cab.

shower

cl.

dn.

railing

BALCONY

cl.

BATH

shelf

walk-in closet

cl.   cl.

lin.

cl.

cl.

H.

cl.

BED RM # 2
17' x 14'-4"

cl.

BED RM # 3
13' x 12'

MASTER SUITE
20' x 13'

PLAN NO. 99600

LUXURY IS ALWAYS POPULAR

- ❏ FIRST FLOOR — 2,579 SQ. FT.
- ❏ SECOND FLOOR — 997 SQ. FT.
- ❏ BASEMENT — 2,579 SQ. FT.
- ❏ GARAGE & STORAGE — 1,001 SQ. FT.

TOTAL LIVING AREA — 3,576 SQ. FT.

- ❏ Step down to repose in sunken Great Room featuring bar, fireplace, and built-in cabinets for TV and stereo
- ❏ Fully-equipped Kitchen enjoys sweeping view of patio and opens to stunning Breakfast Nook
- ❏ Luxurious Master Bedroom offers quiet solitude featuring sunny Sitting Room with bay window away from noisy living area
- ❏ 3-car Garage includes extra storage space
- ❏ Two additional Bedrooms upstairs feature private Baths and walk-in closets
- ❏ Bridge-like Balcony on second level overlooks Dining Room to the rear and Foyer on the front
- ❏ Unusual ceiling treatments in most rooms completes the fabulous impressiveness of this home
- ❏ His-n-hers walk-in closets offer plenty of storage space in Master Bedroom

No. 10531
A Karl Kreeger Design

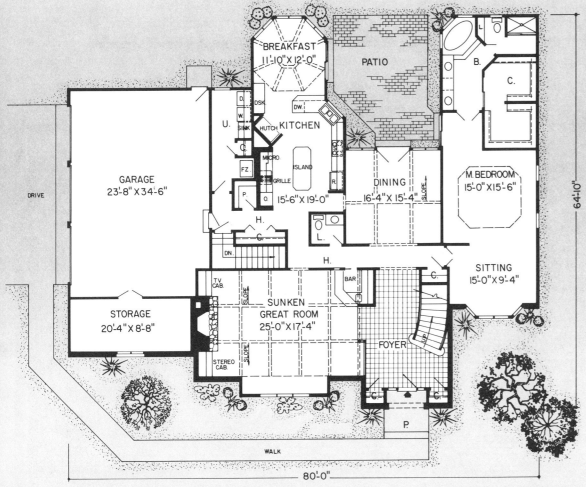

DRIVE

GARAGE
23'-8" X 34'-6"

STORAGE
20'-4" X 8'-8"

BREAKFAST
11'-10" X 12'-0"

PATIO

KITCHEN

D.
DSK.
DW
U.
W
SINK
HUTCH
C.
MICRO.
FZ
ISLAND
GRILLE
O.
R
15'-6" X 19'-0"
P.

DINING
16'-4" X 15'-4"
SLOPE

B.
C.

M. BEDROOM
15'-0" X 15'-6"

H.
C.
DN.
L.
H.

T.V.
CAB.
SLOPE
SUNKEN
GREAT ROOM
25'-0" X 17'-4"
SLOPE
STEREO
CAB.

BAR
C.
UP

SITTING
15'-0" X 9'-4"

FOYER
C.
C.
P.

WALK

80'-0"

64'-0"

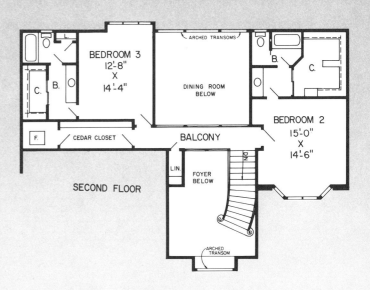

SECOND FLOOR

BEDROOM 3
12'-8"
X
14'-4"

ARCHED TRANSOMS

DINING ROOM
BELOW

B.
C.

C.
B.
F.
CEDAR CLOSET

BALCONY

LIN.
FOYER
BELOW

DN.

BEDROOM 2
15'-0"
X
14'-6"

ARCHED
TRANSOM

PLAN No. 10531

185

FIRST FLOOR — 2,389 SQ. FT.

SECOND FLOOR — 673 SQ. FT.

BASEMENT — 1,348 SQ. FT.

GARAGE — 2-CAR

TOTAL LIVING AREA — 3,062 SQ. FT.

SPECIAL TOUCH

Front projections and gables give custom look justifying special interior finishes and flourishes

Impressive Foyer with view through to backyard features angular staircase

Invite guests to step down into vaulted Parlor

Uniquely-shaped Kitchen includes modern conveniences

Breakfast alcove juts out between Kitchen and Family Room for early morning repast

Vast Family Room with vaulted ceiling, fireplace, and wetbar offers perfect place to entertain friends

Library located in quiet side of house can double as Guest Room with ample closet space

Master Suite has adjoining Sitting Room and secluded luxury Bath and walk-in wardrobe

Second floor houses two additional Bedrooms with individual closets and shared Bath

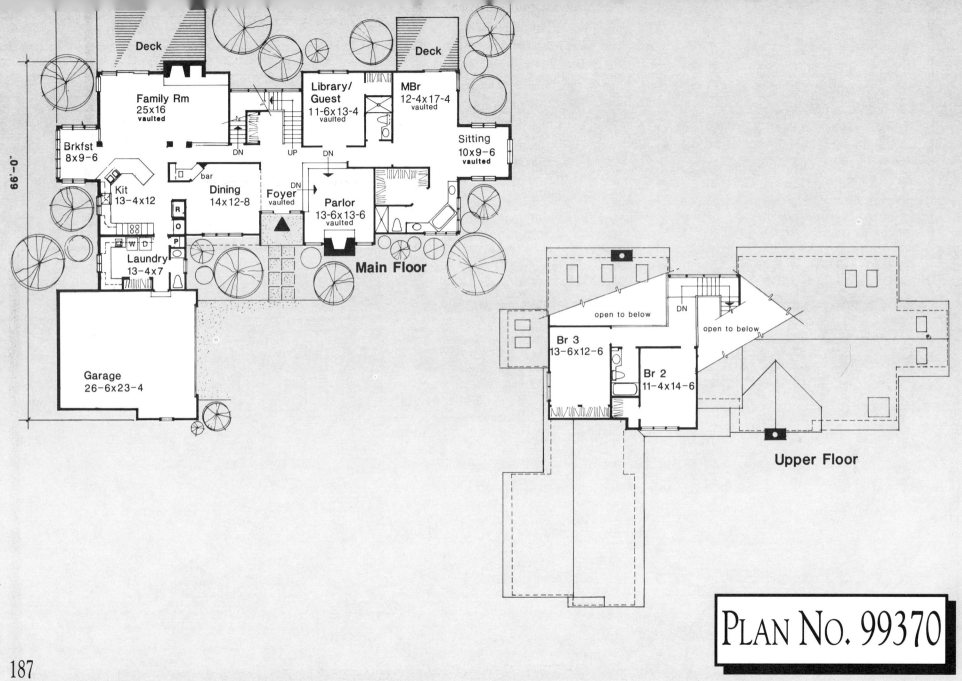

Deck

Deck

Family Rm
25x16
vaulted

Library/
Guest
11-6x13-4
vaulted

MBr
12-4x17-4
vaulted

Brkfst
8x9-6

Sitting
10x9-6
vaulted

66'-0"

Kit
13-4x12

bar

Dining
14x12-8

Foyer
vaulted

Parlor
13-6x13-6
vaulted

DN

UP

DN

DN

R
O
P

Laundry
13-4x7

W D

Main Floor

Garage
26-6x23-4

open to below

DN

open to below

Br 3
13-6x12-6

Br 2
11-4x14-6

Upper Floor

PLAN No. 99370

187

DESIGNED FOR ELEGANT LIVING

- ❑ Magnificent home creates formidable impression after dark
- ❑ Numerous arched windows glowing with light extend warm welcome to visitors
- ❑ Inside find skylights, vaulted ceilings, and multiple levels rendering an interior equally as exciting as exterior
- ❑ Step from skylit central Foyer into vaulted Dining Room, cozy Parlor, and fireplaced Family Room with built-in bar

- ❑ Walk down book-lined hallway to island Kitchen, Breakfast Nook with built-in desk and unique curved glass wall overlooking backyard patio
- ❑ Master Suite complemented by elegant pan vaulted ceiling, fireplace for romantic evenings, private deck, and garden spa
- ❑ At either end of upstairs Balcony, find Bedrooms each with individual Bath and spacious closets

- ❑ FIRST FLOOR — 1,807 SQ. FT.
- ❑ SECOND FLOOR — 1,359 SQ. FT.
- ❑ BASEMENT — 1,807 SQ. FT.
- ❑ GARAGE — 840 SQ. FT.

TOTAL LIVING AREA — 3,166 SQ. FT.

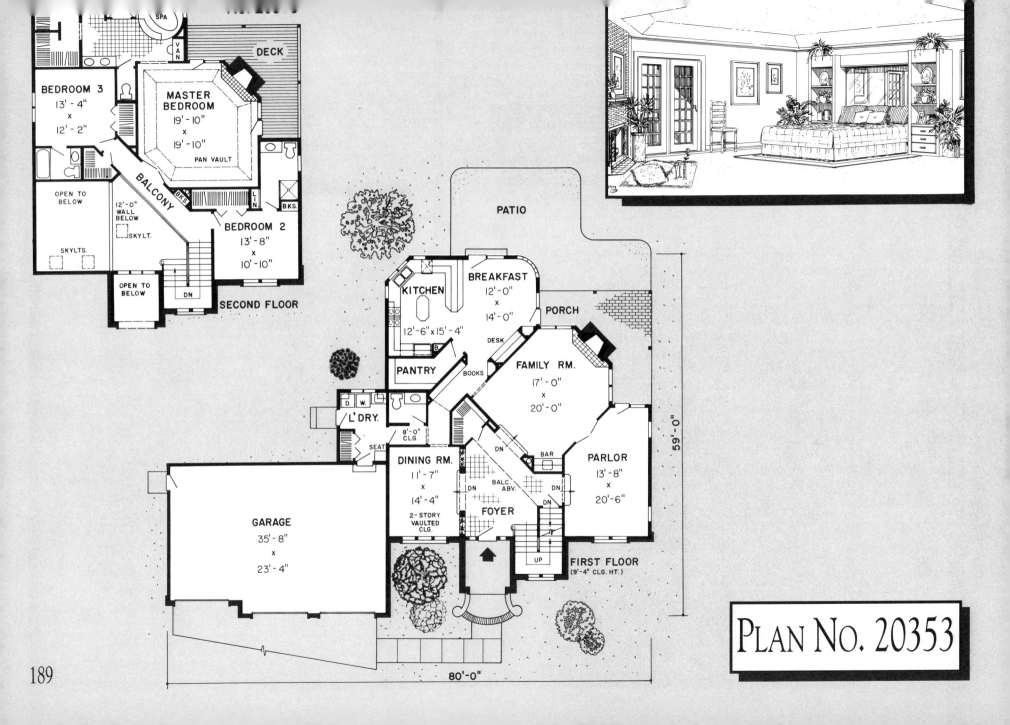

SPA

BEDROOM 3
13'-4"
x
12'-2"

MASTER
BEDROOM
19'-10"
x
19'-10"

DECK

VAN.

PAN VAULT

BALCONY

OPEN TO
BELOW

12'-0"
WALL
BELOW

SKYLT.

SKYLTS.

OPEN TO
BELOW

LIN.

BKS.

BEDROOM 2
13'-8"
x
10'-10"

DN

SECOND FLOOR

PATIO

BREAKFAST
12'-0"
x
14'-0"

KITCHEN
12'-6" x 15'-4"

PORCH

DESK

PANTRY

BOOKS

FAMILY RM.
17'-0"
x
20'-0"

D. W.

L'DRY.

8'-0"
CLG.

SEAT

DINING RM.
11'-7"
x
14'-4"

2-STORY
VAULTED
CLG.

DN

BAR

DN

BALC.
ABV.

DN

DN

FOYER

UP

PARLOR
13'-8"
x
20'-6"

GARAGE
35'-8"
x
23'-4"

FIRST FLOOR
(9'-4" CLG. HT.)

59'-0"

80'-0"

PLAN NO. 20353

BRICK ARCH ADDS CHARM

- Savor lavish view of barrel vaulted Entry with grand staircase, hanging chandalier, and display of windows surrounding front entrance door

- Three bedrooms reside on second floor each with spacious closet, sloping ceilings, and access to full Bath

- Exceptional window design framing fireplace allows natural light to bathe Living Room with cathedral ceiling

- Immense island Kitchen opens to bright Breakfast Room for convenience

- Wood-paneled Study with beamed ceilings and floor-to-ceiling bookcases located just off Gallery

- Classy detailing in Master Bath with plant ledge, skylight, and tall ceiling entices occupants to linger

- Vast Family Room with corner bar features windows overlooking covered patio in backyard

- FIRST FLOOR — 2,635 SQ. FT.
- SECOND FLOOR — 1,005 SQ. FT.
- BASEMENT — 2,573 SQ. FT.
- GARAGE — 3-CAR

TOTAL LIVING AREA — 3,640 SQ. FT.

Plant Ledge

MstrBath Below

Sloping Clg.

Skylight

Plant Ledge

No. 92202

73' - 0"

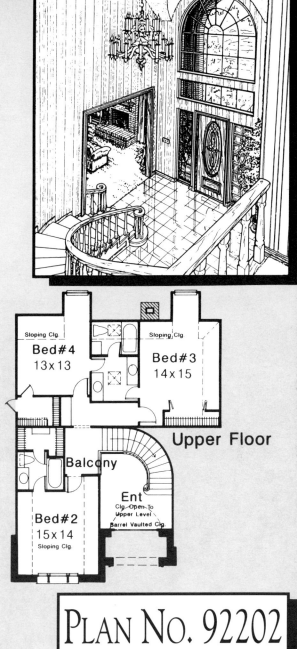

59' - 10"

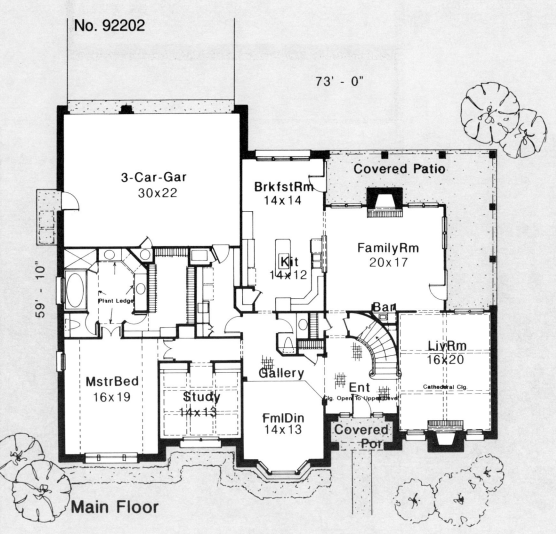

3-Car-Gar
30x22

BrkfstRm
14x14

Covered Patio

Kit
14x12

FamilyRm
20x17

Bar

MstrBed
16x19

Study
14x13

Gallery

Ent
Clg. Open To Upper Level

LivRm
16x20

Cathedral Clg.

FmlDin
14x13

Covered Por

Plant Ledge

Main Floor

Upper Floor

Sloping Clg.   Sloping Clg.

Bed#4
13x13

Bed#3
14x15

Balcony

Bed#2
15x14
Sloping Clg.

Ent
Clg. Open To
Upper Level
Barrel Vaulted Clg.

PLAN No. 92202

BRIDGE FORMS FOCAL POINT

- Bridge forms connection between stairway and second-floor Bedrooms, crossing open space created by two-story ceilings of Family Room and Entry

- Family Room is well-lit by double-hung windows covering both stories of the back wall and has access to the covered patio

- Fireplaced Living Room shares open space with bayed Dining Room for great entertaining

- Kitchen features angled snack bar, pantry and sunny Breakfast Nook

- Master Suite, on first floor, enjoys large dressing area and walk-in closet in its private five-piece Bath

- Bedroom Two, also on first floor, has private Bath and large bay window and serves well as a guest room

- All upstairs Bedrooms feature walk-in closets and share a double-vanitied Bath

- FIRST FLOOR — 2,445 SQ. FT.
- SECOND FLOOR — 898 SQ. FT.
- GARAGE — 687 SQ. FT.
- COVERED PATIOS — 244 SQ. FT.

TOTAL LIVING AREA — 3,343 SQ. FT.

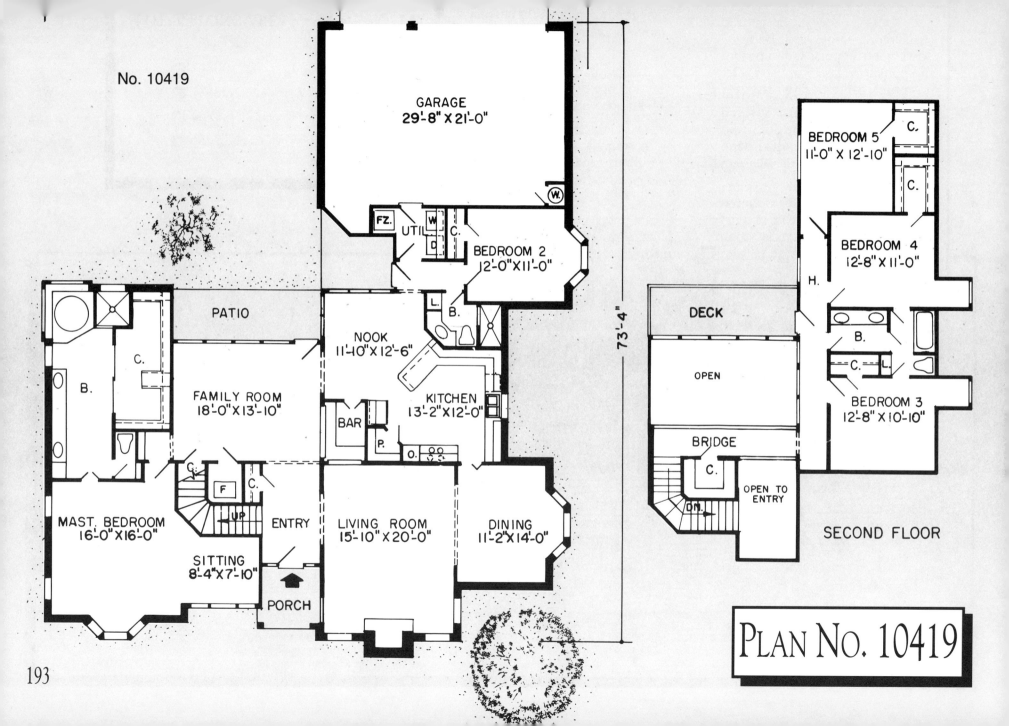

No. 10419

GARAGE
29'-8" X 21'-0"

FZ.

UTIL

W

C.

D

BEDROOM 2
12'-0" X 11'-0"

PATIO

NOOK
11'-10" X 12'-6"

L.

B.

FAMILY ROOM
18'-0" X 13'-10"

C.

B.

BAR

KITCHEN
13'-2" X 12'-0"

P.

O.

C.

F

C.

MAST. BEDROOM
16'-0" X 16'-0"

UP

ENTRY

LIVING ROOM
15'-10" X 20'-0"

DINING
11'-2" X 14'-0"

SITTING
8'-4" X 7'-10"

PORCH

73'-4"

DECK

OPEN

BRIDGE

C.

DN.

OPEN TO
ENTRY

BEDROOM 5
11'-0" X 12'-10"

C.

C.

BEDROOM 4
12'-8" X 11'-0"

H.

B.

C.

L.

BEDROOM 3
12'-8" X 10'-10"

SECOND FLOOR

PLAN No. 10419

193

BLEND OF TUDOR AND QUEEN ANNE STYLING

- ☐ Mullioned bay windows varied in shape provide visual interest and tasteful touch of elegance across wide brick facade

- ☐ Living Room and Dining Room traditionally placed with twin columned entries on left and right sides of Foyer

- ☐ Corner of L-shaped cooking island/eating bar in Kitchen juts into Family Room visually connecting the two

- ☐ Two bedrooms upstairs spacious enough for several children

- ☐ Bathed in light from windows, doors, and skylights, high-ceilinged Family Room acts as natural magnet for friends and family

- ☐ Garden window over Kitchen sink offers perfect environment for nurturing flowering plants and herbs year-round

- ☐ Elaborate Master Suite features large walk-in closet, oversized tub tucked in bay window nook, two vanities, cedar closet, and opens onto deck

- ☐ FIRST FLOOR — 2,267 SQ. FT.
- ☐ SECOND FLOOR — 705 SQ. FT.
- ☐ BASEMENT — 2,267 SQ. FT.
- ☐ GARAGE — 763 SQ. FT.

TOTAL LIVING AREA — 2,972 SQ. FT.

No. 91731

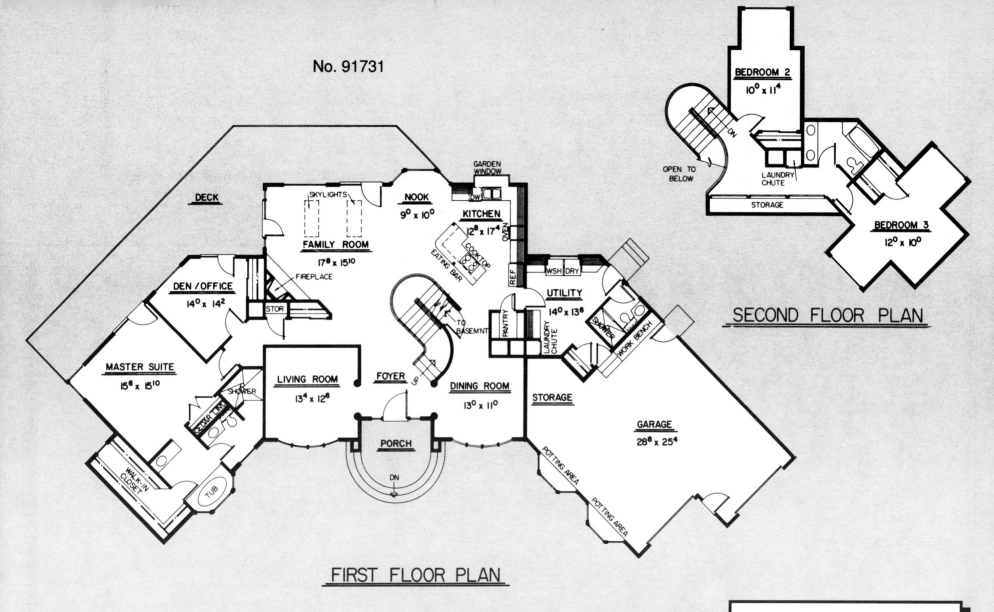

DECK

SKYLIGHTS

FAMILY ROOM
17⁸ x 15¹⁰

FIREPLACE

GARDEN
WINDOW

DW

NOOK
9⁰ x 10⁰

KITCHEN
12⁸ x 17⁴

OVEN

EATING BAR

COOKTOP

DEN / OFFICE
14⁰ x 14²

STOR

REF

WSH DRY

UTILITY
14⁰ x 13⁶

PANTRY

LAUNDRY
CHUTE

SHOWER

WORK BENCH

MASTER SUITE
15⁶ x 15¹⁰

LIVING ROOM
13⁴ x 12⁸

FOYER

UP

TO
BASEM'NT

DINING ROOM
13⁰ x 11⁰

STORAGE

GARAGE
28⁸ x 25⁴

SHOWER

WALK-IN
CLOSET

CEDAR LINED

TUB

PORCH

DN

POTTING AREA

POTTING AREA

FIRST FLOOR PLAN

BEDROOM 2
10⁰ x 11⁴

OPEN TO
BELOW

DN

LAUNDRY
CHUTE

STORAGE

BEDROOM 3
12⁰ x 10⁰

SECOND FLOOR PLAN

PLAN NO. 91731

195

Two-Story Daylight Basement Design

- ❑ Step-down 3-car Garage on side hidden by graceful arched window treatment
- ❑ Secluded Study with corner window affords peaceful atmosphere
- ❑ Exceptional Family Room has elegant corner fireplace and additional light floods in from door to deck
- ❑ Island Kitchen features pantry for extra storage and bright sunny Nook with access to rear deck

- ❑ Recreation Room with wetbar, private Bath including convenient shower stall, luxurious hot tub, and angled vanity features Pool Room
- ❑ Private Guest room with ample closet space opens to expansive patio
- ❑ Basement complemented by handyman Shop located next to Recreation Room with access to backyard patio

---

- ❑ First floor — 1,888 sq. ft.
- ❑ Second floor — 1,613 sq. ft.
- ❑ Basement — 1,365 sq. ft.
- ❑ Shop — 543 sq. ft.
- ❑ Garage — 955 sq. ft.

Total living area — 4,866 sq. ft.

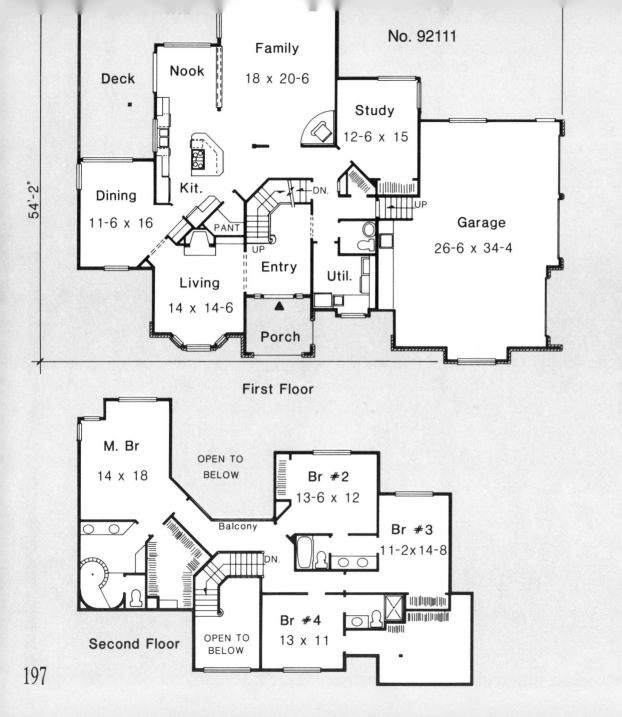

Deck

Nook

Family
18 x 20-6

Study
12-6 x 15

Dining
11-6 x 16

Kit.

PANT

UP

DN.

UP

Garage
26-6 x 34-4

Entry

Util.

Living
14 x 14-6

54'-2"

Porch

First Floor

M. Br
14 x 18

OPEN TO
BELOW

Br #2
13-6 x 12

Balcony

DN.

Br #3
11-2 x 14-8

Br #4
13 x 11

OPEN TO
BELOW

Second Floor

197

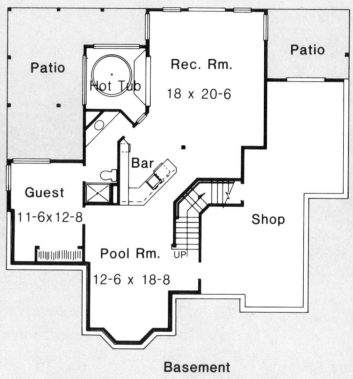

Patio

Hot Tub

Rec. Rm.
18 x 20-6

Patio

Bar

Guest
11-6 x 12-8

Shop

Pool Rm.
12-6 x 18-8

UP

Basement

PLAN No. 92111

SPECTACULAR STUCCO

- ☐ Magnificent Entry set aglow by recessed lighting and enhanced by curved suspended staircase
- ☐ Vaulted Dining Room well-angled to obtain best available lighting
- ☐ Open floor plan in well-equipped island Kitchen heads into brightly lighted Nook and side pantry
- ☐ Quiet Library adds to elegance and charm of Living Room featuring window over gas fireplace

- ☐ Spacious fireplaced Family Room leads out to cleverly curved patio
- ☐ Master Bedroom offers fireplace, full luxury Bath amenities, and extra-roomy closet space
- ☐ Practical Playroom with added beauty of dormers gives that just right touch for additional space
- ☐ Rear staircase eases movement for family members
- ☐ Enter house from oversized 3-car Garage through convenient Utility Room and half Bath

- ☐ FIRST FLOOR — 1,924 SQ. FT.
- ☐ SECOND FLOOR — 1,424 SQ. FT.
- ☐ GARAGE — 836 SQ. FT.

TOTAL LIVING AREA — 3,348 SQ. FT.

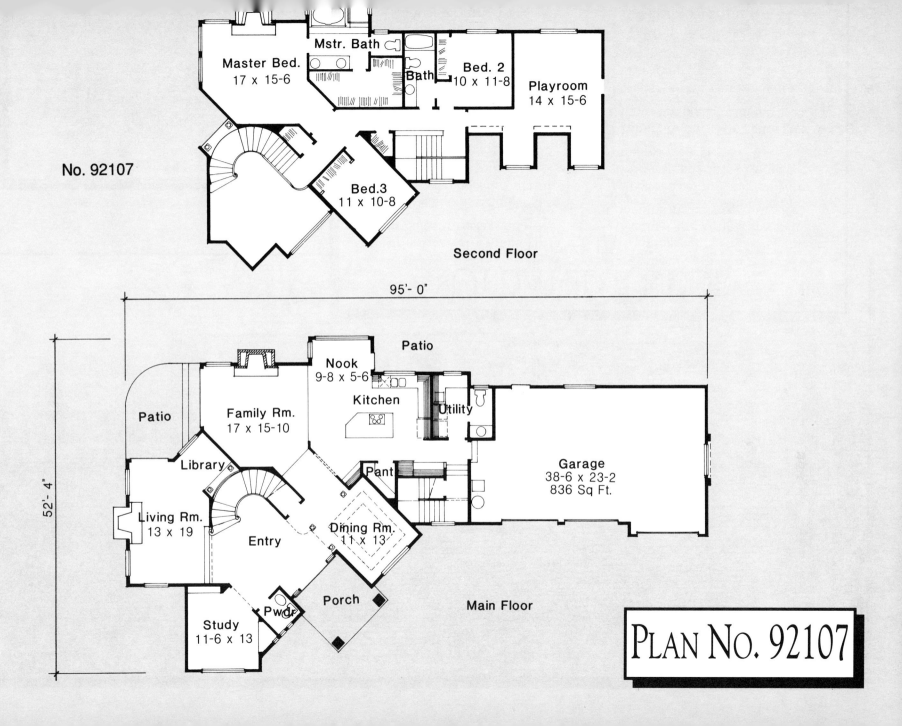

No. 92107

Master Bed.
17 x 15-6

Mstr. Bath

Bath

Bed. 2
10 x 11-8

Playroom
14 x 15-6

Bed.3
11 x 10-8

Second Floor

95'- 0"

Patio

Nook
9-8 x 5-6

Patio

Family Rm.
17 x 15-10

Kitchen

Utility

Library

Pant

Garage
38-6 x 23-2
836 Sq Ft.

Living Rm.
13 x 19

Dining Rm.
11 x 13

52'- 4"

Entry

Study
11-6 x 13

Pwdr

Porch

Main Floor

PLAN NO. 92107

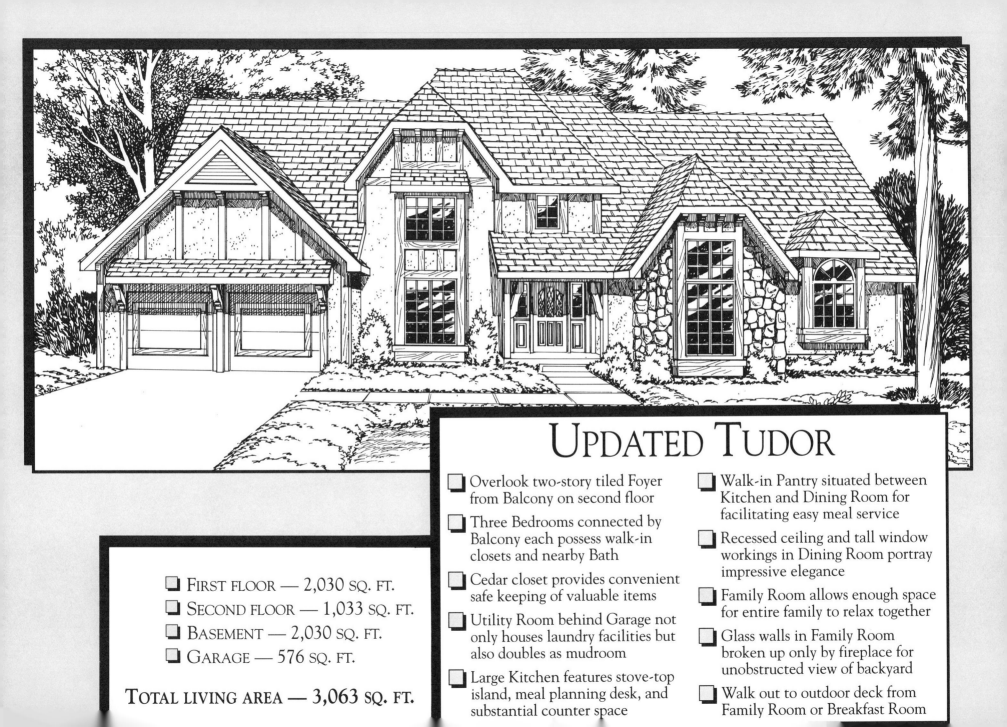

UPDATED TUDOR

- FIRST FLOOR — 2,030 SQ. FT.
- SECOND FLOOR — 1,033 SQ. FT.
- BASEMENT — 2,030 SQ. FT.
- GARAGE — 576 SQ. FT.

TOTAL LIVING AREA — 3,063 SQ. FT.

- Overlook two-story tiled Foyer from Balcony on second floor
- Three Bedrooms connected by Balcony each possess walk-in closets and nearby Bath
- Cedar closet provides convenient safe keeping of valuable items
- Utility Room behind Garage not only houses laundry facilities but also doubles as mudroom
- Large Kitchen features stove-top island, meal planning desk, and substantial counter space

- Walk-in Pantry situated between Kitchen and Dining Room for facilitating easy meal service
- Recessed ceiling and tall window workings in Dining Room portray impressive elegance
- Family Room allows enough space for entire family to relax together
- Glass walls in Family Room broken up only by fireplace for unobstructed view of backyard
- Walk out to outdoor deck from Family Room or Breakfast Room

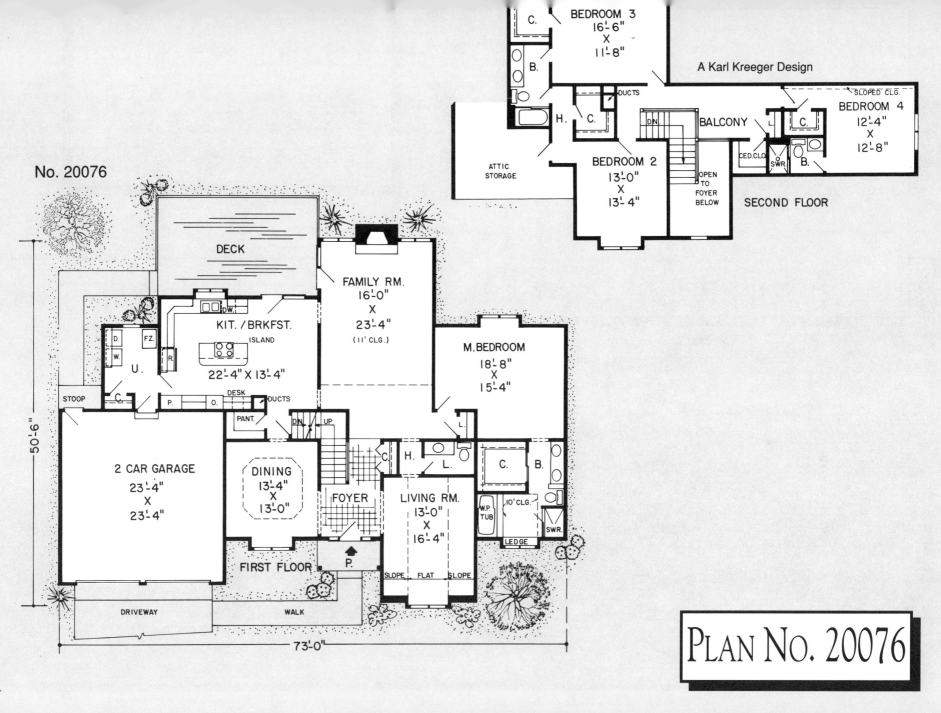

No. 20076

BEDROOM 3
16'-6"
X
11'-8"

A Karl Kreeger Design

C.

B.

SLOPED CLG.
BEDROOM 4
12'-4"
X
12'-8"

H.

C.

DUCTS

DN.

BALCONY

L.

C.

CED.CLO.

SWR.

B.

ATTIC
STORAGE

BEDROOM 2
13'-0"
X
13'-4"

OPEN
TO
FOYER
BELOW

SECOND FLOOR

DECK

FAMILY RM.
16'-0"
X
23'-4"
(11' CLG.)

D.   FZ.
W.   R.
U.
C.

KIT./BRKFST.

ISLAND

22'-4" X 13'-4"

DW.

M.BEDROOM
18'-8"
X
15'-4"

STOOP

P.   O.   DESK   DUCTS

PANT.

DN.   UP

C.   H.   L.

L.

C.

B.

2 CAR GARAGE
23'-4"
X
23'-4"

DINING
13'-4"
X
13'-0"

FOYER

LIVING RM.
13'-0"
X
16'-4"

W.P.
TUB

10' CLG.

SWR.

FIRST FLOOR

P.

LEDGE

SLOPE   FLAT   SLOPE

DRIVEWAY

WALK

50'-6"

73'-0"

PLAN NO. 20076

CLASSIC BRICK HOME

- ❏ Enter through covered porch with unusual brick detailing into open Entry

- ❏ Gallery with decorative columns separates Dining Room and Living Room

- ❏ U-shaped Kitchen designed for efficiency features food preparation island and plenty of counter space

- ❏ Comfortable Family Room extends genial invitation for complete relaxation

- ❏ Sleeping quarters located in separate wing away from busy living areas

- ❏ Highlights of Master Suite include vaulted ceiling, two individual vanities, and skylights over raised tub

- ❏ King-sized walk-around closet in Master Suite supplies room for even the largest wardrobe

- ❏ Two additional Bedrooms share full Bath with skylight and twin basin vanity

---

- ❏ LIVING AREA — 3,157 SQ. FT.
- ❏ GARAGE — 3-CAR

TOTAL LIVING AREA — 3,157 SQ. FT.

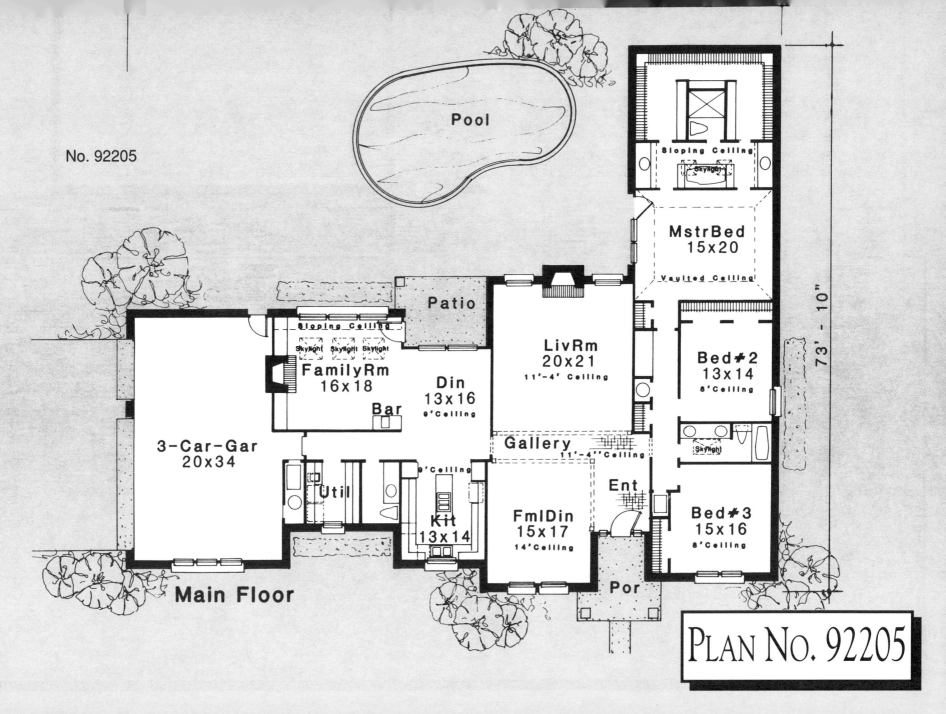

No. 92205

Pool

MstrBed
15x20
Vaulted Ceiling

Sloping Ceiling

Skylight

Patio

LivRm
20x21
11'-4" Ceiling

Bed #2
13x14
8' Ceiling

Sloping Ceiling

Skylight Skylight Skylight

FamilyRm
16x18

3-Car-Gar
20x34

Bar

Din
13x16
8' Ceiling

Gallery
11'-4" Ceiling

Skylight

Util

Kit
13x14

9'Ceiling

FmlDin
15x17
14' Ceiling

Ent

Bed #3
15x16
8' Ceiling

Por

73' - 10"

Main Floor

PLAN No. 92205

AMPLE ROOM TO GROW

- ☐ Hip-roofed covered porch enters to Foyer with interesting staircase and open floor plan offset by convenient Powder Room

- ☐ Enormous island Kitched features large Pantry, well-lighted Nook, cabinets galore and built-in desk for convenient meal-planning

- ☐ Fireplaced Family Room flooded with light from extravagant window wall blends to Kitchen area

- ☐ Master Bath with double vanities, shower, tub, and private water closet leads to walk-in closet

- ☐ Bedroom Three and Bedroom Four both feature plenty of windows, walk-in closet, and each have their own vanity in shared full Bath

- ☐ Upstairs hallway has second staircase for convenience and opens to Foyer below

- ☐ Huge Bonus Room with walk-in closet on second floor gives space for future expansion

- ☐ FIRST FLOOR — 1,703 SQ. FT.
- ☐ SECOND FLOOR — 1,739 SQ. FT.
- ☐ BONUS ROOM — 291 SQ. FT.
- ☐ GARAGE — 3-CAR

TOTAL LIVING AREA — 3,733 SQ. FT.

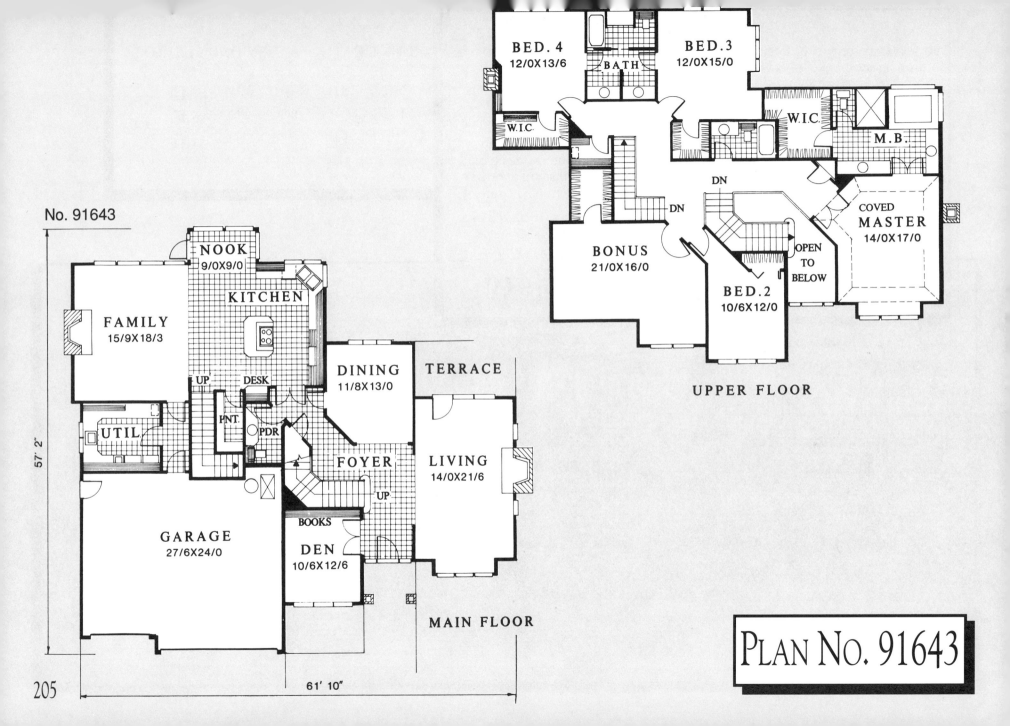

No. 91643

FAMILY
15/9X18/3

NOOK
9/0X9/0

KITCHEN

DINING
11/8X13/0

TERRACE

UP

DESK

UTIL

PNT.

PDR

FOYER

LIVING
14/0X21/6

UP

GARAGE
27/6X24/0

BOOKS

DEN
10/6X12/6

57' 2"

61' 10"

MAIN FLOOR

BED. 4
12/0X13/6

BATH

BED. 3
12/0X15/0

W.I.C.

W.I.C.

M.B.

DN

COVED
MASTER
14/0X17/0

BONUS
21/0X16/0

DN

OPEN
TO
BELOW

BED. 2
10/6X12/0

UPPER FLOOR

PLAN No. 91643

205

Majestic Columnar Manor

- ☐ First floor — 2,143 sq. ft.
- ☐ Second floor — 1,035 sq. ft.
- ☐ Garage — 560 sq. ft.

Total living area — 3,178 sq. ft.

- ☐ Foyer has sidelights for extra light, elegant staircase and leads to convenient Powder Room
- ☐ Family Room, with access to rear patio features fireplace, built-in bookshelves and convenient wetbar
- ☐ Kitchen with ample cabinet and counter space allows choice use of Dining Area or Formal Dining Room for entertainment
- ☐ Second-floor Study enjoys feeling of quiet solitude

- ☐ Master Bedroom features extra long windows for added light, private Study, and opens to Master Bath with double vanity, angled tub, and twin walk-in closets
- ☐ Enormous Living Room may be entered from either Foyer or Family Room and offers plenty of wall space for easy placement of furnishings
- ☐ Balcony on second floor landing culminates in balcony overlooking front entrance

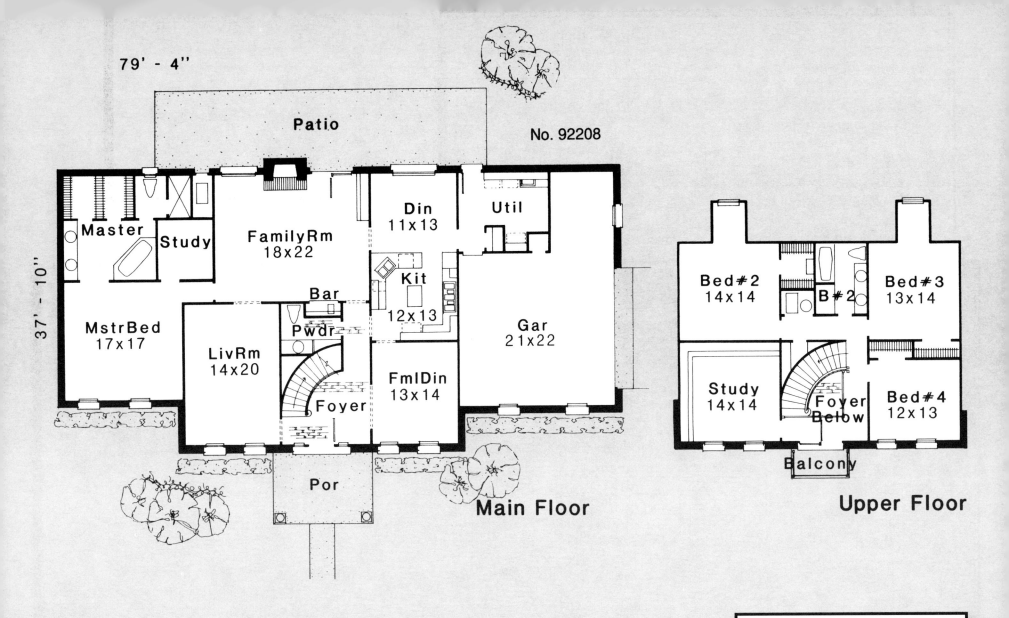

79' - 4"

Patio

No. 92208

37' - 10"

Master

Study

FamilyRm
18x22

Din
11x13

Util

MstrBed
17x17

Bar

Kit
12x13

Gar
21x22

LivRm
14x20

Pwdr

Foyer

FmlDin
13x14

Por

Main Floor

Bed#2
14x14

B#2

Bed#3
13x14

Study
14x14

Foyer
Below

Bed#4
12x13

Balcony

Upper Floor

PLAN No. 92208

BEAUTY WITH A BONUS

- ☐ Vaulted Entry flowing into Living Room and Dining Room creates expansive formal area accentuated by huge windows and cozy fireplace
- ☐ Island Kitchen with room-sized pantry adjoins sunny Breakfast Nook
- ☐ Enjoy family barbeques on grill outdoors on patio just steps away from Kitchen
- ☐ Step down to sunken Family Room with additional fireplace

- ☐ Inviting Den offers seclusion for solitary entertainment
- ☐ Angular stairway dominating Entry leads to magnificant Master Suite with bay Sitting Area
- ☐ Two additional Bedrooms enjoy individual walk-in closets and basins, and share Bath facilities
- ☐ Separate staircase leads from 3-car Garage to special retreat set apart from rest of house for private office

---

- ☐ FIRST FLOOR — 1,706 SQ. FT.
- ☐ SECOND FLOOR — 1,162 SQ. FT.
- ☐ OFFICE — 205 SQ. FT.
- ☐ BASEMENT — 1,062 SQ. FT.
- ☐ GARAGE — 3-CAR

TOTAL LIVING AREA — 3,073 SQ. FT.

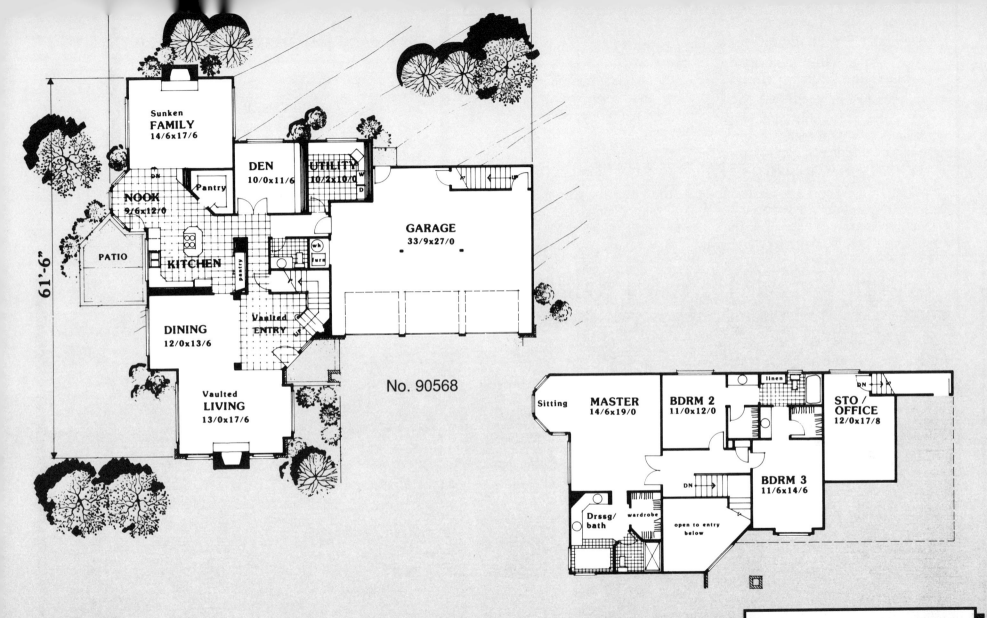

Sunken
FAMILY
14/6x17/6

DEN
10/0x11/6

UTILITY
10/2x10/0

Pantry

NOOK
9/6x12/0

GARAGE
33/9x27/0

PATIO

KITCHEN

pantry

61'-6"

DINING
12/0x13/6

Vaulted
ENTRY

Vaulted
LIVING
13/0x17/6

No. 90568

Sitting

MASTER
14/6x19/0

BDRM 2
11/0x12/0

linen

**STO /
OFFICE**
12/0x17/8

BDRM 3
11/6x14/6

DN

Drssg/
bath

wardrobe

open to entry
below

PLAN NO. 90568

Victorian Touches Grace Exterior

- ☐ Richly embellished covered porches sweep across majority of front while turrets and gables adorn every turn

- ☐ Unique to this home, Kitchen and Entryway have vaulted ceilings

- ☐ Octagon-shaped eating Nook brightens any mealtime with windows at ground level, another row above, and ceiling stretching to window-lined turret overhead

- ☐ Huge Kitchen features range and oven located in work island, lots of counter space, and trash recycling center

- ☐ Circular Sitting room partially surrounded by captain's walk balcony leads up to observatory on higher level

- ☐ Two upstairs bedrooms feature private balconies while third includes step-in closet

- ☐ Large Work shop supplies room for conversion to Garage if desired

- ☐ First floor — 3,031 sq. ft.
- ☐ Second floor — 1,578 sq. ft.
- ☐ Garage — 514 sq. ft.

Total living area — 4,609 sq. ft.

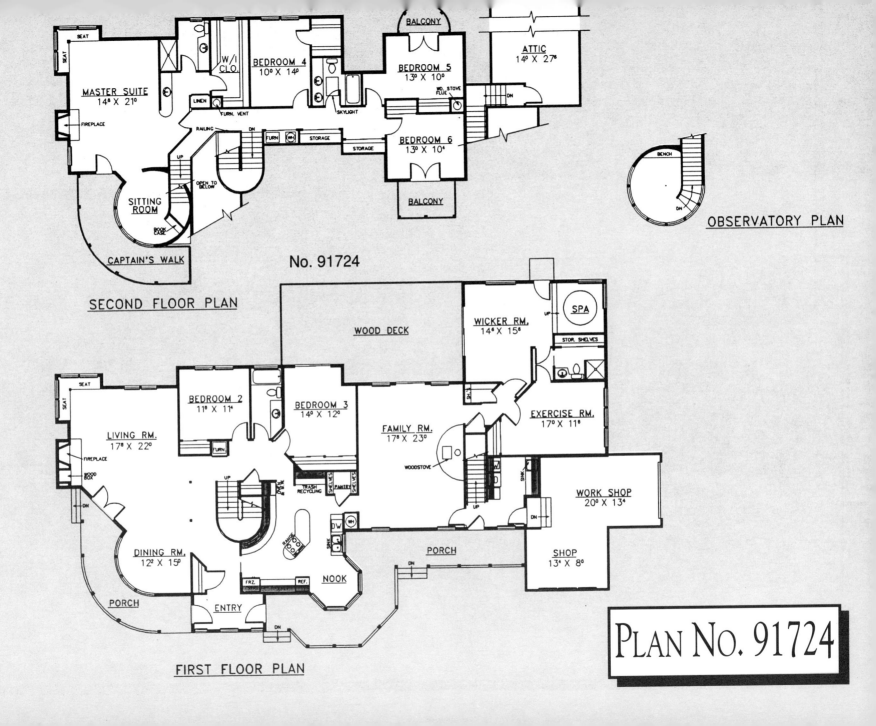

MASTER SUITE
14⁸ X 21⁰

SEAT

SEAT

W/I CLO.

BEDROOM 4
10⁰ X 14⁰

BALCONY

BEDROOM 5
13⁰ X 10⁰

ATTIC
14⁰ X 27⁸

WD. STOVE FLUE

FIREPLACE

LINEN

FURN. VENT

SKYLIGHT

BEDROOM 6
13⁰ X 10⁴

DN

RAILING

DN

FURN

WH

STORAGE

STORAGE

UP

OPEN TO BELOW

SITTING ROOM

BOOK CASE

BALCONY

CAPTAIN'S WALK

No. 91724

BENCH

DN

OBSERVATORY PLAN

SECOND FLOOR PLAN

WICKER RM.
14⁸ X 15⁰

SPA

UP

WOOD DECK

STOR. SHELVES

SEAT

SEAT

BEDROOM 2
11⁸ X 11⁴

BEDROOM 3
14⁰ X 12⁰

FAMILY RM.
17⁸ X 23⁰

EXERCISE RM.
17⁰ X 11⁸

LIVING RM.
17⁸ X 22⁰

FIREPLACE

WOOD BOX

DN

FURN.

UP

WOODSTOVE

WORK SHOP
20⁰ X 13⁴

SHELVES

PANTRY

SHELVES

SNK

TRASH RECYCLING

DW

WH

UP

DN

RANGE

SNK

DINING RM.
12² X 15⁰

PORCH

FRZ.

REF.

NOOK

DN

PORCH

SHOP
13⁴ X 8⁰

PORCH

ENTRY

DN

FIRST FLOOR PLAN

PLAN NO. 91724

211

Floor-to-Ceiling Window Treatment

- Unique front porch with elegant brick angled wall makes grand entrance to gracious Foyer

- Daylight basement Recreation Room affords efficient uniqueness of full Kitchen, Bar, and Wine Storage, and exit to spacious patio

- Curved staircase from another era in Foyer combines with open concept allowing for ease in entertaining

- Book-shelved Library has interesting window treatment and extends to full Bath

- Kitchen with island surrounded by cabinets features Pantry and opens to sunny Nook which steps onto wrap-around bi-level Deck

- Master Bedroom features fireplace, double windows and sliding glass door leading to private deck

- Three-car angled Garage steps up to enter roomy Utility Area with separate linen closet

- First floor — 1,587 sq. ft.
- Second floor — 905 sq. ft.
- Basement — 1,289 sq. ft.
- Garage — 1,020 sq. ft.

Total living area — 3,781 sq. ft.

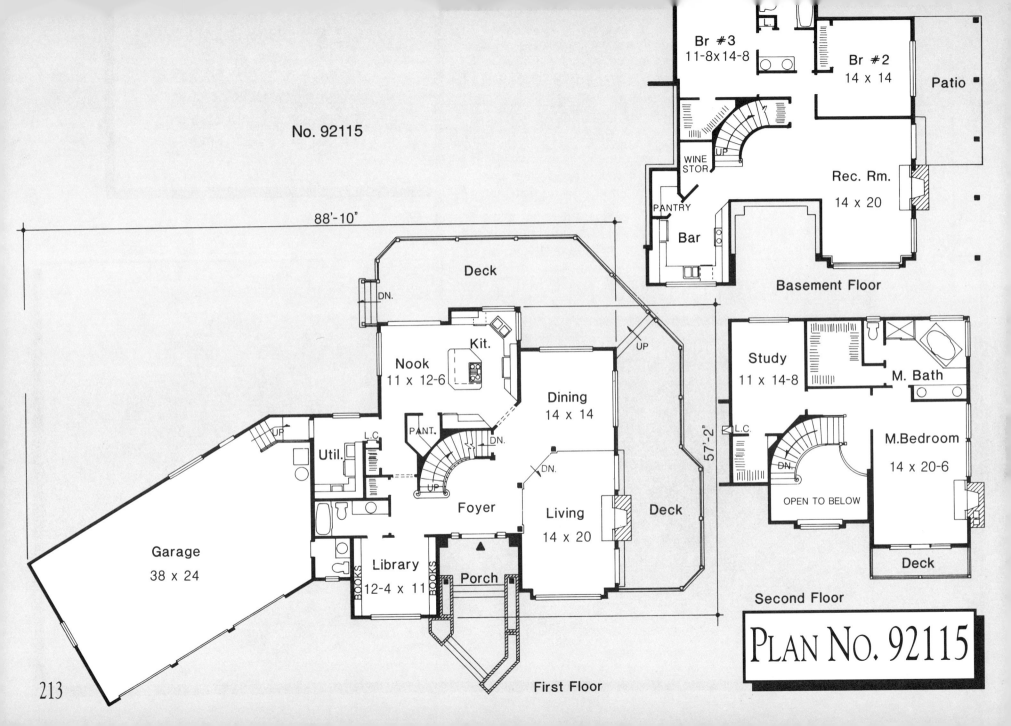

QUOINED CORNERS EMBELLISH STUCCO

- Greet guests entering through portico in impressive tiled Foyer with grand angled stairway

- Fireplaced Living Room features floor-to-ceiling window for full aesthetic affect

- French doors lead into Den for private conversation or just quiet solitude

- Open Kitchen with food-preparation island blends into cordial Nook with bay windows for plenty of natural light

- Fireplaced Family Room merges into eating areas for spacious appearance

- Step up to conveniently located Utility Room and entrance to 3-car Garage

- Extravagent Master Suite features vaulted ceiling and double doors leading into Master Bath and walk-in closet

- Three additional Bedrooms on second floor share full Bath complete with twin sink vanity

- FIRST FLOOR — 1,714 SQ. FT.
- SECOND FLOOR — 1,424 SQ. FT.
- BONUS ROOM — 352 SQ. FT.
- GARAGE — 3-CAR

TOTAL LIVING AREA — 3,138 SQ. FT.

No. 91663

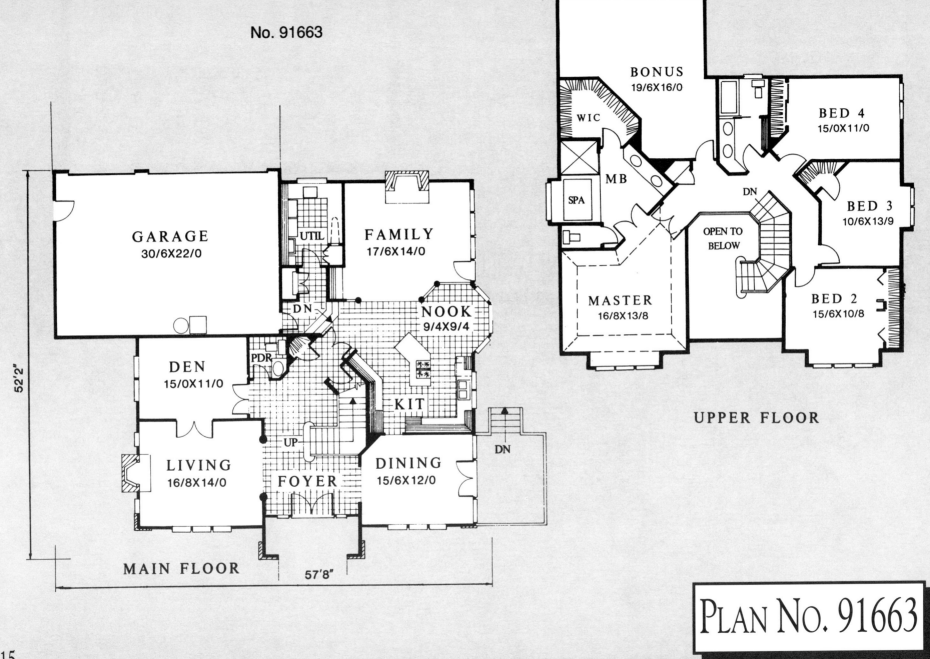

GARAGE
30/6X22/0

UTIL

FAMILY
17/6X14/0

DN

NOOK
9/4X9/4

DEN
15/0X11/0

PDR

KIT

UP

DN

LIVING
16/8X14/0

FOYER

DINING
15/6X12/0

52'2"

MAIN FLOOR

57'8"

BONUS
19/6X16/0

WIC

BED 4
15/0X11/0

SPA

MB

DN

BED 3
10/6X13/9

OPEN TO
BELOW

MASTER
16/8X13/8

BED 2
15/6X10/8

UPPER FLOOR

PLAN No. 91663

215

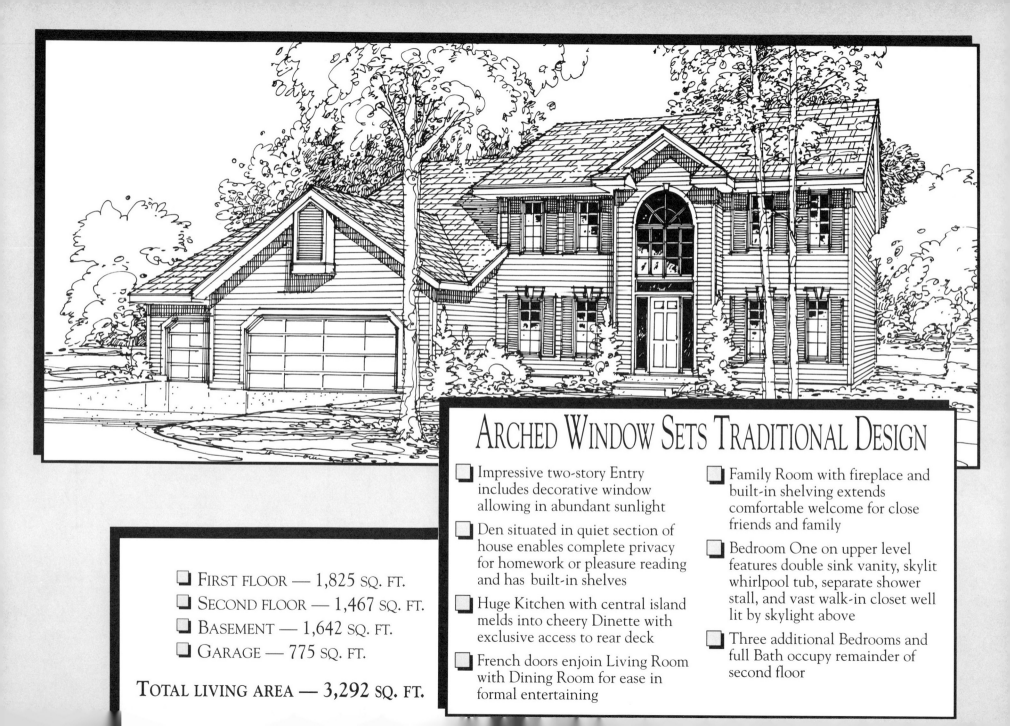

Arched Window Sets Traditional Design

- ☐ Impressive two-story Entry includes decorative window allowing in abundant sunlight

- ☐ Den situated in quiet section of house enables complete privacy for homework or pleasure reading and has built-in shelves

- ☐ Huge Kitchen with central island melds into cheery Dinette with exclusive access to rear deck

- ☐ French doors enjoin Living Room with Dining Room for ease in formal entertaining

- ☐ Family Room with fireplace and built-in shelving extends comfortable welcome for close friends and family

- ☐ Bedroom One on upper level features double sink vanity, skylit whirlpool tub, separate shower stall, and vast walk-in closet well lit by skylight above

- ☐ Three additional Bedrooms and full Bath occupy remainder of second floor

- ☐ First floor — 1,825 sq. ft.
- ☐ Second floor — 1,467 sq. ft.
- ☐ Basement — 1,642 sq. ft.
- ☐ Garage — 775 sq. ft.

Total living area — 3,292 sq. ft.

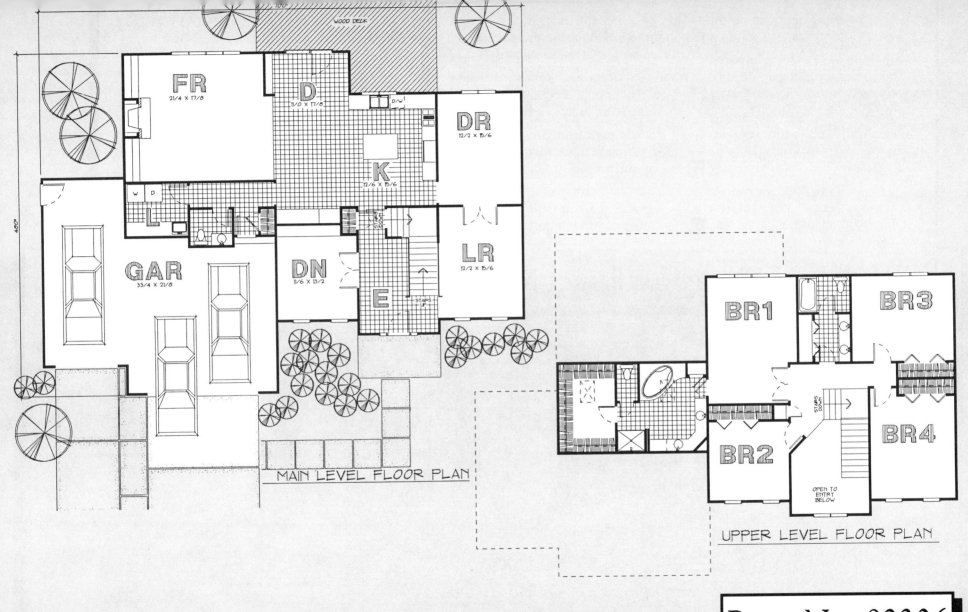

WOOD DECK

FR
21/4 X 17/8

D
11/0 X 17/8

D/W

DR
12/2 X 15/6

K
12/6 X 15/6

W D

GAR
33/4 X 21/8

DN
11/6 X 13/2

STAIRS DOWN

E

STAIRS UP

LR
12/2 X 15/6

MAIN LEVEL FLOOR PLAN

BR1

BR3

BR2

STAIRS DOWN

BR4

OPEN TO ENTRY BELOW

UPPER LEVEL FLOOR PLAN

PLAN No. 92306

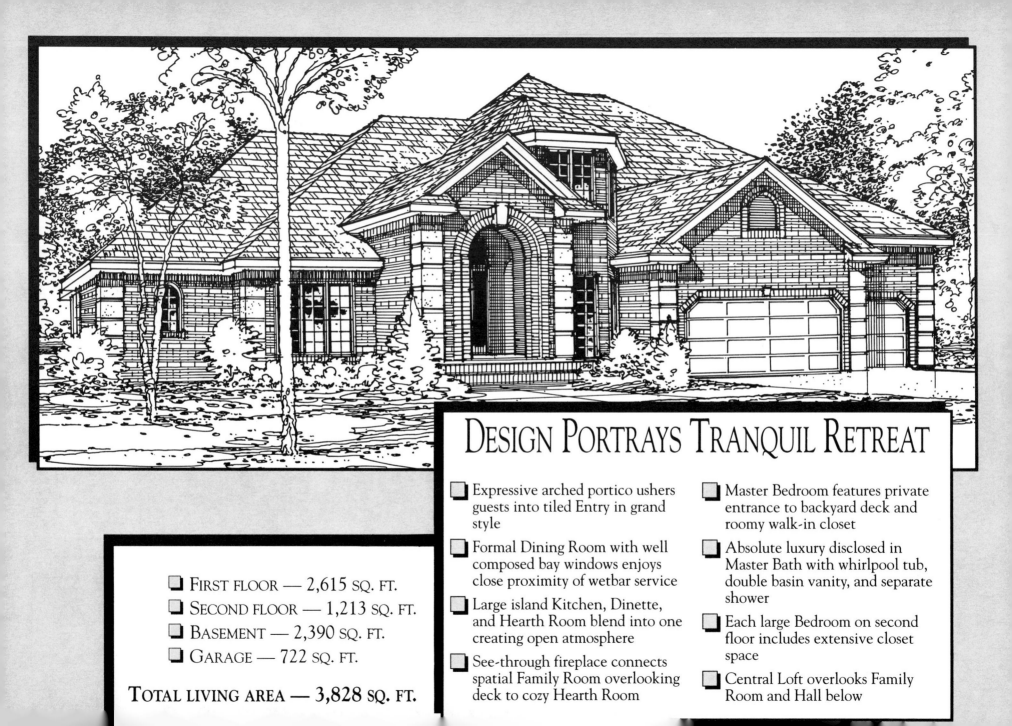

DESIGN PORTRAYS TRANQUIL RETREAT

- ❏ Expressive arched portico ushers guests into tiled Entry in grand style

- ❏ Formal Dining Room with well composed bay windows enjoys close proximity of wetbar service

- ❏ Large island Kitchen, Dinette, and Hearth Room blend into one creating open atmosphere

- ❏ See-through fireplace connects spatial Family Room overlooking deck to cozy Hearth Room

- ❏ Master Bedroom features private entrance to backyard deck and roomy walk-in closet

- ❏ Absolute luxury disclosed in Master Bath with whirlpool tub, double basin vanity, and separate shower

- ❏ Each large Bedroom on second floor includes extensive closet space

- ❏ Central Loft overlooks Family Room and Hall below

- ❏ FIRST FLOOR — 2,615 SQ. FT.
- ❏ SECOND FLOOR — 1,213 SQ. FT.
- ❏ BASEMENT — 2,390 SQ. FT.
- ❏ GARAGE — 722 SQ. FT.

TOTAL LIVING AREA — 3,828 SQ. FT.

No. 92302

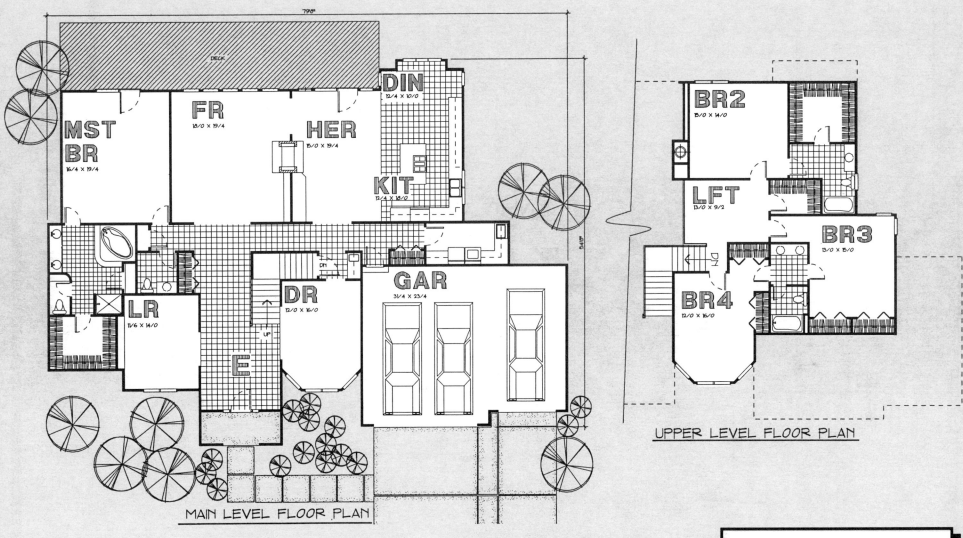

MST BR
16/4 x 19/4

FR
18/0 x 19/4

HER
13/0 x 19/4

DIN
12/4 x 10/0

KIT
12/4 x 18/0

LR
11/6 x 14/0

DR
12/0 x 16/0

GAR
31/4 x 23/4

MAIN LEVEL FLOOR PLAN

BR2
13/0 x 14/0

LFT
13/0 x 9/2

BR3
13/0 x 13/0

BR4
12/0 x 16/0

UPPER LEVEL FLOOR PLAN

PLAN No. 92302

219

ENGLUND

CONTEMPORARY DRAMA

☐ Special dramatics focused on grand stairway and balcony above Great Room

☐ Columned arcade directs traffic from Vestibule to Master Suite and Library wing on right; Family and Kitchen areas on left

☐ Entrance offers impressive view to double-height Great Room with detailed fireplace wall

☐ Dining Room is open, yet in its own alcove, to savor same spatial elegance

☐ Vast Master Suite has walk-in closet and whirlpool tub with twin vanities in Master Bath

☐ Private access through Master Suite allows intimate evenings relaxing in hot tub on deck

☐ L-shaped Kitchen opens to Breakfast Area with sliding glass doors to second deck

☐ Three additional Bedrooms on second level each sport personal Baths and plenty of closet space

☐ FIRST FLOOR — 3,900 SQ. FT.
☐ SECOND FLOOR — 1,720 SQ. FT.
☐ BASEMENT — 2,505 SQ. FT.
☐ GARAGE — 3-CAR

TOTAL LIVING AREA — 5,620 SQ. FT.

No. 99366

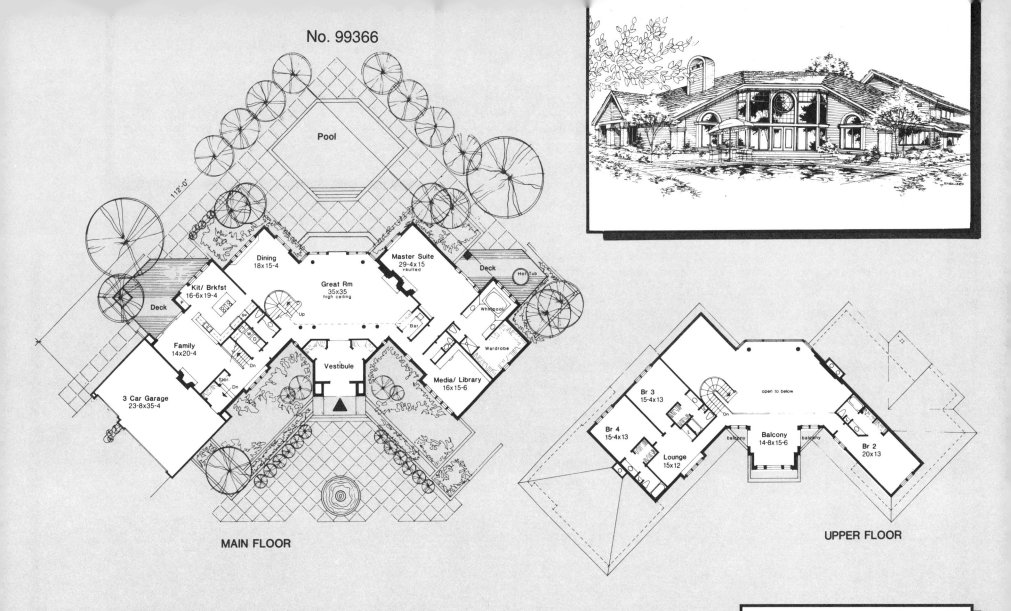

Pool

112'-0"

Dining
18 x 15-4

Kit/ Brkfst
16-6 x 19-4

Deck

Family
14 x 20-4

3 Car Garage
23-8 x 35-4

Great Rm
35 x 35
high ceiling

Up

Dn

Stor.

Dn

W D

Vestibule

Master Suite
29-4 x 15
vaulted

Deck

Hot Tub

Whirlpool

Bar

Wardrobe

Media/ Library
16 x 15-6

MAIN FLOOR

Br 3
15-4 x 13

open to below

Dn

Br 4
15-4 x 13

Lounge
15 x 12

balcony

Balcony
14-8 x 15-6

balcony

Br 2
20 x 13

UPPER FLOOR

PLAN No. 99366

221

LUNCH BY THE POOL

- ☐ Colossal walk-in closet in Master Suite includes two built-in chests
- ☐ Skylight above whirlpool bath dispenses cheerful sunlight into roomy Master Bath
- ☐ Book-lined Study provides tranquil retreat for concentration
- ☐ Fully-equipped island Kitchen flows into Breakfast Room bathed with light streaming through numerous windows
- ☐ Immense pantry adjacent to Kitchen offers substantial shelf room
- ☐ Master Bedroom occupying entire wing of home includes comfortable Sitting Room with fireplace looking out over pool area
- ☐ Cozy Library at top of stairs overlooks Foyer below
- ☐ Three additional Bedrooms and two Baths extend throughout the remainder of the second floor

- ☐ FIRST FLOOR — 3,252 SQ. FT.
- ☐ SECOND FLOOR — 873 SQ. FT.
- ☐ GARAGE — 746 SQ. FT.

TOTAL LIVING AREA — 4,125 SQ. FT.

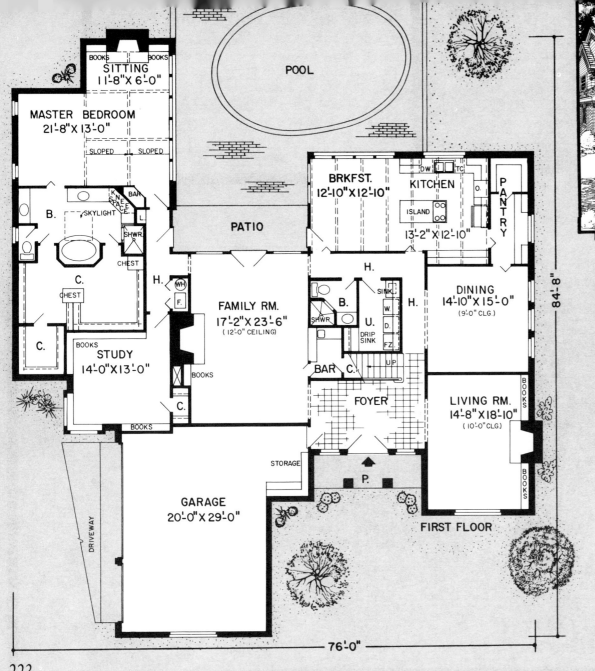

SITTING
11'-8" X 6'-0"

BOOKS

BOOKS

MASTER BEDROOM
21'-8" X 13'-0"

POOL

SLOPED   SLOPED

KNEE SPACE

BAR

B.

SKYLIGHT

L

CHEST

SHWR

C.

CHEST

C.

H.

WH

F.

PATIO

FAMILY RM.
17'-2" X 23'-6"
(12'-0" CEILING)

BOOKS

STUDY
14'-0" X 13'-0"

BOOKS

C.

BOOKS

BRKFST.
12'-10" X 12'-10"

DW   TC

KITCHEN

ISLAND

O.

PANTRY

13'-2" X 12'-10"

H.

SINK

B.

SHWR

U.

W.

D.

DRIP SINK

FZ.

H.

DINING
14'-10" X 15'-0"
(9'-0" CLG.)

BAR   C.

UP

FOYER

LIVING RM.
14'-8" X 18'-10"
(10'-0" CLG.)

BOOKS

BOOKS

STORAGE

GARAGE
20'-0" X 29'-0"

P.

DRIVEWAY

BOOKS

FIRST FLOOR

84'-8"

76'-0"

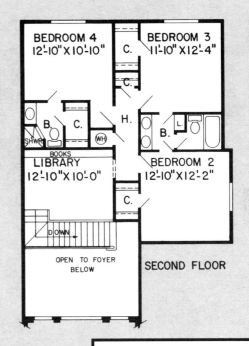

BEDROOM 4
12'-10" X 10'-10"

C.

BEDROOM 3
11'-10" X 12'-4"

C.

B.

C.

H.

SHWR

WH

B.

L

BOOKS

LIBRARY
12'-10" X 10'-0"

BEDROOM 2
12'-10" X 12'-2"

C.

DOWN

OPEN TO FOYER
BELOW

SECOND FLOOR

PLAN NO. 10696

FANCY BRICKWORK ADORNS FACADE

☐ First floor — 1,638 sq. ft.
☐ Second floor — 1,668 sq. ft.
☐ Basement — 1,525 sq. ft.
☐ Garage — 1,066 sq. ft.

Total living area — 3,306 sq. ft.

☐ Striking angled staircase dominating two-story Foyer greets guests entering through rich arched portico

☐ Formal Dining Room and bayed Living Room blend into one lavish room for spacious impression

☐ Access three-season porch through fireplaced Great Room for additional entertaining space

☐ Dinette offers easy access to wood deck for effortless barbeques

☐ Enter home from 3-car Garage through roomy Laundry Room housing washer, dryer, freezer, etc.

☐ Three-quarter Bath situated near outdoor side entrance proves beneficial for muddy days

☐ Bedroom One on upper level functioning as master suite features ample walk-in closet, double vanities, and whirlpool tub

☐ Three additional Bedrooms on second floor share two full Baths and plenty of living space

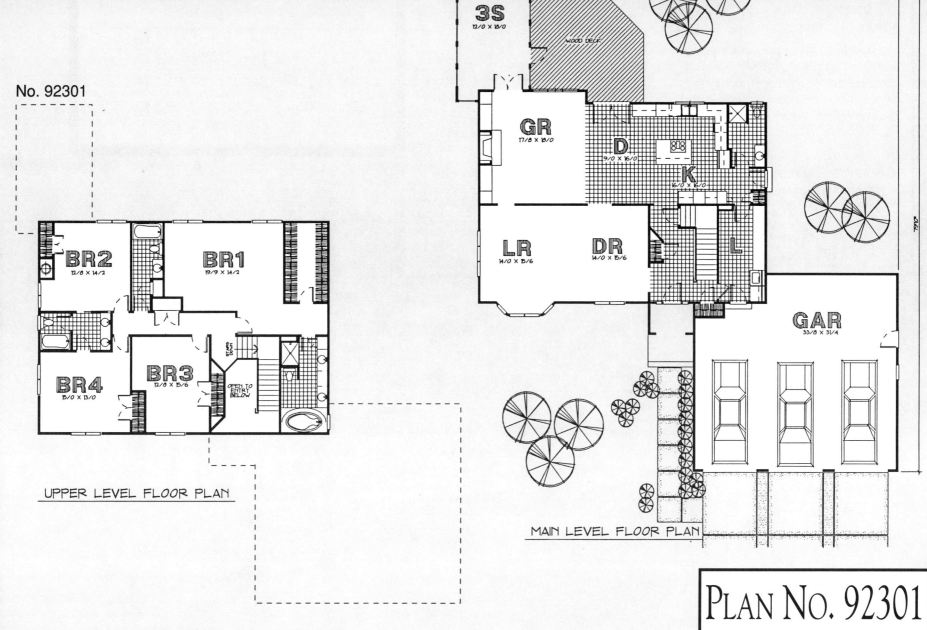

No. 92301

3S
12/0 x 19/0

WOOD DECK

GR
17/8 x 19/0

D
9/0 x 16/0

K
16/0 x 16/0

LR
14/0 x 13/6

DR
14/0 x 13/6

L

GAR
33/8 x 31/4

MAIN LEVEL FLOOR PLAN

BR2
12/8 x 14/2

BR1
19/9 x 14/2

BR4
13/0 x 13/0

BR3
12/8 x 13/6

STAIRS DOWN

OPEN TO ENTRY BELOW

UPPER LEVEL FLOOR PLAN

PLAN NO. 92301

Two-Story Farmhouse

- ☐ First floor — 1,590 sq. ft.
- ☐ Second floor — 1,344 sq. ft.
- ☐ Basement — 1,271 sq. ft.
- ☐ Garage — 2-car

Total living area — 2,934 sq. ft.

- ☐ Wrap-around covered porch gives good old-fashioned air of comfort and relaxation
- ☐ Welcoming Foyer features angled staircase, huge closet, built-in curio shelves and access to convenient Powder Room
- ☐ Extra-large Workshop has built-in workbench for tool organization
- ☐ Oversized Master Bedroom opens to Dressing Room with make-up vanity, old-fashioned window seat and his-and-hers walk-in closets
- ☐ Spacious Kitchen with plenty of cabinet and counter space, and cook-top opens to bright sunny Breakfast Room overlooking backyard terrace
- ☐ Exceptionally large Family Room with fireplace and convenient pass-thru to Kitchen exits to patio or steps down to Mud Room with Washroom and handy built-in desk
- ☐ Three Bedrooms share a full Bath with double vanity, tub, linen closet and extra towel storage

No. 99205

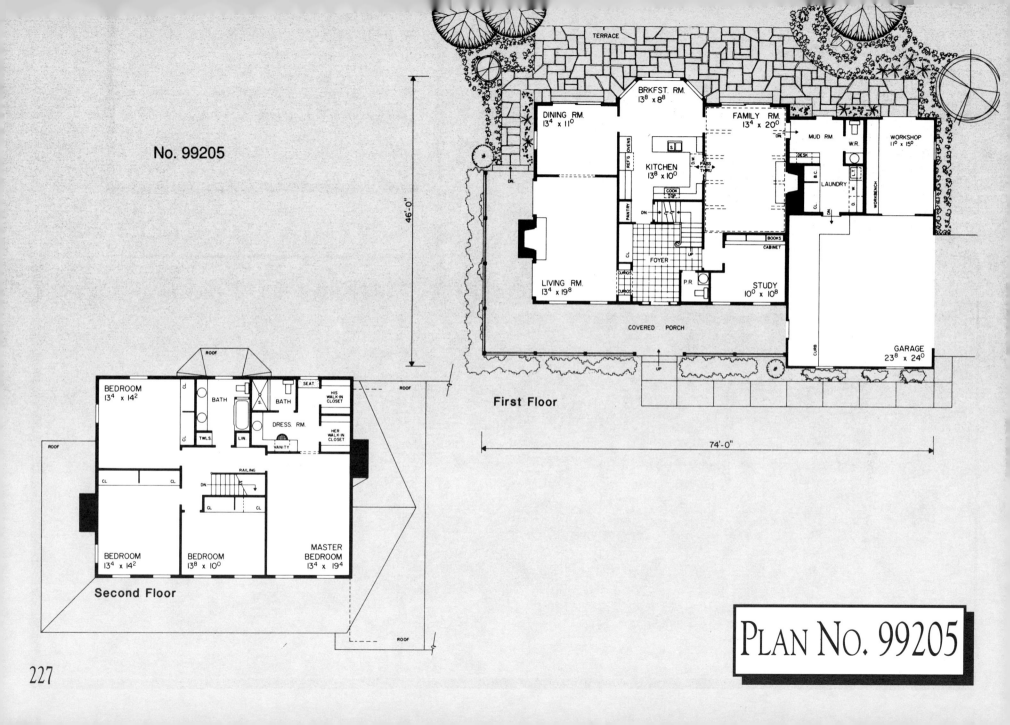

TERRACE

BRKFST. RM.
13⁸ x 8⁸

DINING RM.
13⁴ x 11⁰

FAMILY RM.
13⁴ x 20⁰

MUD RM.

WORKSHOP
11⁰ x 15⁰

W.R.

KITCHEN
13⁸ x 10⁰

OVENS

REF'G

D.W.

PASS THRU

DESK

B.C.

LAUNDRY

D

WORKBENCH

COOK TOP

PANTRY

DN

S

BOOKS

CABINET

CL

LIVING RM.
13⁴ x 19⁸

CL

FOYER

UP

CURIOS

STUDY
10⁰ x 10⁸

CURIOS

P.R.

COVERED PORCH

CURB

GARAGE
23⁸ x 24⁰

UP

46'-0"

74'-0"

First Floor

ROOF

BEDROOM
13⁴ x 14²

BATH

S.

BATH

SEAT

HIS WALK-IN CLOSET

ROOF

ROOF

TWLS.

LIN

DRESS. RM.

HER WALK-IN CLOSET

VANITY

CL

CL

RAILING

DN

CL

CL

BEDROOM
13⁴ x 14²

BEDROOM
13⁸ x 10⁰

MASTER BEDROOM
13⁴ x 19⁴

ROOF

Second Floor

ORNATE WINDOWS COMPLEMENT EXTERIOR

- ☐ Tiled Entry greets all who enter with two-story grandeur overlooked by Gallery above

- ☐ Den with sliders to side deck offers quiet solitude for readers

- ☐ Enormous Great Room offers corner fireplace, enclosed wetbar, and access to both 3-season porch and wood deck for top notch entertaining

- ☐ Enjoy backyard vistas while enjoying informal family meals in Dinette with bay windows

- ☐ Large island Kitchen featuring plenty of counter space borders formal Dining Room

- ☐ Bedroom One on upper level functioning as master suite demonstrates superb luxury with bay window, personal fireplace, huge walk-in closet, and well equipped Bath

- ☐ Three additional Bedrooms on second floor includes private access to a full bath and individual walk-in closets

- ☐ FIRST FLOOR — 1,612 SQ. FT.
- ☐ SECOND FLOOR — 2,312 SQ. FT.
- ☐ BASEMENT — 1,450 SQ. FT.
- ☐ GARAGE — 973 SQ. FT.

TOTAL LIVING AREA — 3,924 SQ. FT.

No. 92300

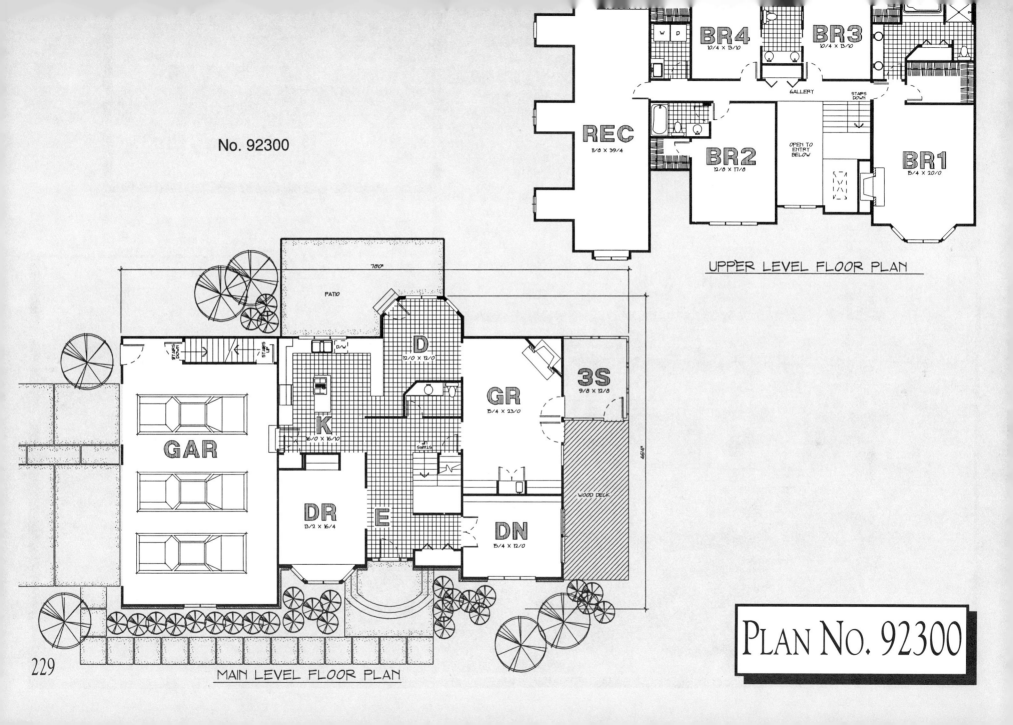

BR4
10/4 x 13/0

BR3
10/4 x 13/0

GALLERY

STAIRS DOWN

REC
11/8 x 39/4

BR2
12/8 x 17/8

OPEN TO ENTRY BELOW

BR1
13/4 x 20/0

UPPER LEVEL FLOOR PLAN

PATIO

STAIRS DOWN

STAIRS UP

D
12/0 x 12/0

GR
13/4 x 23/0

3S
9/8 x 12/8

K
16/0 x 16/0

GAR

DR
13/2 x 16/4

E

STAIRS

WOOD DECK

DN
13/4 x 12/0

229

MAIN LEVEL FLOOR PLAN

PLAN No. 92300

STUCCO SPLENDOR

- Massive stucco columns combine with floor-to-ceiling glass walls to create fascinating home

- Impressive Foyer affords view of Den enhanced by French doors

- Cove ceilings add flair to this fireplaced, well-lit Living Room which opens into equally beautiful Dining Room

- Carefully-detailed island Kitchen has luxurious glass-walled Nook for fantastic view of backyard and offset pantry

- Impressive fireplaced Family Room with benefit of wetbar leads to backyard porch

- Reach upper levels on elegant staircase that arcs over Foyer, or U-shaped staircase off Kitchen

- Enchanting Master Suite features private sitting room, fabulous spa Bath and more than ample walk-in closet

- Intriguing Bonus Room adds charm and extra space

- FIRST FLOOR — 2,268 SQ. FT.
- SECOND FLOOR — 1,484 SQ. FT.
- BONUS ROOM — 300 SQ. FT.
- GARAGE — 3-CAR

TOTAL LIVING AREA — 4,052 SQ. FT.

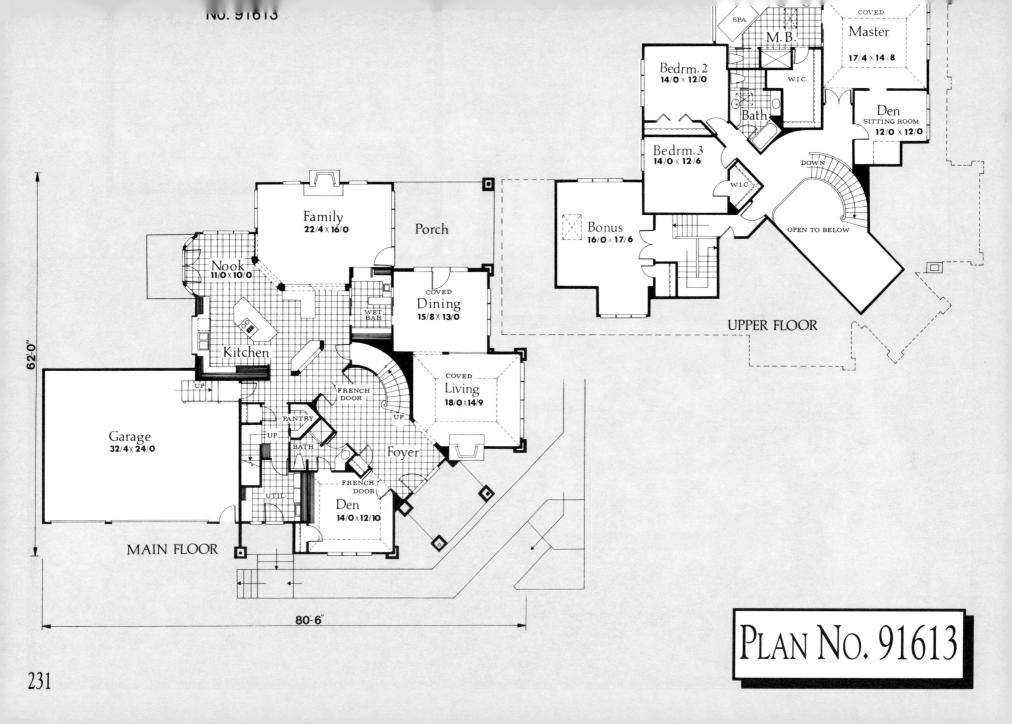

No. 91613

Family
22/4 × 16/0

Porch

Nook
11/0 × 10/0

COVED
Dining
15/8 × 13/0

WET
BAR

Kitchen

UP

FRENCH
DOOR

UP

PANTRY

BATH

COVED
Living
18/0 × 14/9

UP

UTIL.

Foyer

FRENCH
DOOR

Den
14/0 × 12/10

Garage
32/4 × 24/0

62'-0"

80'-6"

MAIN FLOOR

231

SPA

COVED

M. B.

Master
17/4 × 14/8

Bedrm. 2
14/0 × 12/0

W.I.C.

Bath

Den
SITTING ROOM
12/0 × 12/0

Bedrm. 3
14/0 × 12/6

DOWN

W.I.C.

Bonus
16/0 × 17/6

OPEN TO BELOW

UPPER FLOOR

PLAN No. 91613

- First floor — 2,107 sq. ft.
- Second floor — 1,223 sq. ft.
- Exercise room — 598 sq. ft.
- Basement — 928 sq. ft.
- Garage — 863 sq. ft.

Total living area — 3,330 sq. ft.

Views From Every Major Living Area

- Overlook dramatic circular staircase in Foyer from second floor landing
- Extra space behind Utility Room allows for second staircase accessing unfinished Basement as well as second floor unfinished Exercise Room
- Gigantic Family Room features fireplace with handy log storage bin, access to backyard covered porch and includes sunny Nook with elegant bay window
- Spacious Dining Room has double windows for extra light
- Enjoy spectacular view from immense multi-windowed fireplaced Living Room featuring glass doors
- More-than-generous Master Bedroom includes twin walk-in closets and opens to private Bath including shower stall, corner-spa tub, and double vanity
- Two large Bedrooms with full Bath complete second story

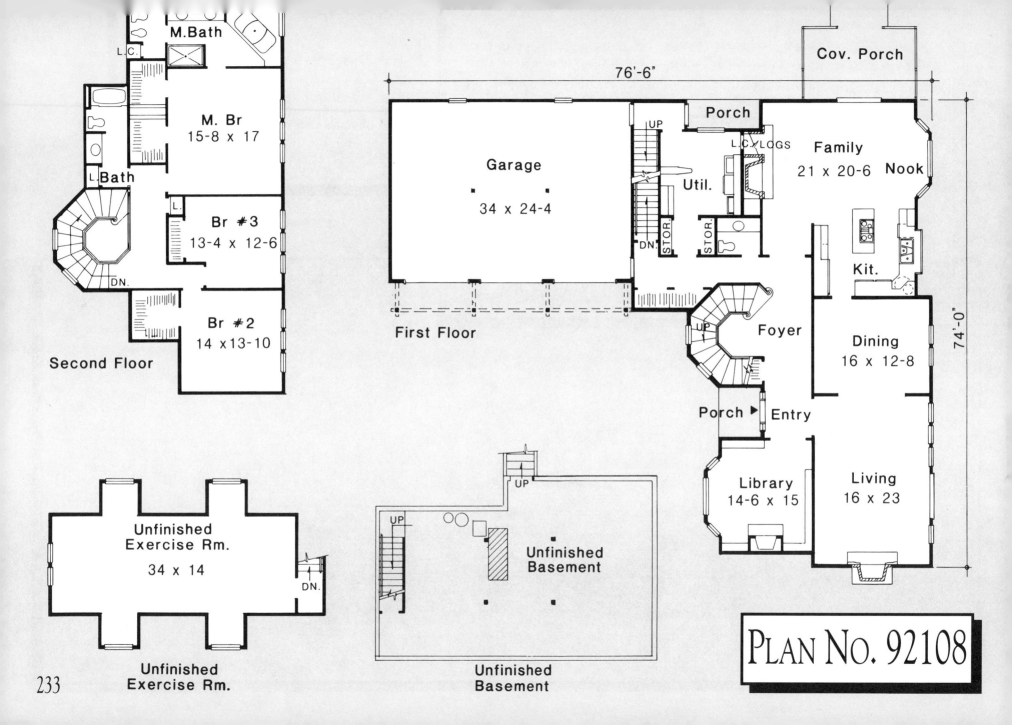

M.Bath

L.C.

M. Br
15-8 x 17

L.Bath

L.

Br #3
13-4 x 12-6

DN.

Br #2
14 x 13-10

Second Floor

Unfinished Exercise Rm.
34 x 14

DN.

Unfinished Exercise Rm.

233

76'-6"

Cov. Porch

Porch

UP

Garage
34 x 24-4

L.C./LOGS

Family
21 x 20-6

Nook

Util.

STOR.

STOR.

DN.

Kit.

First Floor

UP

Foyer

Dining
16 x 12-8

74'-0"

Porch ▶ **Entry**

UP

Unfinished Basement

Library
14-6 x 15

Living
16 x 23

Unfinished Basement

PLAN No. 92108

SPRAWLING SUNCATCHER

- Circular Foyer opens to every area of house

- Three Bedrooms down skylit hall include Master Bedroom featuring garden spa, double vanities, and room-sized walk-in closet

- Full Bath adjoins remaining Bedrooms

- Columns separate fireplaced Living Room and octagonal, vaulted Dining Room

- Kitchen is chef's delight with twin ovens, rangetop island, and built-ins galore

- Just over counter, Nook and fireplaced Family Room offer informal comfort with cheerful atmosphere

- From 3-car Garage step up to large Laundry room with built-in ironing board

- French doors open to backyard patio from cozy Den

- LIVING AREA — 3,160 SQ. FT.
- GARAGE — 3-CAR

TOTAL LIVING AREA — 3,160 SQ. FT.

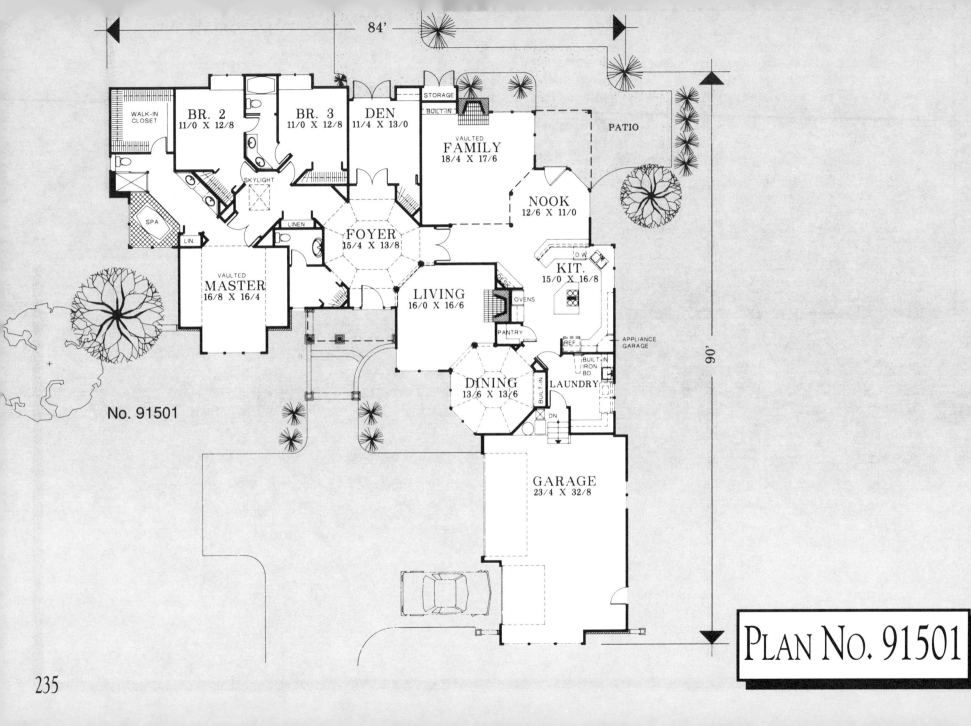

84'

90'

WALK-IN CLOSET

BR. 2
11/0 X 12/8

BR. 3
11/0 X 12/8

DEN
11/4 X 13/0

STORAGE

BUILT-IN

VAULTED
FAMILY
18/4 X 17/6

PATIO

SKYLIGHT

SPA

LIN.

LINEN

FOYER
15/4 X 13/8

NOOK
12/6 X 11/0

D.W.

KIT.
15/0 X 16/8

VAULTED
MASTER
16/8 X 16/4

LIVING
16/0 X 16/6

OVENS

PANTRY

REF.

APPLIANCE GARAGE

BUILT-IN IRON BD

No. 91501

DINING
13/6 X 13/6

BUILT-IN

LAUNDRY

DN

GARAGE
23/4 X 32/8

PLAN No. 91501

Sherman R Shook

LUXURY RESIDENCE FOR EXECUTIVE FAMILY

- ☐ Main floor zoned into three main living areas: formal, informal, and Master Suite

- ☐ Enter formal living/entertaining area from impressive Foyer which opens into Dining Room with efficient serving pantry

- ☐ Second floor features a loft and three bedrooms each with personal Baths and walk-in closets

- ☐ Informal zone centers around large island Kitchen with built-in desk and handy access to 3-car Garage past Laundry and Mudroom

- ☐ Kitchen also oversees Breakfast and Sunroom eating areas as well as sunken Family Room

- ☐ Master Suite located in private wing includes vaulted Sitting Room, personal Exercise Room, sunken whirlpool tub, and twin walk-in closets

- ☐ FIRST FLOOR — 3,798 SQ. FT.
- ☐ SECOND FLOOR — 1,244 SQ. FT.
- ☐ BASEMENT — 3,798 SQ. FT.
- ☐ GARAGE — 3-CAR

TOTAL LIVING AREA — 5,042 SQ. FT.

No. 99369

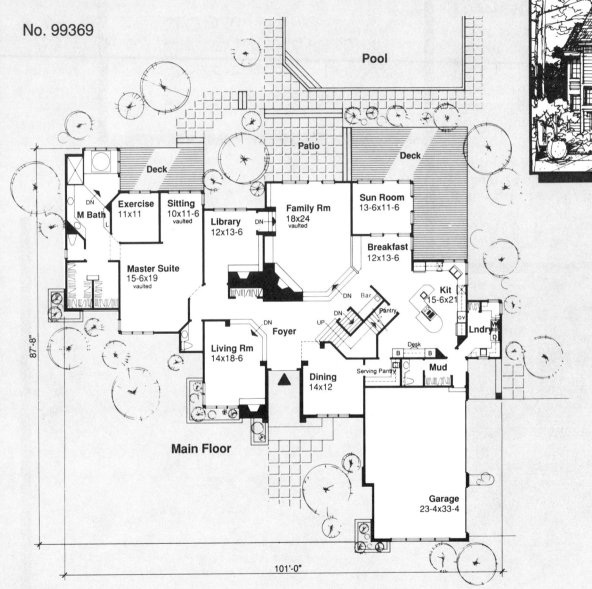

Pool

Patio

Deck

Deck

Exercise
11x11

Sitting
10x11-6
vaulted

Library
12x13-6

Family Rm
18x24
vaulted

Sun Room
13-6x11-6

DN

M Bath

DN

DN

Breakfast
12x13-6

Master Suite
15-6x19
vaulted

Kit
15-6x21

Bar

Pantry

DN

UP

Lndry

Foyer

DN

Living Rm
14x18-6

Desk

B   B

Mud

Serving Pantry

ov

Dining
14x12

Main Floor

Garage
23-4x33-4

87'-8"

101'-0"

**Guest /
Bedroom 4**
13-6x16

open to below

DN

Bedroom 3
15-6x12

Skylight

Loft
12-4x9

Bedroom 2
14x13-6

Upper Floor

PLAN NO. 99369

237

ENGLUND

TRADITIONAL DESIGN OFFERS LIVING APPEAL

- ☐ Super-sized Family Room with vaulted ceiling and transom glass area beside imposing fireplace wall
- ☐ Serve-through bar in perfect location for big gatherings and smaller family groups
- ☐ Ample Hobby Room provides undisturbed area for special projects for entire family
- ☐ Deluxe Master Suite focuses on luxurious Bath and large closet divided into his/hers sides

- ☐ Bump-out window in Dining Room lends appropriate character for formal entertaining
- ☐ Living Room gains height and interest with raised tray ceiling
- ☐ Ascend stairs to find three bedrooms with adjoining baths and a Study
- ☐ Family/Eating Room with direct access to backyard deck conveniently situated adjacent to large Kitchen with stove-top island

- ☐ FIRST FLOOR — 2,464 SQ. FT.
- ☐ SECOND FLOOR — 1,646 SQ. FT.
- ☐ BASEMENT — 2,464 SQ. FT.
- ☐ GARAGE — 3-CAR

TOTAL LIVING AREA — 4,110 SQ. FT.

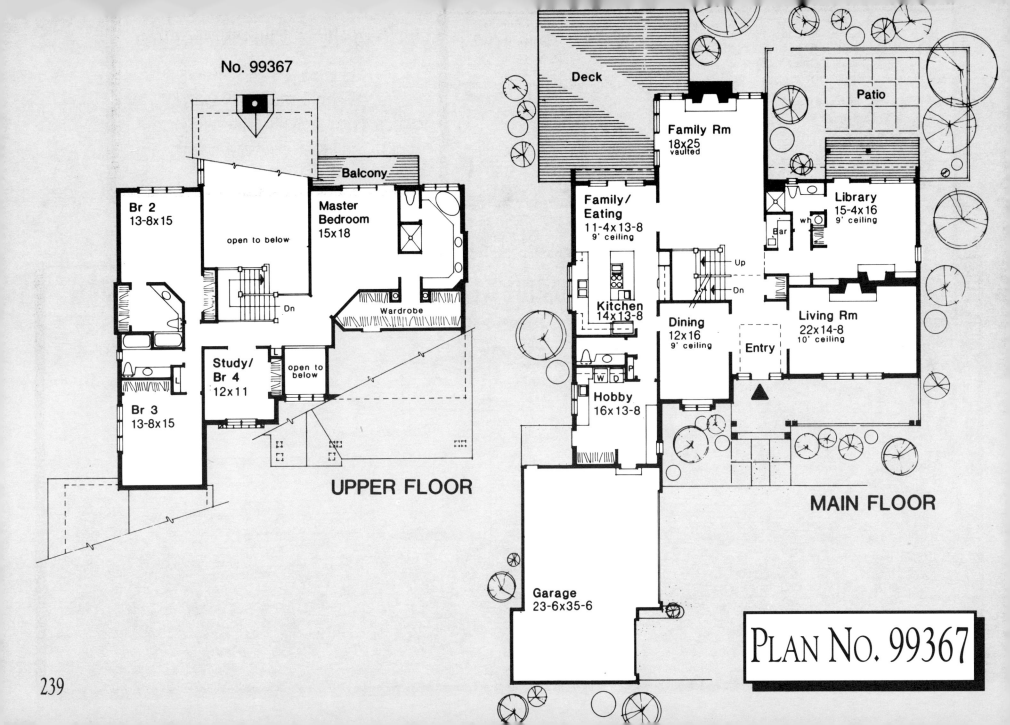

No. 99367

UPPER FLOOR

Br 2
13-8x15

Balcony

Master Bedroom
15x18

open to below

Study/
Br 4
12x11

open to below

Wardrobe

Br 3
13-8x15

MAIN FLOOR

Deck

Patio

Family Rm
18x25
vaulted

Family/
Eating
11-4x13-8
9' ceiling

Library
15-4x16
9' ceiling

Bar

wh

Kitchen
14x13-8

Up

Dn

Dining
12x16
9' ceiling

Living Rm
22x14-8
10' ceiling

Entry

Hobby
16x13-8

W D P

Garage
23-6x35-6

PLAN NO. 99367

239

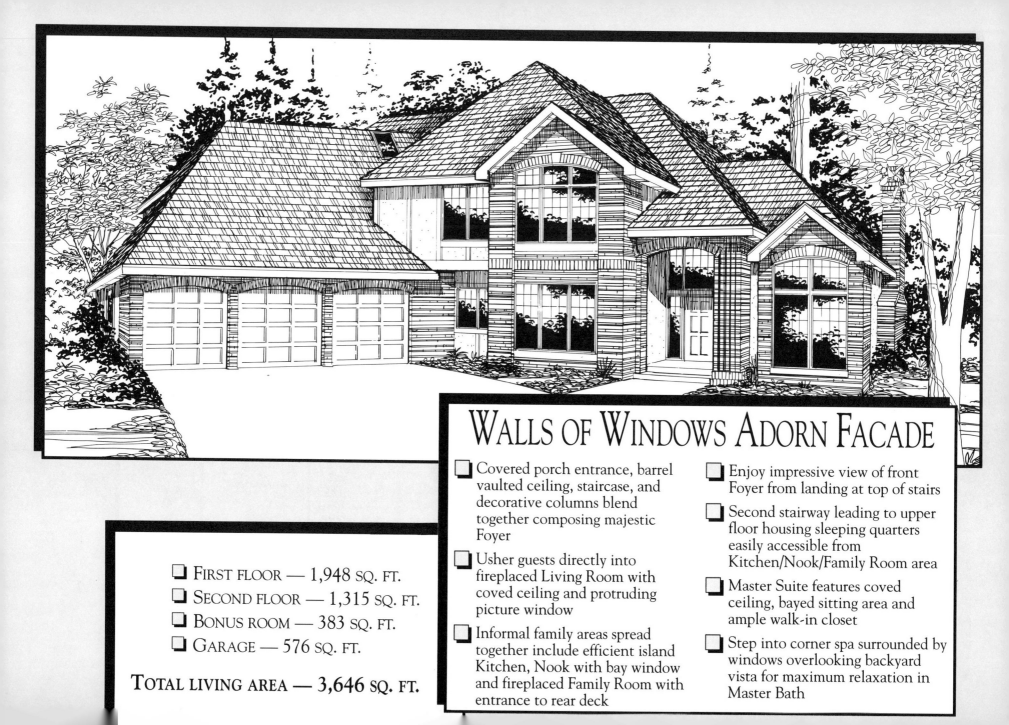

WALLS OF WINDOWS ADORN FACADE

- ☐ Covered porch entrance, barrel vaulted ceiling, staircase, and decorative columns blend together composing majestic Foyer

- ☐ Usher guests directly into fireplaced Living Room with coved ceiling and protruding picture window

- ☐ Informal family areas spread together include efficient island Kitchen, Nook with bay window and fireplaced Family Room with entrance to rear deck

- ☐ Enjoy impressive view of front Foyer from landing at top of stairs

- ☐ Second stairway leading to upper floor housing sleeping quarters easily accessible from Kitchen/Nook/Family Room area

- ☐ Master Suite features coved ceiling, bayed sitting area and ample walk-in closet

- ☐ Step into corner spa surrounded by windows overlooking backyard vista for maximum relaxation in Master Bath

- ☐ FIRST FLOOR — 1,948 SQ. FT.
- ☐ SECOND FLOOR — 1,315 SQ. FT.
- ☐ BONUS ROOM — 383 SQ. FT.
- ☐ GARAGE — 576 SQ. FT.

TOTAL LIVING AREA — 3,646 SQ. FT.

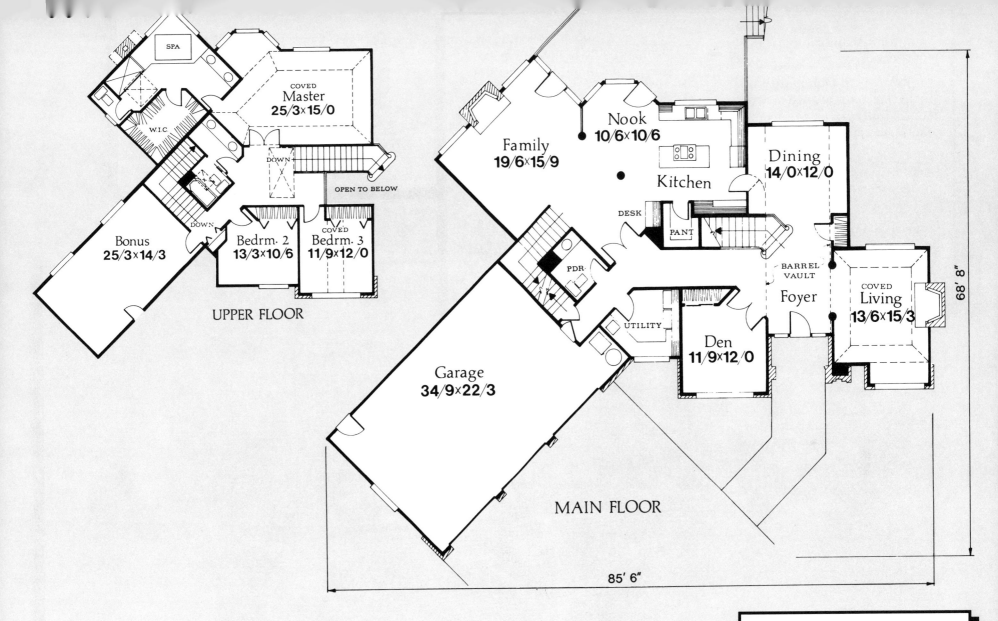

SPA

W.I.C.

DOWN

OPEN TO BELOW

DOWN

COVED
Master
25/3×15/0

Bonus
25/3×14/3

Bedrm. 2
13/3×10/6

COVED
Bedrm. 3
11/9×12/0

UPPER FLOOR

Family
19/6×15/9

Nook
10/6×10/6

Kitchen

Dining
14/0×12/0

DESK

PANT

BARREL
VAULT

Foyer

COVED
Living
13/6×15/3

PDR

UTILITY

Den
11/9×12/0

Garage
34/9×22/3

MAIN FLOOR

68' 8"

85' 6"

PLAN No. 91664

241

STUNNING MANOR SOURCE OF DELIGHT

- ☐ Distinctive covered porch escorts guests to the Entry highlighted by double curved staircase and 19-foot ceiling
- ☐ Fireplaced Library with built-in shelving for extensive collection of books
- ☐ Enormous Family Room extends cordial welcome to informal gatherings and private family relaxation with built-in entertainment center, fireplace, and full-sized wetbar

- ☐ Spacious island Kitchen with huge walk-in pantry separated from Dinnette by eating bar
- ☐ Access to swimming pool via covered patio through Dinnette or Family Room
- ☐ Enter Master Suite through double French doors to discover personal fireplace, private study and skylit Bath with double sink vanity
- ☐ Three additional Bedrooms on second floor feature adjoining Baths

- ☐ FIRST FLOOR — 2,745 SQ. FT.
- ☐ SECOND FLOOR — 2,355 SQ. FT.
- ☐ BASEMENT — 1,400 SQ. FT.
- ☐ GARAGE — 3-CAR

TOTAL LIVING AREA — 5,100 SQ. FT.

No. 92210

Pool

90' - 10"

Upper Floor

Bed#3
17 x 18

MstrBed
23 x 21

Study
17 x 11

Balcony

DN   DN

Bed#2
17 x 12

Ent Below

Bed#4
17 x 14

53' - 8"

Covered Patio

Entertainment Center

FamilyRm
32 x 22
10'Clg.

Bar

Din
13 x 17
10'Clg.

Kit
15 x 17

3-Car-Gar
22 x 31

Basement
DN 4"

Library
17 x 23
10'-4"Clg.

UP   UP

FmlDin
17 x 17
10'-4" Clg.

W
D

Util

DN 4"

Ent
19' Clg.

DN 4"

Covered Por

Main Floor

PLAN No. 92210

ANGULAR ELEGANCE

- ☐ Majestic two-story Foyer, complete with gently curving staircase leads directly into spacious Den

- ☐ Vaulted Living Room has unique mini-gazebo look, efficiency of fireplace, and columns form separation from Dining Room

- ☐ Island Kitchen has added feature of roomy Nook that leads directly to patio for backyard views

- ☐ Bonus room nestled above Garage serves as multi-purpose room

- ☐ Oversized, fireplaced Family Room allows extra light through interesting window works

- ☐ Master Bedroom features lovely garden spa, bay window, and huge walk-in closet

- ☐ Skylight and double vanities add desired light and convenience to hall Bath

- ☐ Three-bay Garage conveniently angled to allow easy entrance to home has extra beauty of side windows

---

- ☐ FIRST FLOOR — 1,675 SQ. FT.
- ☐ SECOND FLOOR — 1,032 SQ. FT.
- ☐ BONUS ROOM — 450 SQ. FT.
- ☐ PARTIAL BASEMENT — 702 SQ. FT.
- ☐ GARAGE — 3-CAR

TOTAL LIVING AREA — 2,707 SQ. FT.

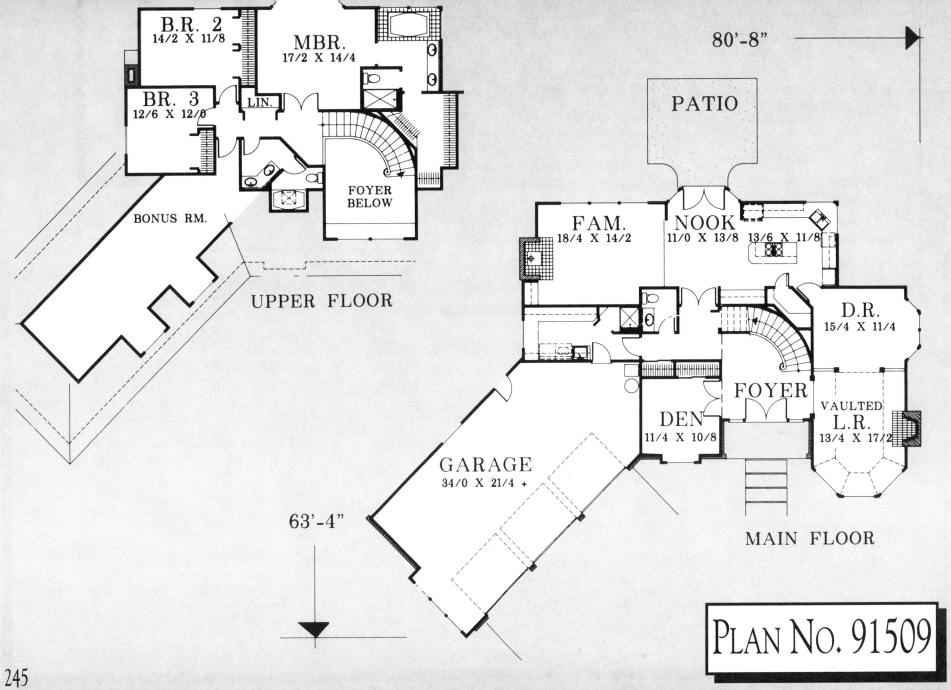

B.R. 2
14/2 X 11/8

MBR.
17/2 X 14/4

B.R. 3
12/6 X 12/0

LIN.

BONUS RM.

FOYER
BELOW

UPPER FLOOR

80'-8"

PATIO

FAM.
18/4 X 14/2

NOOK
11/0 X 13/8

13/6 X 11/8

D.R.
15/4 X 11/4

FOYER

DEN
11/4 X 10/8

VAULTED
L.R.
13/4 X 17/2

GARADE
34/0 X 21/4 +

63'-4"

MAIN FLOOR

PLAN No. 91509

245

PLENTY OF GROWING ROOM

- ☐ Central Foyer creates dazzling impression on all who enter with towering ceilings pierced by skylights and angular staircase

- ☐ Fireplaced Master Suite with unique ceiling lines incorporates Bath, walk-in closet, and sole access to skylit "Secret" Room

- ☐ Two additional Bedrooms on second floor provide ample room for growing family

- ☐ Enter home via ample Laundry Room from 3-car Garage

- ☐ Utilize elegant Dining Room and formal Living Room overlooking front yard for entertaining

- ☐ Retire to sunken Family Room with fireplace, built-in bar and bookcases for brief respite from busy routines

- ☐ Enjoy informal barbeques on rear deck easily accessible from Family Room

- ☐ Island Kitchen designed for modern family includes pantry and desk for convenient meal planning

---

- ☐ FIRST FLOOR — 1,522 SQ. FT.
- ☐ SECOND FLOOR — 1,545 SQ. FT.
- ☐ BASEMENT — 1,500 SQ. FT.
- ☐ GARAGE — 778 SQ. FT.

TOTAL LIVING AREA — 3,067 SQ. FT.

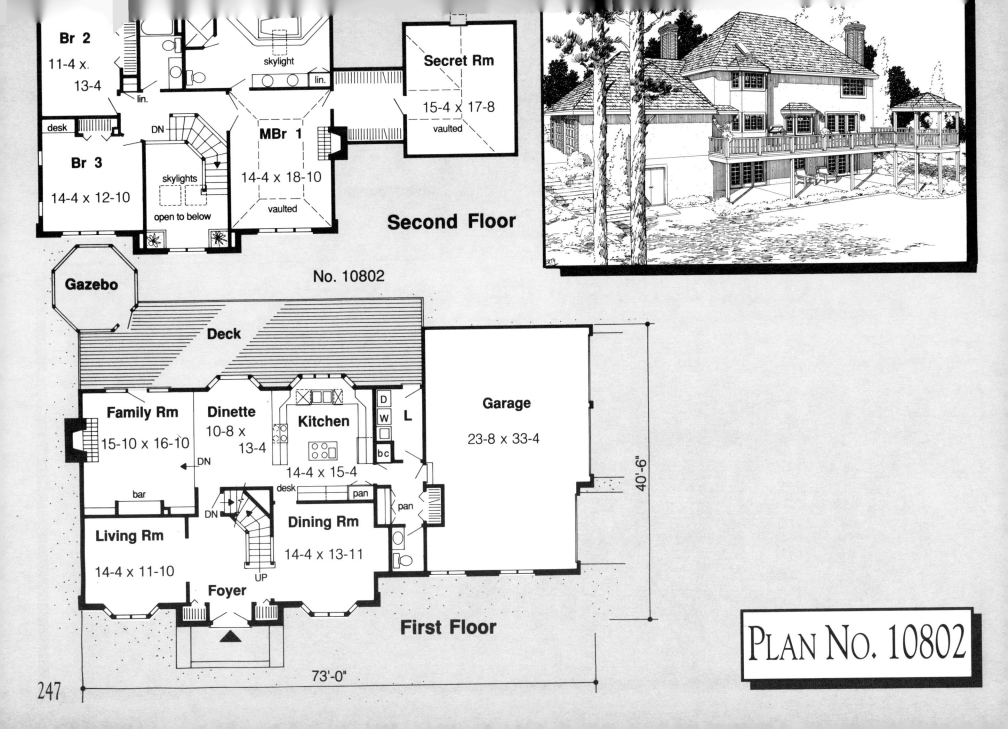

Br 2
11-4 x. 13-4

lin.

desk

Br 3
14-4 x 12-10

DN

skylights

open to below

skylight

lin.

MBr 1
14-4 x 18-10
vaulted

Secret Rm
15-4 x 17-8
vaulted

Second Floor

Gazebo

No. 10802

Deck

Family Rm
15-10 x 16-10

Dinette
10-8 x 13-4

Kitchen
14-4 x 15-4

D

W

bc

L

Garage
23-8 x 33-4

bar

DN

DN

desk

pan

pan

Dining Rm
14-4 x 13-11

Living Rm
14-4 x 11-10

UP

Foyer

First Floor

40'-6"

73'-0"

PLAN NO. 10802

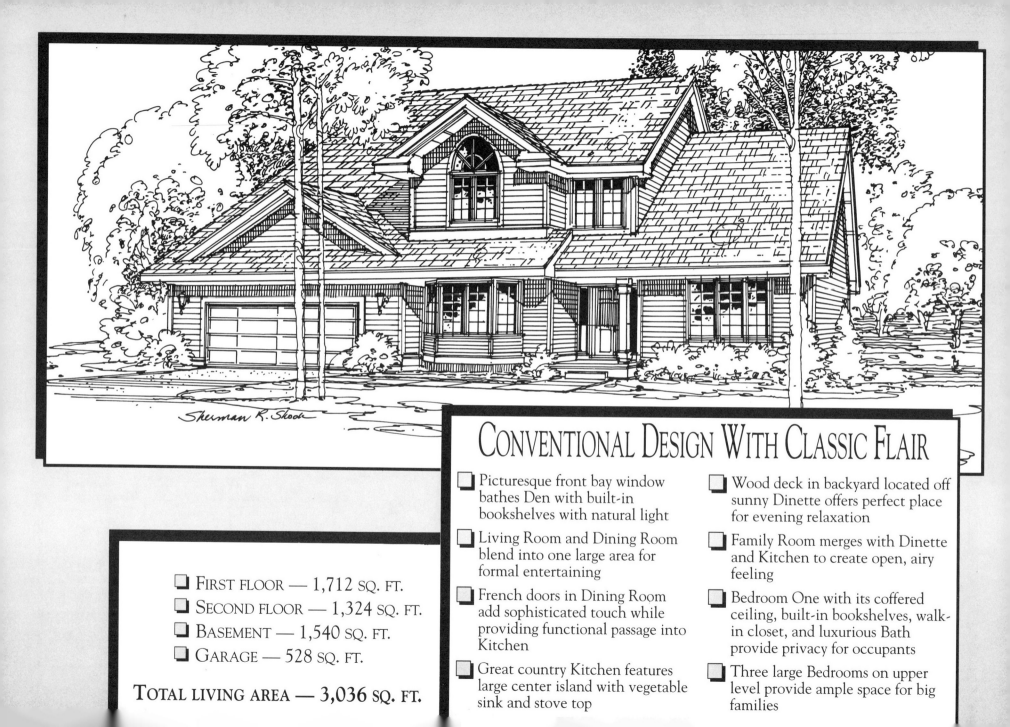

Sherman R. Shook

CONVENTIONAL DESIGN WITH CLASSIC FLAIR

- ☐ Picturesque front bay window bathes Den with built-in bookshelves with natural light
- ☐ Living Room and Dining Room blend into one large area for formal entertaining
- ☐ French doors in Dining Room add sophisticated touch while providing functional passage into Kitchen
- ☐ Great country Kitchen features large center island with vegetable sink and stove top
- ☐ Wood deck in backyard located off sunny Dinette offers perfect place for evening relaxation
- ☐ Family Room merges with Dinette and Kitchen to create open, airy feeling
- ☐ Bedroom One with its coffered ceiling, built-in bookshelves, walk-in closet, and luxurious Bath provide privacy for occupants
- ☐ Three large Bedrooms on upper level provide ample space for big families

- ☐ FIRST FLOOR — 1,712 SQ. FT.
- ☐ SECOND FLOOR — 1,324 SQ. FT.
- ☐ BASEMENT — 1,540 SQ. FT.
- ☐ GARAGE — 528 SQ. FT.

TOTAL LIVING AREA — 3,036 SQ. FT.

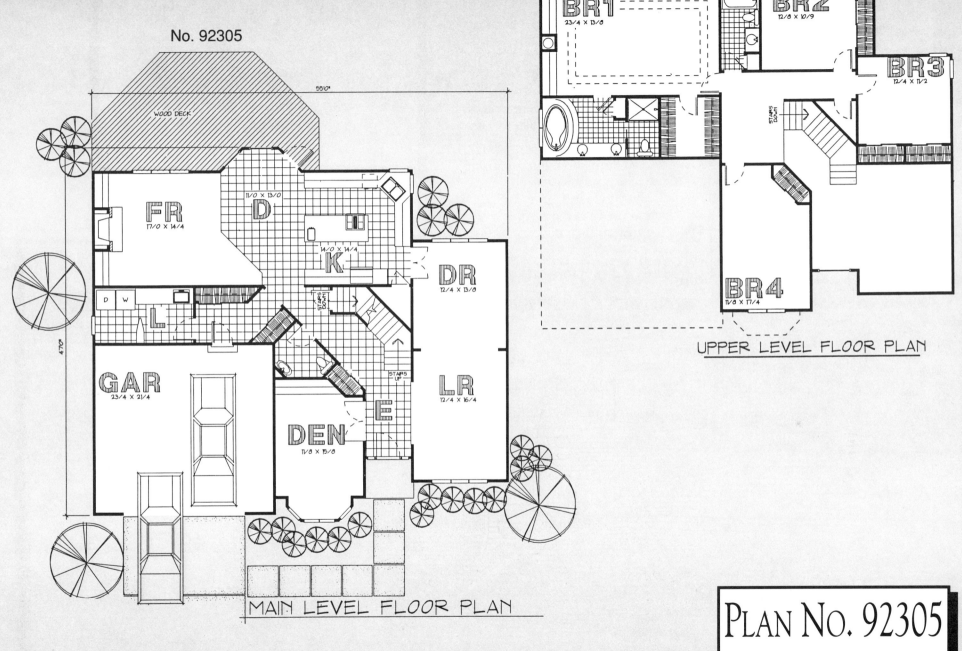

No. 92305

55'0"

WOOD DECK

FR
17/0 X 14/4

D
11/0 X 13/0

K
14/0 X 14/4

DR
12/4 X 13/8

GAR
23/4 X 21/4

DEN
11/8 X 15/8

LR
12/4 X 16/4

STAIRS DOWN

STAIRS UP

D W

47'0"

MAIN LEVEL FLOOR PLAN

BR1
23/4 X 13/8

BR2
12/8 X 10/9

BR3
12/4 X 11/2

BR4
11/8 X 11/4

STAIRS DOWN

UPPER LEVEL FLOOR PLAN

PLAN NO. 92305

FIRST FLOOR — 2,230 SQ. FT.
SECOND FLOOR — 1,204 SQ. FT.
BASEMENT — 2,230 SQ. FT.
GARAGE — 881 SQ. FT.

TOTAL LIVING AREA — 3,434 SQ. FT.

CONTEMPORARY HOME WITH COUNTRY FLAVOR

Country Kitchen features work island, long eating bar with built-in cooktop and grill, appliance center, double ovens, trash compactor and more

Huge Family Room bathed in beams of light streaming through skylights in high vaulted ceilings

Long hearth stretching across entire far end of Family room draws attention to fireplace

His-n-hers walk-in closets providing sound insulation between sleeping area and water closet in Master Suite

Sliding door in toilet area maintains privacy in Master Bath, but shower, spa and double vanities are wide open

Home Office located across hall from Master Suite

Steps away to left of two-story vaulted Entry takes you directly into Living Room

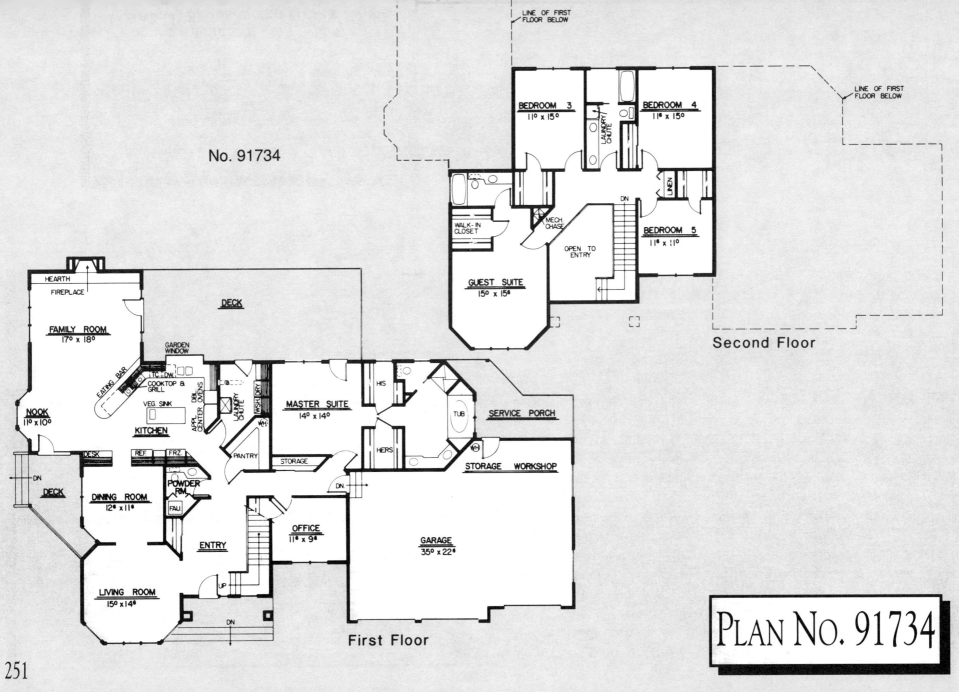

No. 91734

Second Floor

BEDROOM 3
11⁰ x 15⁰

BEDROOM 4
11⁸ x 15⁰

LAUNDRY CHUTE

LINEN

WALK-IN CLOSET

MECH. CHASE

DN

OPEN TO ENTRY

BEDROOM 5
11⁸ x 11⁰

GUEST SUITE
15⁰ x 15⁸

LINE OF FIRST FLOOR BELOW

LINE OF FIRST FLOOR BELOW

First Floor

HEARTH
FIREPLACE

FAMILY ROOM
17⁰ x 18⁰

DECK

GARDEN WINDOW

EATING BAR

TC DW.

COOKTOP & GRILL

VEG. SINK

KITCHEN

DBL. CENTER OVENS

APPL.

LAUNDRY CHUTE

WSH DRY

WH

MASTER SUITE
14⁰ x 14⁰

HIS

HERS

TUB

WH

SERVICE PORCH

NOOK
11⁰ x 10⁰

DESK

REF.

FRZ.

PANTRY

STORAGE

STORAGE WORKSHOP

DN

DINING ROOM
12⁸ x 11⁸

POWDER RM.

FAU

DECK

DN

ENTRY

OFFICE
11⁸ x 9⁸

DN

GARAGE
35⁰ x 22⁸

LIVING ROOM
15⁰ x 14⁸

UP

DN

PLAN No. 91734

251

You've picked your dream home!

You can already see it standing on your lot... you can see yourselves in your new home... enjoying family, entertaining guests, celebrating holidays. All that remains ahead are the details. That's where we can help.

Whether you plan to build-it-yourself, be your own contractor, or hand your plans over to an outside contractor, your Garlinghouse blueprints provide the perfect beginning for putting yourself in your dream home right away.

We even make it simple for you to make professional design modifications. We can also provide a materials list for greater economy.

My grandfather, L.F. Garlinghouse, started a tradition of quality when he founded this company in 1907. For over 85 years, homeowners and builders have relied on us for accurate, complete, professional blueprints. Our plans help you get results fast... and save money, too! These pages will give you all the information you need to order. So get started now... I know you'll love your new Garlinghouse home!

Sincerely,

Everything you need to make your dream come true!

You pay only a fraction of the original cost for home designs by respected professionals.

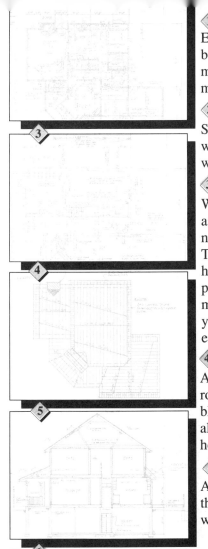

① Exterior Elevations

Exact scale views of the front, rear, and both sides of your home, showing exterior materials, details, and all necessary measurements.

② Detailed Floor Plans

Showing the placement of all interior walls, the dimensions of rooms, doors, windows, stairways, and other details.

③ Foundation Plan

With footings and all load-bearing points as applicable to your home, including all necessary notations and dimensions. The foundation style supplied varies from home to home. Local conditions and practices will determine whether a basement, crawl-space, or a slab is best for you. Your professional contractor can easily make the necessary adaption.

④ Roof Plan

All information necessary to construct the roof for your home is included. Many blueprints contain framing plans showing all of the roof elements, so you'll know how these details look and fit together.

⑤ Typical Cross-Section

A detailed, full cross-sectional view through the entire house, as if the house was cut from top to bottom. This eleva- stand the interconnections of the construction components.

⑥ Typical Wall Sections

Detailed views of your exterior wall, as though sliced from top to bottom. These drawings clarify exterior wall construction, insulation, flooring, and roofing details.

Depending on your specific geography and climate, your home will be built with either 2x4 or 2x6 exterior walls. Most professional contractors can easily adapt plans for either requirement.

⑦ Kitchen & Bath Cabinet Details

These plans, or, in some cases, elevations, show the specific details and placement of the cabinets in your kitchen and bathrooms as applicable. Customizing these areas is simpler beginning with these details.

⑧ Fireplace Details

When your home includes one or more fireplaces, these detailed drawings will help your mason with their construction and appearance. It is easy to review details with professionals when you have the plans for reference.

⑨ Stair Details

If stairs are part of the design you selected, specific plans are included for their construction and details.

⑩ Schematic Electrical Layouts

The suggested locations for all of your switches, outlets, and fixtures are indicated on these drawings. They are practical as they are, but they are also a solid taking-off point for any personal adaptions.

Also available, is a money-saving Materials List.

Plus...

FREE
Specifications and Contract Form

FREE
14-page Energy Conservation Guide.

TURN THE PAGE FOR THE EASY STEPS TO COMPLETE YOUR DREAM HOME ORDER!

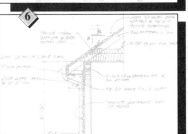
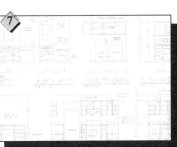

253

Reversed Plans Can Make Your Dream Home Just Right!

"That's our dream home... if only the garage were on the other side!"

You could have exactly the home you want by flipping it end-for-end. Check it out by holding your dream home page of this book up to a mirror. Then simply order your plans "reversed". We'll send you one full set of mirror-image plans (with the writing backwards) as a master guide for you and your builder.

The remaining sets of your order will come as shown in this book so the dimensions and specifications are easily read on the job site... but they will be specially stamped "REVERSED" so there is no construction confusion.

We can only send reversed plans with multiple-set orders. But, there is no extra charge for this service.

Normal OR Reversed

Modifying Your Garlinghouse Home Plan

Easy modifications to your dream home... minor non-structural changes, simple materials substitutions... can be made between you and your builder.

However, if you are considering making major changes to your design, we strongly recommend that you use an architect or a professional designer. And, since you have already started with our complete detailed blueprints, the cost of those expensive professional services will be significantly less.

Our Reproducible Paper Sepias Make Modifications Easier

They provide a design professional with the right way to make changes directly to your Garlinghouse home plans and then print as many copies of the modified plans as you need. The price is $395.00 plus shipping.

Call 1-800-235-5700 to find out more.

Remember To Order Your Materials List

It'll help you save money. Available at a modest additional charge, the Materials List gives the quantity, dimensions, and specifications for the major materials needed to build your home. You will get faster, more accurate bids from your contractors and building suppliers — and avoid paying for unused materials and waste. Materials Lists are available for all home plans except as otherwise indicated, but can only be ordered with a set of home plans. Due to differences in local building codes, regional requirements, and home-owner/ builder preferences... electrical, plumbing & heating/air conditioning equipment requirements aren't provided.

Questions?

Call our customer service number at
1-203-632-0500

How Many Sets Of Plans Will You Need?

The Standard 8-Set Construction Package

Our experience shows that you'll speed every step of construction and avoid costly building errors by ordering enough sets to go around. Each tradesperson wants a set — the general contractor and all subcontractors; foundation, electrical, plumbing, heating/air conditioning, drywall, finish carpenters, and cabinet shop. Don't forget your lending institution, building deparment and, of course, a set for yourself.

The Minimum 5-Set Construction Package

If you're comfortable with arduous follow-up, this package can save you a few dollars by giving you the option of passing down plan sets as work progresses. You might have enough copies to go around if work goes exactly as scheduled and no plans are lost or damaged. But for only $30 more, the 8-set package eliminates these worries.

The Single-Set Decision-Maker Package

We offer this set so you can study the blueprints to plan your dream home in detail. But remember... one set is never enough to build your home... and they're copyrighted.

An important note:

All plans are drawn to conform to one or more of the industry's major national building standards. However, due to the variety of local building regulations, your plan may need to be modified to comply with local requirements — snow loads, energy loads, seismic zones, etc. Do check them fully and consult your local building officials.

A few states require that all building plans used be drawn by an architect registered in that state. While having your plans reviewed and stamped by such an architect may be prudent, laws requiring non-conforming plans like ours to be completely redrawn forces you to unnecessarily pay very large fees. If your state has such a law, we strongly recom-

Your order is processed immediately. Allow 10 working days from our receipt of your order for normal UPS delivery. Save time with your credit card and our "800" number. UPS *must* have a street address or Rural Route Box number — never a post office box. Use a work address if no one is home during the day.

Orders being shipped to Alaska, Hawaii, APO, FPO or Post Office Boxes must go via First Class Mail. Please include the proper postage.

Canadian Orders and Shipping:

To our friends in Canada, we have a plan design affiliate in Kitchener, Ontario. This relationship will help you avoid the delays and charges associated with shipments from the United States. Moreover, our affiliate is familiar with the building requirements in your community and country.

We prefer payments in U.S. Currency. If you,

to the prices of the plans and shipping fees.
Please submit all Canadian plan orders to:
The Garlinghouse Company, Inc.
20 Cedar Street North
Kitchener, Ontario N2H, 2W8
(519) 743-4169

Mexico and Other Countries:

If you are ordering from outside the United States, please note that your check, money orders, or international money transfers **must be payable in US currency**. For speed, we ship international orders Air Parcel Post. Please refer to the chart for the correct shipping cost.

Blueprint Price Schedule *(stated in U.S. dollars)*	
Standard Construction Package (8 sets)	$255.00
Minimum Construction Package (5 sets)	225.00
Single-Set Package (no reverses)	180.00
Each Additional Set (ordered w/one above)	20.00
Materials List (with plan order only)	25.00

Prices subject to change without notice.

Domestic Shipping (stated in U.S. dollars)

UPS Ground Service	$ 7.00
First Class Mail	$ 8.50
Express Delivery Service Call For Details 1-800-235-5700	

International Shipping	**One Set**	**Mult. Sets**
Canada	$ 7.25	$ 12.50
Caribbean Nations & Mexico	$16.50	$ 39.50
All Other Nations	$18.50	$ 50.00

Canadian orders are now Duty Free.

ORDER TOLL FREE — 1-800-235-5700
Monday-Friday 8:00am to 5:00pm Eastern Time
or FAX your Credit Card order to 203-632-0712
Connecticut, Alaska, Hawaii, and all foreign residents call 1-203-632-0500.
Please have ready:
1. Your credit card number
2. The plan number
3. The order code number

Before ordering **PLEASE READ** *all ordering information*

Blueprint Order Form

Order Code #H2LX2

GARLINGHOUSE

Plan No. _____

❑ As Shown ❑ Reversed *(mult. set pkgs. only)*

	Each	Amount
8 set pkg.	$255.00	$
5 set pkg.	$225.00	$
1 set pkg.*(no reverses)*	$180.00	$
___(Qty.) Add. sets @	$20.00 ea.	$
Material List	$25.00	$
Shipping — see chart		$
Subtotal		$
Sales Tax (CT residents add 6% sales tax, KS residents add 5.9% sales tax)		$
Total Amount Enclosed		$

Send your check, money order or credit card information to:
Garlinghouse Company, 34 Industrial Park Place, P.O. Box 1717, Middletown, CT 06457

Bill To: *(address must be as it appears on credit card statement)*

Name_____ Daytime Phone (___) _____
        (Please Print)

Address_____ City/State _____ Zip _____

Ship To *(if different from Bill to)***:**

Name_____

Address_____ City/State _____ Zip _____
        (UPS will not ship to P.O. Boxes)

Credit Card Information

Charge To: ❑ Visa ❑ Mastercard ❑ Discover

Card # | | | | | | | | | | | | | | | | | |

Signature _____ Exp. ____ / ____

Thank you for your order!

Garlinghouse plans are copyright protected. Purchaser hereby agrees that the home plan construction drawings being purchased will not be used for the construction of more than one single dwelling, and that these drawings will not be reproduced either in whole or in part by any means whatsoever.

Canadian book orders should be submitted to:
The Garlinghouse Company, Inc.
20 Cedar Street North
Kitchener, Ontario   N2H 2W8
(519) 743-4169

Cover Photography by John Ehrenclou

☐ Cover Plan, number 10436, is shown on pages 16 and 17

☐ Plan shown on top of back cover, number 10531, is shown on pages 84 and 85

☐ Plan shown on bottom of back cover, number 10419, is shown on pages 192 and 193